Concealment and Exposure

CONCEALMENT AND EXPOSURE

And Other Essays

Thomas Nagel

OXFORD

UNIVERSITY PRESS

2002

OXFORD
UNIVERSITY PRESS

Oxford   New York
Auckland   Bangkok   Buenos Aires   Cape Town   Chennai
Dar es Salaam   Delhi   Hong Kong   Istanbul   Karachi   Kolkata
Kuala Lumpur   Madrid   Melbourne   Mexico City   Mumbai   Nairobi
São Paulo   Shanghai   Singapore   Taipei   Tokyo   Toronto

and an associated company in Berlin

Copyright © 2002 by Oxford University Press, Inc.

Published by Oxford University Press, Inc.
198 Madison Avenue, New York, New York 10016

www.oup.com

Oxford is a registered trademark of Oxford University Press

Library of Congress Cataloging-in-Publication Data
Nagel, Thomas, 1937–
Concealment and exposure : and other essays / Thomas Nagel.
p. cm.
Includes bibliographical references and index.
ISBN 0-19-515293-X
1. Philosophy of mind. 2. Ethics, Modern. 3. Privacy. I. Title.
B945.N333 C66 2002
100—dc21   2002025758

2 4 6 8 9 7 5 3 1

Printed in the United States of America
on acid-free paper

To Bernard and Patricia Williams

Preface

These essays, written over the past few years, do not form a natural unity, but they do form three groups, corresponding to my main philosophical concerns during the period: (1) the relations between private and public life, especially with regard to sexual privacy; (2) the right form of a liberal outlook in moral and political theory; (3) the understanding of objective reality in the face of various forms of subjectivism. Those concerns found expression equally in independent essays and in book reviews, so I have included both. The long final essay on the mind-body problem stands a bit apart, but as a flagrant example of metaphysical realism, I include it in the third category.

    I have revised nearly all the essays to some extent.

New York   T. N.
March 2002

Acknowledgments

Earlier versions of these essays appeared in the following places:

1. *Philosophy & Public Affairs*, 27, no. 1 (1998).
2. *Times Literary Supplement*, August 14, 1998.
3. *Philosophy & Public Affairs*, 24, no. 2 (1995).
4. *Times Literary Supplement*, June 18, 1999.
5. *The New Republic*, March 8, 1999.
6. *The New Republic*, May 7, 2001.
7. *The New Republic*, October 25, 1999.
8. Samuel Freeman, ed., *The Cambridge Companion to Rawls* (Cambridge: Cambridge University Press, 2002).
9. *Times Literary Supplement*, June 23, 2000.
10. *Oxford Journal of Legal Studies*, 17, no. 2 (1997).
11. *London Review of Books*, September 22, 1994.
12. *London Review of Books*, October 14, 1999.
13. *London Review of Books*, February 4, 1999.
14. *Times Literary Supplement*, August 28, 1998.
15. *The New Republic*, October 12, 1998.
16. Lewis Hahn, ed., *The Philosophy of Donald Davidson* (Chicago: Open Court, 1999).
17. *London Review of Books*, September 20, 2001.
18. Paul Boghossian and Christopher Peacocke, eds., *New Essays on the A Priori* (Oxford: Clarendon, 2000).

Contents

PART I
Public and Private

1

Concealment and Exposure

I

Everyone knows that something has gone wrong in the United States with the conventions of privacy. Increased tolerance for variation in sexual life seems to have brought with it a sharp increase in prurient and censorious attention to the sexual lives of public figures and famous persons, past and present. The culture seems to be growing more tolerant and more intolerant at the same time.

Sexual taboos a generation ago were also taboos against saying much about sex in public, and this had the salutary side effect of protecting persons in the public eye from invasions of privacy by the mainstream media. It meant that the sex lives of politicians were rightly treated as irrelevant to the assessment of their qualifications and that one learned only in rough outline, if at all, about the sexual conduct of prominent creative thinkers and artists of the past. Now, instead, there is open season on all this material. The public, followed sanctimoniously by the media, feels entitled to know the most intimate details of the life of any public figure, as if it were part of the price of fame that you exposed everything about yourself to view and not just the achievement or performance that has brought you to public attention. Because of the way life is, this results in real damage to the condition of the public sphere: Many people cannot take that kind of exposure, and many are discredited or tarnished in ways that have nothing to do with their real qualifications or achievements.

One might think, in a utopian vein, that we could carry our toleration a bit further and, instead of trying to reinstitute the protection of privacy, cease to regard all this personal information as important. Then

3

pornographic films of presidential candidates could be available in video stores and it wouldn't matter. But it isn't as simple as that. Boundaries between what is publicly exposed and what is not exist for a reason. We will never reach a point at which nothing that anyone does disgusts anyone else. We can expect to remain in a sexual world deeply divided by various lines of imaginative incomprehension and disapproval. So conventions of reticence and privacy serve a valuable function in keeping us out of each other's faces. But they also serve to give each of us some control over the face we present to the world. We don't want to expose ourselves completely to strangers even if we don't fear their disapproval, hostility, or disgust. Naked exposure itself, whether or not it arouses disapproval, is disqualifying. The boundary between what we reveal and what we do not, and some control over that boundary, is among the most important attributes of our humanity. Someone who for special reasons becomes a public or famous figure should not have to give it up.

This particular problem is part of a larger topic, namely, the importance of concealment as a condition of civilization. Concealment includes not only secrecy and deception but also reticence and nonacknowledgment. There is much more going on inside us all the time than we are willing to express, and civilization would be impossible if we could all read each other's minds. Apart from everything else there is the sheer chaotic, tropical luxuriance of the inner life. To quote Simmel: "All we communicate to another individual by means of words or perhaps in another fashion—even the most subjective, impulsive, intimate matters—is a selection from that psychological-real whole whose absolutely exact report (absolutely exact in terms of content and sequence) would drive everybody into the insane asylum."[1] As children we have to learn gradually not only to express what we feel but also to keep many thoughts and feelings to ourselves in order to maintain relations with other people on an even keel. We also have to learn, especially in adolescence, not to be overwhelmed by a consciousness of other people's awareness of and reaction to ourselves—so that our inner lives can be carried on under the protection of an exposed public self over which we have enough control to be able to identify with it, at least in part.

There is an analogy between the familiar problem that liberalism addresses in political theory—of how to join together individuals with conflicting interests and a plurality of values under a common system of law that serves their collective interests equitably without destroying their autonomy—and the purely social problem of defining conventions of reticence and privacy that allow people to interact peacefully in public without exposing themselves in ways that would be emotionally

1. Kurt H. Wolff, ed. *The Sociology of Georg Simmel* (New York: Free Press, 1950), pp. 311–12; translated from Georg Simmel, *Soziologie* (1908).

traumatic or would inhibit the free operation of personal feeling, fantasy, imagination, and thought. It is only an analogy: One can be a political liberal without being a social individualist, as liberals never tire of pointing out. But I think there is a natural way in which a more comprehensive liberal respect for individual autonomy would express itself through social conventions, as opposed to legal rules. In both cases a delicate balance has to be struck, and it is possible in both cases to err in the direction of too much or too little restraint. I believe that in the social domain, the restraints that protect privacy are not in good shape. They are weakest where privacy impinges on the political domain, but the problem is broader than that. The grasp of the public sphere and public norms has come to include too much. That is the claim I want to defend in this essay—in a sense it is a defense of the element of restraint in a liberal social order.

In practice, it is hard to know what to do about a problem like this. Once a convention of privacy loses its grip, there is a race to the bottom by competing media of publicity. What I would like to do here is to say something about the broader phenomenon of boundaries and to consider more particularly what would be a functional form of restraint in a culture like ours, where the general level of tolerance is high and the portrayal of sex and other intimate matters in general terms is widely accepted—in movies, magazines, and literature. Knowing all that we do, what reason is there still to be reticent?

While sex is a central part of the topic, the question of reticence and acknowledgment is much broader. The fact is that once we leave infancy and begin to get a grip on the distinction between ourselves and others, reticence and limits on disclosure and acknowledgment are part of every type of human relation, including the most intimate. Intimacy creates personal relations protected from the general gaze, permitting us to lose our inhibitions and expose ourselves to one another. But we do not necessarily share all our sexual fantasies with our sexual partners, or all our opinions of their actions with our closest friends. All interpersonal contact goes through the visible surface, even if it penetrates fairly deep, and managing what appears on the surface—both positively and negatively—is the constant work of human life.[2]

This is one topic of Freud's *Civilization and Its Discontents*, the problem of constructing on an animal base human beings capable of living together in harmony. But the additional inner life that derives through internalization from civilization itself creates a further need for selection of what will be exposed and what concealed and further demands of self-presentation. I would like to begin by discussing some of the

---

2. Surface management is wonderfully described by Erving Goffman. See, for example, "On Face-Work," in his collection of essays, *Interaction Ritual* (New York: Anchor Books, 1967).

conventions of uniformity of surface that may seem dishonest to the naive but that make civilized life possible.

II

The first and most obvious thing to note about many of the most important forms of reticence is that they are not dishonest, because the conventions that govern them are generally known. If I don't tell you everything I think and feel about you, that is not a case of deception since you don't expect me to do so and would probably be appalled if I did. The same is true of many explicit expressions that are literally false. If I say, "How nice to see you," you know perfectly well that this is not meant as a report of my true feelings: Even if it happens to be true, I might very well say it even if you were the last person I wanted to see at just that moment, and that is something you know as well as I.[3] The point of polite formulae and broad abstentions from expression is to leave a great range of potentially disruptive material unacknowledged and therefore out of play. It is material that everyone who has been around knows is there—feelings of hostility, contempt, derision, envy, vanity, boredom, fear, sexual desire, or aversion, plus a great deal of simple self-absorption.

Part of growing up is developing an external self that fits smoothly into the world with others that have been similarly designed. One expresses one's desires, for example, only to the extent that they are compatible with the publicly acknowledged desires of others, or at least in such a way that any conflict can be easily resolved by a commonly accepted procedure of decision. One avoids calling attention to one's own obsessions or needs in a way that forces others either to attend to them or too conspicuously to ignore them, and one avoids showing that one has noticed the failings of others in order to allow them to carry on without having to respond to one's reactions of amusement or alarm. These forms of tact are conspicuously absent in childhood, whose social brutality we can all remember.

At first it is not easy to take on these conventions as a second skin. In adolescence one feels transparent and unprotected from the awareness of others, and one is likely to become defensively affected or else secretive and expressionless. The need for a publicly acceptable persona also has too much resonance in the interior, and until one develops a sure habit of division, external efforts to conform will result in inner falsity, as one tries hopelessly to become wholly the self one has to present to the world. But if the external demands are too great, this problem may become permanent. Clearly an external persona will always make some

3. Paul Grice once observed to me that in Oxford, when someone says, "We must have lunch some time," it means, "I don't care if I never see you again in my life."

demands on the inner life, and it may require serious repression or distortion on the inside if it doesn't fit smoothly or comfortably enough. Ideally the social costume shouldn't be too thick.

Above all it should not be confused with the whole self. To internalize too much of one's social being and regard inner feelings and thoughts that conflict with it as unworthy or impure is disastrous. Everyone is entitled to commit murder in the imagination once in a while, not to mention lesser infractions. There may be those who lack a good grip on the distinction between fantasy and reality, but most people who enjoy violent movies, for example, are simply operating in a different gear from the one in which they engage with other people. The other consequence of the distinction is that one has to keep a firm grip on the fact that the social self that others present to us is not the whole of their personality either, and that this is not a form of deception because it is meant to be understood by everyone. Everyone knows that there is much more going on than what enters the public domain, but the smooth functioning of that domain depends on a general nonacknowledgment of what everyone knows.

Admittedly, nonacknowledgment can sometimes also serve the purpose of deceiving those, like children or outsiders, who do not know the conventions. But its main purpose is usually not to deceive but to manage the distinction between foreground and background, between what invites attention and a collective response and what remains individual and may be ignored. The possibility of combining civilized interpersonal relations with a relatively free inner life depends on this division.

Exactly how this works is not easy to explain. One might well ask how it is that we can remain on good terms with others when we know that behind their polite exteriors they harbor feelings and opinions that we would find unacceptable if they were expressed publicly. In some cases, perhaps, good manners do their work by making it possible for us to believe that things are not as they are and that others hold us in the regard that they formally display. If someone is inclined toward self-deception, that is certainly an option. But anyone who is reasonably realistic will not make that use of the conventions, and if others engage in flattery that is actually meant to be believed, it is offensive because it implies that they believe you require this kind of deception as a balm to your vanity.

No, the real work is done by leaving unacknowledged things that are known, even if only in general terms, on all sides. The more effective the conventions controlling acknowledgment, the more easily we can handle our knowledge of what others do not express and their knowledge of what we do not express. One of the remarkable effects of a smoothly fitting public surface is that it protects one from the sense of exposure without having to be in any way dishonest or deceptive, just as clothing does not conceal the fact that one is naked underneath. The mere sense that the gaze of others, and their explicit reactions, are conventionally discouraged from penetrating this surface, in spite of their unstated awareness of much that lies beneath it, allows a sense of freedom to lead one's inner life as if it were invisible, even though it is not. It is enough that it is firmly excluded from direct public view and that only what one puts out into the public domain is a legitimate object of explicit response from others.

Even if public manners are fairly relaxed and open, they can permit the exposure of only a small fraction of what people are feeling. Toleration of what people choose to do or say can go only so far: To really accept people as they are requires an understanding that there is much more to them than could possibly be integrated into a common social space. The single most important fact to keep in mind in connection with this topic is that each of the multifarious individual souls is an enormous and complex world in itself, but the social space into which they must all fit is severely limited. What is admitted into that space has to be constrained both to avoid crowding and to prevent conflict and offense. Only so much freedom is compatible with public order: The bulk of toleration must be extended to the private sphere, which will then be left in all its variety behind the protective cover of public conventions of reticence and discretion.

One of our problems, as liberal attitudes become more prevalent, is how to draw the line between public and private tolerance. It is always risky to raise the stakes by attempting to take over too much of the limited social space. If in the name of liberty one tries to institute a free-for-all, the result will be a revival of the forces of repression, a decline of social peace and perhaps eventually of generally accepted norms of toleration. I think we have seen some of this in recent cultural battles in the United States. The partial success of a cultural revolution of tolerance for the expression of sexual material that was formerly kept out of public view has provoked a reaction that includes the breakdown of barriers of privacy even for those who are not eager to let it all hang out. The same developments have also fueled the demand from another quarter for a return to public hypocrisy in the form of political correctness. The more crowded the public arena gets, the more people want to control it.

Variety is inevitable, and it inevitably includes elements that are in strong potential conflict with one another. The more complicated people's lives become, the more they need the protection of separate private domains. The idea that everything should be out in the open is childish and represents a misunderstanding of the mutually protective function of conventions of restraint, which avoid provoking unnecessary conflict. Still more pernicious is the idea that socialization should penetrate to the innermost reaches of the soul, so that one should feel guilty or ashamed of any thoughts or feelings that one would be unwilling to express publicly. When a culture includes both of these elements to a significant degree, the results are very unharmonious, and we find ourselves in the regressed condition of the United States.

In France, a postadolescent civilization, it is simply taken for granted that sex, while important, is essentially a private matter. It is thought inappropriate to seek out or reveal private information against the wishes of the subject; and even when unusual facts about the sexual life of a public figure become known, they do not become a public issue. Everyone knows that politicians, like other human beings, lead sexual lives of great variety, and there is no thrill to be had from hearing the details. In the United States, by contrast, the media and much of the public behave as if they had just learned of the existence of sex and found it both horrifying and fascinating. The British are almost as bad, and this, too, seems a sign of underdevelopment.

This is not an easy subject to treat systematically, but there is the following natural three-way division: (1) Some forms of reticence have a social function, protecting us from one another and from undesirable collisions and hostile reactions. (2) Other forms of reticence have a personal function, protecting the inner life from a public exposure that would cause it to wither or would require too much distortion. (3) As a modification of both these forms of reticence, selective intimacy permits some interpersonal relations to be open to forms of exposure that are needed for the development of a complete life. No one but a maniac will express absolutely everything to anyone, but most of us need someone to whom we can express a good deal that we would not reveal to others.

There are also relations among these phenomena worth noting. For example, why are family gatherings often so exceptionally stifling? Perhaps it is because the social demands of reticence have to keep in check the expression of very strong feelings, and purely formal polite expression is unavailable as a cover because of the modern convention of familial intimacy. If the unexpressed is too powerful and too near the surface, the result can be a sense of total falsity. On the other hand, it can be important what spouses and lovers do not say to one another. The calculated preservation of reticence in the context of intimacy provides Henry James with some of his richest material.

III

The social dimension of reticence and nonacknowledgment is most developed in forms of politeness and deference. We don't want to tell people what we think of them, and we don't want to hear from them what they think of us, though we are happy to surmise their thoughts and feelings and to have them surmise ours, at least up to a point. We don't, if we are reasonable, worry too much about what they may say about us behind our backs, just as we often say things about a third party that

we wouldn't say to his face. Since everyone participates in these practices, they aren't, or shouldn't be, deceptive. Deception is another matter, and sometimes we have reason to object to it, though sometimes we
have no business knowing the truth, even about how someone really
feels about us.

The distinction between mendacity and politeness is blurry, in part
because the listener contributes as much to the formation of the resulting belief as does the speaker, in part because the deceptiveness of any
particular utterance depends on its relation to a wider context of similar
utterances. A visitor to a society whose conventions he does not understand may be deceived if he takes people's performance at face value—
the friendliness of the Americans, the self-abnegation of the Japanese,
the equanimity of the English. Sensitivity to context also operates at the
individual level. Indeed, if someone consistently and flagrantly fails to
tell the truth, he loses the capacity to deceive and becomes paradoxically
less dishonest than someone who preserves a general reputation for
probity or candor and uses it to deceive only on rare occasions. (People
who don't wish to be believed, and who cultivate a reputation for unre-
liability, are not so rare as you might think; the strategy must have its
usefulness.)

What is the point of this vast charade? The answer will differ from
culture to culture, but I believe that the conventions of reticence result
from a kind of implicit social contract, one that, of course, reflects the relations of power among elements of the culture but that serves to some
degree (though unequally) the interests of all—as social conventions
tend to do. An unequal society will have strong conventions of deference to and perhaps flattery of superiors, which presumably do not deceive the well placed into thinking their subordinates admire them, except with the aid of self-deception. My interest, however, is in the design
of conventions governing the give and take among rough social equals
and the influence that a generally egalitarian social ideal should have on
conventions of reticence and acknowledgment. Does equality support
greater exposure or not? One might think a priori that in the absence of
strong hierarchies, we could all afford to tell each other what we think
and show what we feel; but things are not so simple. Although an egalitarian culture can be quite outspoken (this seems to be true of Israel), it
need not be, and I believe there is much to be said for the essentially liberal, rather than communitarian, system whereby equality does not
mean that we share our inner lives, bare our souls, and give voice to all
our opinions—in other words, become like one huge unhappy family.
The real issue is how much of each person's life is everybody else's business, and that is not settled by a conception of equality alone. Equality
can be combined with greater or lesser scope for privacy, lesser or
greater invasion of personal space by the public domain.

What, then, is the social function of acknowledgment or nonacknowledgment with respect to things that are already common knowledge? I believe the answer is this: The essential function of the boundary between what is acknowledged and what is not is to admit or decline to admit potentially significant material into the category of what must be taken into consideration and responded to *collectively* by all parties in the joint enterprise of discourse, action, and justification that proceeds between individuals whenever they come into contact. If something is not acknowledged, then even if it is universally known it can be left out of consideration in the collective social process, though it may play an important role separately in the private deliberations of the individual participants. Without such traffic control, any encounter might turn into a collision.

For example, A and B meet at a cocktail party; A has recently published an unfavorable review of B's latest book, but neither of them alludes to this fact, and they speak, perhaps a bit stiffly, about real estate, their recent travels, or some political development that interests them both. Consider the alternative:

B: You son of a bitch, I bet you didn't even read my book, you're too dimwitted to understand it even if you had read it, and besides you're clearly out to get me, dripping with envy and spite. If you weren't so overweight I'd throw you out the window.

A: You conceited fraud, I handled you with kid gloves in that review; if I'd said what I really thought it would have been unprintable; the book made me want to throw up—and it's by far your best.

At the same party C and D meet. D is a candidate for a job in C's department, and C is transfixed by D's beautiful breasts. They exchange judicious opinions about a recent publication by someone else. Consider the alternative:

C: Groan. . . .

D: Take your eyes off me, you dandruff-covered creep; how such a drooling incompetent can have got tenure, let alone become a department chair, is beyond me.

The trouble with the alternatives is that they lead to a dead end, because they demand engagement on terrain where common ground is unavailable without great effort, and only conflict will result. If C expresses his admiration of D's breasts, C and D have to deal with it as a common problem or feature of the situation, and their social relation must proceed in its light. If, on the other hand, it is just something that C feels and that D knows, from long experience and subtle signs, that he feels, then it can simply be left out of the basis of their joint activity of conversation, even while it operates separately in the background for each of them as a factor in their private thoughts.

What is allowed to become public and what is kept private in any given transaction will depend on what needs to be taken into collective consideration for the purposes of the transaction and what would, on the contrary, disrupt it if introduced into the public space. That doesn't mean that nothing will become public that is a potential source of conflict, because it is the purpose of many transactions to allow conflicts to surface so that they can be dealt with and either collectively resolved or revealed as unresolvable. But if the conventions of reticence are well designed, material will be excluded if the demand for a collective or public reaction to it would interfere with the purpose of the encounter.

In a society with a low tolerance for conflict, not only personal comments but also all controversial subjects, such as politics, money, or religion, will be taboo in social conversation, necessitating the development of a form of conversational wit that doesn't depend on the exchange of opinions. In our present subculture, however, there is considerable latitude for the airing of disagreements and controversy of a general kind, which can be pursued at length, and the most important area of nonacknowledgment is the personal—people's feelings about themselves and about others. It is impolite to draw attention to one's achievements or to express personal insecurity, envy, the fear of death, or strong feelings about those present, except in a context of intimacy in which these subjects can be taken up and pursued. Embarrassing silence is the usual sign that these rules have been broken. Someone says or does something to which there is no collectively acceptable response, so that the ordinary flow of public discourse that usually veils the unruly inner lives of the participants has no natural continuation. Silence, then, makes everything visible, unless someone with exceptional tact rescues the situation:

A: Did you see in the news this morning that X has just won the Nobel prize?

B: I wouldn't accept the Nobel Prize even if they offered it to me.

C: Yes, it's all so political, isn't it? To think that even Nabokov. . . .

In a civilization with a certain degree of maturity people know what needs to be brought out into the open, where it can be considered jointly or collectively, and what should be left to the idiosyncratic, individual responses of each of us. This is the cultural recognition of the complexity of life and of the great variety of essentially ununifiable worlds in which we live. It is the microscopic social analogue of that large-scale acceptance of pluralism that is so important an aspect of political liberalism. We do not have to deal with the full truth about our feelings and opinions in order to interact usefully and effectively: In many respects each of us can carry on with our personal fantasies and attitudes and with our private reactions to what we know about the private reactions of others, while at the same time dealing with one another on a fairly well-defined, limited field of encounter with regard to those matters that demand a more collective reaction.

The liberal idea, in society and culture as in politics, is that no more should be subjected to the demands of public response than is necessary for the requirements of collective life. How much this is will depend on the company and the circumstances. But the idea that everything is fair game and that life is always improved by more exposure, more frankness, and more consensus is a serious mistake. The attempt to impose it leads, moreover, to the kind of defensive hypocrisy and mendacity about one's true feelings that is made unnecessary by a regime of reticence. If your impure or hostile or politically disaffected thoughts are everyone's business, you will have reason to express pure and benevolent and patriotic ones instead. Again, we can see this economy at work in our present circumstances: The decline of privacy brings on the rise of hypocrisy.

Reticence can play an enabling role at every level of interaction, from the most formal to the most intimate. When Maggie in *The Golden Bowl* lets the Prince, her husband, know that she knows everything, by letting him see the broken bowl and describing her encounter with the antiquary from whom she has bought it, they still do not explicitly discuss the Prince's affair with her stepmother, Charlotte. They do not "have it out," as would perhaps have been more likely in a novel written fifty or a hundred years later; the reason is that they both know that they cannot arrive at a common, shared attitude or response to this history. If their uncombinable individual feelings about it are to enable them to go on together, those feelings will have to remain unexpressed, and their intimacy will have to be reconstructed at a shared higher layer of privacy, beneath which deeper individual privacies are permitted to continue to exist. Maggie imagines what lies behind her husband's silence after she lets him know that she knows:

> [T]hough he had, in so almost mystifying a manner, replied to nothing, denied nothing, explained nothing, apologized for nothing, he had somehow conveyed to her that this was not because of any determination to treat her case as not "worth" it . . . she had imagined him positively proposing to her a temporary accommodation. It had been but the matter of something in the depths of the eyes he finally fixed upon her, and she had found in it, the more she kept it before her, the tacitly offered sketch of a working

arrangement. "Leave me my reserve; don't question it—it's all I have just now, don't you see? So that, if you'll make me the concession of letting me alone with it for as long a time as I require I promise you something or other, grown under the cover of it, even though I don't yet quite make out what, as a return for your patience." She had turned away from him with some such unspoken words as that in her ear, and indeed she *had* to represent to herself that she had spritually heard them, had to listen to them still again, to explain her particular patience in face of his particular failure.[4]

It is not enough that the affair should not be acknowledged among all four of the concerned parties—something that would be hard to imagine even in a novel written today. It is essential that it should not be taken up, though known and mutually known to be known, between Maggie and the Prince. If they were really together *faced* with it, if it were out there on the table between them, demanding some kind of joint response, the manifestation of their reactions would lead to a direct collision, filled with reproaches and counterreproaches, guilt and defiance, anger, pity, humiliation, and shame, which their intimacy would not survive. By leaving a great deal unsaid, they can go on without having to arrive together at a resolution of this extreme passage in their lives—without the Prince having either to justify or to condemn himself, and without Maggie having either to condemn or to excuse him.

What we can tolerate having out in the open between us depends on what we think we can handle jointly without crippling our relations for other purposes. Sometimes the only way to find out is to try, particularly when an unacknowledged fact threatens to be crippling in any case. In general it's not a bad idea to stick with the conventions of reticence and to avoid overloading the field of interaction with excess emotional and normative baggage. But sometimes politeness excludes material that, though disruptive, is relevant and whose exclusion affects the results, often in a consistent direction. This is the kind of case in which deliberate obstreperousness can make a difference, as a form of consciousness-raising. Politeness is also a disadvantage when one party to a situation takes advantage of the conventions of mutual restraint to make excessive claims whose excessiveness he knows cannot be publicly pointed out without impoliteness. Politeness leaves us with few weapons against grasping selfishness except exclusion from the society, and that is not always an available option.

It is possible to imagine things being arranged differently, with greater frankness nevertheless not causing social breakdown. But this

4. Henry James, *The Golden Bowl* (1904; New York: Penguin Modern Classics, 1966), chap. 35, p. 448.

would require that people not take up disagreements or criticisms when they surface, and just let them lie there unpursued. It seems more efficient to make explicit acknowledgment function as a signal that something must be collectively dealt with. The likely significance of greater frankness would be that one was in a society of busybodies, who thought everything an individual did was the community's business and that the opinions of others had to be taken into account at every turn. Although this may be necessary in certain extreme circumstances, the more desirable development, as social arrangements come to function smoothly, is to permit different tracks of decision and discourse, from most public to most private, with the former requiring no more than the input strictly needed for the purpose and the latter (finally, the individual's purely individual inner life) taking everything on board and perhaps even expanding to admit material lurking in the unconscious.

This last is a particularly important aspect of a culture of selective reticence: It permits the individual to acknowledge *to himself* a great deal that is not publicly acceptable and to know that others have similar skeletons in their mental closets. Without reticence, repression—concealment even from the self—is more needed as an element in the civilizing process. If everything has to be avowed, what does not fit the acceptable public persona will tend to be internally denied. One of Freud's contributions, by analyzing the process of internal censorship, is to have made it less necessary.

IV

The public-private boundary faces in two directions—keeping disruptive material out of the public arena and protecting private life from the crippling effects of the external gaze. I have been concentrating on the first, social function of reticence and nonacknowledgment. I now turn to the second.

It is very important for human freedom that individuals should not be merely social or political beings. While participation in the public world may be one aspect of human flourishing, and may dominate the lives of certain individuals, it is one of the advantages of large, modern societies that they do not impose a public role on most of their members:

> Since the liberty we need is different from that of the ancients, it needs a different organization from that which suited ancient liberty. In the latter, the more time and energy man dedicated to the exercise of his political rights, the freer he thought himself; in the kind of liberty to which we are drawn, the more time the exercise of political rights leaves us for our private interests, the more precious liberty will be to us.

Hence, the need for the representative system. The representative system is nothing but an organization by means of which a nation charges a few individuals to do what it cannot or does not wish to do itself. Poor men look after their own affairs; rich men hire stewards.[5]

And the inner life, in all its immense variety, requires a social protection of pluralism that can be effective only if much of what is idiosyncratic to the inner fantasies and obsessions and personal relations of individuals remains out of sight.

But it isn't just pluralism that demands privacy. Humans are, so far as I know, the only animals that suffer from self-consciousness—in the ordinary sense, that is, inhibition and embarrassment brought on by the thought that others are watching them. Humans are the only animals that don't as a rule copulate in public. And humans clothe themselves, in one way or another, even if it is only with paint, offering a self-presentation rather than their nakedness to the public gaze. The awareness of how one appears from outside is a constant of human life, sometimes burdensome, sometimes an indispensable resource. But there are aspects of life that require us to be free of it so that we may live and react entirely from the inside. They include sexual life in its most unconstrained form and the more extreme aspects of emotional life—fundamental anxieties about oneself, fear of death, personal rage, remorse, and grief. All these have muted public forms, and sometimes, as with collective grief, they serve an important function for the inner life, but the full private reality needs protection—not primarily from the knowledge but from the direct perception of others.

Why should the direct gaze of others be so damaging, even if what is seen is something already known and not objectionable? If newspapers all over the country published nude photographs of a political candidate, it would be difficult for him to continue with the campaign even if no one could charge him with any fault. The intrusive desire to see people in extremis with their surface stripped away is the other side of the human need for protection from such exposure.

In some respects what is hidden and what is not may be arbitrary. We eat in public and excrete in private, but the obvious fantasy of a reversal of these natural functions is memorably brought to life in Bunuel's film *The Discreet Charm of the Bourgeoisie*. I am also reminded of this rather chilling passage from Gide. He and his wife are in a restaurant in Rome:

5. Benjamin Constant, "De la Liberté des Anciens Comparée a celle des Modernes," *De la liberté chez les modernes: Ecrits politiques* (Paris: Livres de Poche, [1819] 1980) pp. 511–12.

We had barely sat down when there entered a majestic old gentle-
man whose admirable face was set off by a halo of white hair. A bit
short perhaps; but his entire being breathed nobility, intelligence,
serenity. He seemed to see no one; all the waiters in the restaurant
bowed as he passed. The maitre d'hotel hastened to the table
where the Olympian had seated himself; took the order; but re-
turned twice more when summoned, to listen with respect to I
know not what further instructions. Evidently the guest was
someone illustrious. We hardly took our eyes off him and could
observe, as soon as he had the menu in his hands, an extraordinary
alteration in the features of that beautiful face. While placing his
order, he had become a simple mortal. Then, immobile and as if set
in stone, without any sign of impatience, his face had become completely expressionless. He came to life again only when the dish he
had ordered was put before him, and he took leave immediately of
his nobility, his dignity, everything that marked his superiority to
other men. One would have thought that Circe had touched him
with her magic wand. He no longer gave the impression, I don't
say merely of nobility, but even of simple humanity. He bent over
his plate and one couldn't say that he began to eat: He guzzled, like
a glutton, like a pig. It was Carducci.[6]

Learning to eat in a way that others can witness without disgust is one of
our earliest tasks, along with toilet training. Human beings are elaborate
constructions on an animal foundation that always remains part of us.
Most of us can put up with being observed while we eat. But sex and extreme emotion are different.

Ordinary mortals must often wonder how porn stars can manage it.
Perhaps they are people for whom the awareness of being watched is
itself erotic. But most of us, when sexually engaged, do not wish to
be seen by anyone but our partners; full sexual expression and release
leave us entirely vulnerable and without a publicly presentable "face."
Sex transgresses these protective boundaries, breaks us open, and exposes the uncontrolled and unpresentable creature underneath; that is
its essence. We need privacy in order not to have to integrate our sexuality in its fullest expression with the controlled surface we present to the
world. And in general we need privacy to be allowed to conduct ourselves in extremis in a way that serves purely individual demands, the
demands of strong personal emotion.

The public gaze is inhibiting because, except for infants and psy-
chopaths, it brings into effect expressive constraints and requirements of

6. André Gide, *Ainsi Soit-Il* (Paris: Gallimard, 1952), pp. 49–50. The Italian poet and
critic Giosuè Carducci was awarded the Nobel Prize for Literature in 1906.

self-presentation that are strongly incompatible with the natural expression of strong or intimate feeling. And it presents us with a demand to justify ourselves before others that we cannot meet for those things that we cannot put a good face on. The management of one's inner life and one's private demons is a personal task and should not be made to answer to standards broader than necessary. It is the other face of the coin: The public-private boundary keeps the public domain free of disruptive material; but it also keeps the private domain free of insupportable controls. The more we are subjected to public inspection and asked to expose our inner lives, the more the resources available to us in leading those lives will be constrained by the collective norms of the common milieu. Or else we will partially protect our privacy by lying; but if this, too, becomes a social norm, it is likely to create people who also lie to themselves, since everyone will have been lying to them about themselves since childhood.

Still, there is a space between what is open to public view and what people keep to themselves. The veil can be partly lifted to admit certain others, without the inhibiting effect of general exposure. This brings us to the topic of intimacy. Interpersonal spheres of privacy protected from the public gaze are essential for human emotional and sexual life, and I have already said a good deal about this under the heading of individual privacy: Certain forms of exposure to particular others are incompatible with the preservation of a public face.

But intimacy also plays an important part in the development of an articulate inner life, because it permits one to explore unpublic feelings in something other than solitude and to learn about the comparable feelings of one's intimates, including to a degree their feelings toward oneself. Intimacy in its various forms is a partial lifting of the usual veil of reticence. It provides the indispensable setting for certain types of relations, as well as a relief from the strains of public demeanor, which can grow burdensome however habitual it has become. The couple returning home after a social evening will let off steam by expressing to one another the unsociable reactions to their fellow guests that could not be given voice at the time. And it is quite generally useful to be able to express to someone else what cannot be expressed directly to the person concerned—including the things that you may find difficult to bear about some of your closest friends and relations.

Intimacy develops naturally between friends and lovers, but the chief social and legal formalization of intimacy is marriage in its modern bourgeois form. Of course it serves economic and generational purposes as well, but it does provide a special protection for sexual privacy. The conventions of nonacknowledgment that it puts into force have to be particularly effective to leave outside the boundary children living in the same household, who are supposed not to have to think about the sex lives of their parents.

Marriage in the fairly recent past sanctioned and in a curious way concealed sexual activity that was condemned and made more visible outside of it. What went on in bed between husband and wife was not a fit topic for comment or even thought by outsiders. It was exempt from the general prurience that made intimations of adultery or premarital sex so thrilling in American movies of the 1950s—a time when the production code required that married couples always occupy twin beds. Those who felt the transgressive character of even heterosexual married sex could still get reassurance from the thought that it was within a boundary beyond which lay the things that were *really* unacceptable—where everything is turned loose and no holds are barred.

We are now in a more relaxed sexual atmosphere than formerly, but sex remains in essence a form of transgression, in which we take each other apart and disarrange or abandon more than our clothes. The availability of an officially sanctioned and protected form of such transgression, distinguished from other forms that are not sanctioned, plays a significant role in the organization of sexual life. What is permitted is for some people still essentially defined and protected from shame by a contrast with what is forbidden. While the boundaries change, many people still seem to feel the need to think of themselves as sexually "normal," and this requires a contrast. Although premarital sex is by now widely accepted, the institution of heterosexual marriage probably confers a derivative blessing on heterosexual partnerships of all kinds. That is why the idea of homosexual marriage produces so much alarm: It threatens to remove that contrastive protection by turning marriage into a license for anyone to do anything with anybody. There is a genuine conflict here, but it seems to me that the right direction of development is not to expand marriage but to extend the informal protection of intimacy without the need for secrecy to a broader range of sexual relations and to provide robust legal and financial rights to unmarried couples of whatever sex, as has been done in several European countries.

The respect for intimacy and its protection from prurient violation is a useful cultural resource. One sign of our contemporary loss of a sense of the value of privacy is the biographical ruthlessness shown toward public figures of all kinds—not only politicians but also writers, artists, and scientists. It is obligatory for a biographer to find out everything possible about such an individual's intimate personal life, as if he had forfeited all rights over it by becoming famous. Perhaps after enough time has passed, the intrusion will be muted by distance, but with people whose lives have overlapped with ours, there is something excruciating about all this exposure, something wrong with our now having access to Bertrand Russell's desperate love letters, Wittgenstein's agonized expressions of self-hatred, and Einstein's marital difficulties. A creative individual externalizes the best part of himself, producing with incredible effort something better than he is, which can float free of its creator and have a finer existence of its own. But the general admiration for these works seems to nourish a desire to uncover all the dirt about their creators, as if we could possess them more fully by reattaching them to the messy source from which they arose—and perhaps even feel a bit superior. Why not just acknowledge in general terms that we are all human and that greatness is necessarily always partial?

V

After this rather picaresque survey of the territory, let me turn, finally, to normative questions about how the public-private boundary or boundaries should be managed in a pluralistic culture. Those of us who are not political communitarians want to leave each other some space. Some subgroups may wish to use that space to form more intrusive communities whose members leave each other much less space, but the broadest governing norms of publicity and privacy should impose a regime of public restraint and private protection that is compatible with a wide range of individual variation in the inner and intimate life. The conventions that control these boundaries, although not enforced in the same way as laws and judicial decisions, are nevertheless imposed on the individual members of a society, whose lives are shaped by them. They therefore pose questions of justifiability, if not legitimacy. We need to figure out what conventions could justifiably command general acceptance in a society as diverse as ours.

My main point is a conservative one: that we should try to avoid fights over the public space that force into it more than it can contain without the destruction of civility. I say "try," because sometimes this will not be possible, and sometimes starting a cultural war is preferable to preserving civility and the status quo. But I believe that the tendency to "publicize" (this being the opposite of "privatize") certain types of conflict has not been a good thing and that we would be better off if more things were regarded as none of the public's business.

This position could be called cultural liberalism, since it extends the liberal respect for pluralism into the fluid domain of public culture. It is opposed not only to the kind of repressive intolerance of private unconventionality usually associated with conservative cultures. It is opposed also to the kind of control attempted through the imposition of any orthodoxy of professed allegiance—the second best for those who would impose thought control if they could. I do not think the vogue for political correctness is a trivial matter. It represents a strong antiliberal current on the left, the continuation of a long tradition, which is only in part counterbalanced by the even older antiliberalism of the right.

This is the subject of endless fulminations by unsavory characters, but that doesn't make it illegitimate as an object of concern. It shouldn't be just a right-wing issue. The demand for public lip-service to certain pieties and vigilance against telltale signs in speech of unacceptable attitudes or beliefs is due to an insistence that deep cultural conflicts should not simply be tolerated but must be turned into battles for control of the common social space.

The reason this is part of the same topic as our main theme of reticence and concealment is that it involves one of the most effective forms of invasion of privacy—the demand that everyone stand up and be counted. New symbols of allegiance are introduced and suddenly you either have to show the flag or reveal yourself as an enemy of progress. In a way, the campaign against the neutral use of the masculine pronoun, the constant replacement of names for racial groups, and all the other euphemisms are more comic than anything else, but they are also part of an unhealthy social climate, not so distant from the climate that requires demonstrations of patriotism in periods of xenophobia. To some extent it is possible to exercise collective power over people's inner lives by controlling the conventions of expression, not by legal coercion but by social pressure. At its worst, this climate demands that people say what they do not believe in order to demonstrate their commitment to the right side—dishonesty being the ultimate tribute that individual pride can offer to something higher.

The attempt to control public space is importantly an attempt to control the cultural and ideological environment in which young people are formed. Forty years ago the public pieties were patriotic and anticommunist; now they are multicultural and feminist. What concerns me is not the content but the character of this kind of control: Its effect is to make it difficult to breathe, because the atmosphere is so thick with significance and falsity. And the atmosphere of falsity is independent of the truth or falsity of the orthodoxy being imposed. It may be entirely true, but if it is presented as what one is supposed to believe and publicly affirm if one is on the right side, it becomes a form of mental suffocation.

Those who favor the badges of correctness believe that it is salutary if the forms of discourse and the examples chosen serve as reminders that women and members of minorities can be successful doctors, lawyers, scientists, soldiers, and so on. They also favor forms for the designation of oppressed or formerly oppressed groups that express, in the eyes of members of those groups, an appropriate respect. But all this is dreadfully phony and, I think, counterproductive. It should be possible to address or refer to people without expressing either respect or disrespect for their race and to talk about law without inserting constant little reminders that women can be judges. And it ought to be possible to carry out one's responsibilities in the role of a teacher of English or philosophy or physics without at the same time advancing the cause of racial or sexual equality or engaging in social consciousness-raising.

The avoidance of what is offensive is one thing; the requirement to include visible signals of respect and correct opinion is another. It is like
pasting an American flag on your rear windshield. We used to have a
genuinely neutral way of talking, but the current system forces everyone to decide, one way or the other, whether to conform to the pattern
that is contending for orthodoxy—so everyone is forced to express
more, in one direction or another, than should be necessary for the purposes of communication, education, or whatever. One has to either go
along with it or resist, and there is no good reason to force that choice on
people just by virtue of their being speakers of the language—no reason
to demand external signs of inner conformity. In the abyss at the far end
of the same road, one finds anticommunist loyalty oaths for teachers or
civil servants and declarations of solidarity with the workers and peasants in the antifascist and anti-imperialist struggle.

The radical response to orthodoxy is to smash it and dump the pieces
into the dustbin of history. The liberal alternative does not depend on
the defeat of one orthodoxy by another—not even a multicultural orthodoxy. Liberalism should favor the avoidance of forced choices and tests
of purity and the substitution of a certain reticence behind which potentially disruptive disagreements can persist without breaking into the
open and without requiring anyone to lie. The disagreements needn't be
a secret—they can just remain quiescent. In my version, the liberal ideal
is not content with the legal protection of free speech for fascists but also
includes a social environment in which fascists can keep their counsel if
they choose.

I suspect that this refusal to force the issue unless it becomes necessary is what many people hate about liberalism. But even if one finds it
attractive as an ideal, there is a problem of getting there from a situation
of imposed orthodoxy without engaging in a bit of revolutionary
smashing along the way. It is not easy to avoid battles over the public
terrain that end up reducing the scope of the private unnecessarily. Genuine pluralism is difficult to achieve.

The recent sexual revolution is an instructive case. The fairly puritanical climate of the 1950s and early 1960s was displaced not by a tacit admission of sexual pluralism and withdrawal of the enforcement of orthodoxy but by a frontal public attack, so that explicit sexual images and
language and open extramarital cohabitation and homosexuality became part of everyday life. Unfortunately this was apparently inseparable from an ideology of sexual expressiveness that made the character of
everyone's sexual inner life a matter of public interest and something
that one could be expected to reveal. This is undesirable, in fact, because
sexual attitudes are not universally compatible, and the deepest desires
and fantasies of some are inevitably offensive to others.

Not only that, but sex has unequal importance to different people. It
is now embarrassing for anyone to admit that he doesn't care much

about sex—as it was forty years ago embarrassing to admit that sex was the most important thing in one's life—but both things are true of many people, and I suspect that it has always been so. The current public understanding, like that of the past, is an imposition on those whom it does not fit.

We should stop trying to achieve a common understanding in this area and leave people to their mutual incomprehension, under the cover of conventions of reticence. We should also leave people their privacy, which is so essential for the protection of inner freedom from the stifling effect of the demands of face. I began by referring to contemporary prurience about political figures. President Clinton seems to have survived it so far,[7] but the press remains committed to satisfying the curiosity of the most childish elements of the public. Outside of politics, the recent discharge of a woman pilot for adultery and then the disqualification of a candidate for chairmanship of the Joint Chiefs of Staff on grounds of "adultery" committed thirteen years ago while separated from his wife, on the way to a divorce, are ridiculous episodes. The insistence by defenders of the woman that the man also be punished just to preserve equal treatment was morally obtuse: If it was wrong to punish her, it was also wrong to penalize him.

A more inflammatory case: Clarence Thomas's nomination to the Supreme Court could have been legitimately rejected by the Senate on grounds of competence and judicial philosophy, but I believe the challenge on the basis of his sexual victimization of Anita Hill was quite unjustified, even though I'm sure it was all true. At the time I was ambivalent; like a lot of people, I would have been glad to see Thomas rejected for any reason. But that is no excuse for abandoning the private-public distinction: This sort of bad personal conduct is completely irrelevant to the occupation of a position of public trust, and if the press hadn't made an issue of it, the Senate Judiciary Committee might have been able to ignore the rumors. There was no evidence that Thomas didn't believe in the equal rights of women. It is true that Hill was his professional subordinate, but his essential fault was being personally crude and offensive: It was no more relevant than would have been a true charge of serious maltreatment from his ex-wife.

But consider the situation we are in: The *only* way to avoid damage to someone's reputation by facts of this kind, in spite of their irrelevance to qualification for public office, is through a powerful convention of nonacknowledgment. If this is rejected as a form of male mutual self-protection, then we are stuck with masses of irrelevant and titillating material that clog up our public life and the procedures for selection of public officials and shrink the pool of willing and viable candidates for

7. This was written before the Lewinsky scandal broke. He survived that, too, but barely.

responsible positions. I'm not objecting to the regulation of conduct at the individual level. It is a good thing that sexual coercion of an employee or a student should be legally actionable and that the transgression of civilized norms should be an occasion for personal rebuke. What is unfortunate is the expansion of control beyond this by a broadening of the conception of sexual harrassment to include all forms of unwelcome or objectionable sexual attention and the increasingly vigilant enforcement of expressive taboos. Too much in the personal conduct of individuals is being made a matter for public censure, either legally or through the force of powerful social norms. As Mill pointed out in *On Liberty*, the power of public opinion can be as effective an instrument of coercion as law in an intrusive society.

Formerly the efforts to impose orthodoxy in the public sphere and to pry into the private came primarily from the forces of political and social conservatism; now they come from all directions, resulting in a battle for control that no one is going to win. We have undergone a genuine and very salutary cultural revolution over the past thirty years. There has been an increase in what people can do in private without losing their jobs or going to jail, and a decrease in arbitrary exercises of power and inequality of treatment. There is more tolerance of plurality in forms of life. But revolution breeds counterrevolution, and it is a good idea to leave the public space of a society comfortably habitable, without too much conflict, by the main incompatible elements that are not about to disappear.

Before the current period we had nearly achieved this in the area of religion. Although national political candidates were expected to identify themselves as belonging to some religion or other, loud professions of faith were not expected, and it was considered very poor form to criticize someone's religion. In fact, there was no shortage of silent anticlericalism and silent hostility between communicants of different religions in the United States, but a general blanket of mutual politeness muffled all public utterance on the subject. The political activism of the religious right has changed all that, and it is part of the conservative backlash against the sexual revolution. We would be better off if we could somehow restore a state of truce, behind which healthy mutual contempt could flourish in its customary way.

There are enough issues that have to be fought out in the public sphere, issues of justice, of economics, of security, of defense, of the definition and protection of public goods. We should try to avoid forcing the effort to reach collective decisions or dominant results when we don't have to. Privacy supports plurality by eliminating the need for collective choice or an official public stance. I believe the presence of a deeply conservative religious and cultural segment of American society can be expected to continue and should be accommodated by those who are radically out of sympathy with it—not in the inevitable conflicts over central political issues, but in regard to how much of the public space will be subjected to cultural contestation. We owe it to one another to want the public space to preserve a character neutral enough to allow those from whom we differ radically to inhabit it comfortably—and that means a culture that is publicly reticent, if possible, and not just tolerant of diversity. Pluralism and privacy should be protected not only against legal interference but also, more informally, against the invasiveness of a public culture that insists on settling too many questions.

The natural objection to this elevation of reticence is that it is too protective of the status quo and that it gives a kind of cultural veto to conservative forces who will resent any disruption. Those who favor confrontation and invasion of privacy think it necessary to overthrow pernicious conventions like the double standard of sexual conduct and the unmentionability of homosexuality. To attack harmful prejudices, it is necessary to give offense by overturning the conventions of reticence that help to support them.

Against this, my position is in a sense conservative, though it is motivated by liberal principles. While we should insist on the protection of individual rights of personal freedom, I believe we should not insist on confrontation in the public space over different attitudes about the conduct of personal life. To the extent possible, and the extent compatible with the protection of private rights, it would be better if these battles for the soul of the culture were avoided and no collective response required. Best would be a regime of private freedom combined with public or collective neutrality.

The old liberal distinction between toleration and endorsement may be applicable here. One case in which I think it supports restraint is the issue of public support for the arts. Even though art that is extremely offensive to many people should certainly not be censored, it is entirely reasonable to withhold public financial support from the more extreme productions of Robert Mapplethorpe, Andres Serrano, and Karen Finley. Even when the allocation of public funds is delegated to experts, there has to be some rough political consensus in the background about the kind of thing that is worthy of government support, and it is inappropriate to storm the barricades by insisting that the National Endowment for the Arts repudiate that consensus. The trouble with public support is that it increases the importance of public agreement in artistic domains where individualistic pluralism is essential. The consequence may be unexpected, but the liberal defense of the public-private boundary should not be limited to cases that favor broader liberal sympathies.

What I have offered is not legal analysis but social criticism—trying to describe desirable and undesirable ways of handling the conflicts that pervade our society through conventions of reticence and acknowledgement and management of the limited and easily disrupted public space in which we must encounter all those with whom we may differ profoundly. It is an anticommunitarian vision of civility. And it is entirely compatible with the strict protection of the individual rights of persons to violate the conditions of civility in the context of collective political deliberation, that is, a strong legal protection of freedom of expression.[8] Finally, the same public-private division that tries to avoid unnecessary clashes in the public sphere leaves room for the legal protection of enormous variety in the private, from pornography to religious millenarianism. It is wonderful how much disagreement and mutual incomprehension a liberal society can contain in solution without falling to pieces, provided we are careful about what issues we insist on facing collectively.

Communitarianism—the ambition of collective self-realization—is one of the most persistent threats to the human spirit. The debate over its political manifestations has been sustained and serious. But it is also a cultural issue, one whose relation to the values of political liberalism has been clouded by the fact that some of those values seem such natural candidates for collective public promotion. My claim has been that liberals should not be fighting for control of the culture—that they should embrace a form of cultural restraint comparable to that which governs the liberal attitude to law—and that this is the largest conception of the value of privacy. No one should be in control of the culture, and the persistence of private racism, sexism, homophobia, religious and ethnic bigotry, sexual puritanism, and other such private pleasures should not provoke liberals to demand constant public affirmation of the opposite values. The important battles are about how people are required to treat each other, how social and economic institutions are to be arranged, and how public resources are to be used. The insistence on securing more agreement in attitudes than we need for these purposes, and on including more of the inner life in the purview of even informal public authority, just raises the social stakes unnecessarily.

---

8. See Robert C. Post, *Constitutional Domains* (Cambridge, Mass.: Harvard University Press, 1995), pp. 146–47, on what he calls the "paradox of public discourse"—that the law may not be used to enforce the civility rules that make rational deliberation possible.

2

The Shredding of Public Privacy

The shameful farce now being played out in Washington[1] has many contributing causes: the Supreme Court, which refused to permit the Paula Jones lawsuit to be deferred until the end of President Clinton's term in office; the panel of federal judges in Washington that approved Kenneth Starr's request to extend his Whitewater investigation to the president's sex life; the sinister and obsessionally puritanical Starr himself and the independent prosecutor statute that created his almost limitless power to persecute the president; the lurid and poisonous Linda Tripp; the fetishistic and infantile Monica Lewinsky; and the president himself, for falling on this land mine disguised as a cream puff.

But it is also the culmination of a disastrous erosion of the precious but fragile conventions of personal privacy in the United States over the past ten or twenty years. If the president and Miss Lewinsky really had sex in the White House, the only decent thing for them to do if anybody asked was to deny it, as they initially did. But they are not going to be permitted this elementary form of privacy because the machinery of the law is being used to shred every ordinary boundary between matters of public concern and matters that are the business of no one but the parties involved, in the name of the ostensible value to the nation of getting at The Truth. Not only Republican senators but sanctimonious editorial writers at the *New York Times* are urging the president to bare his soul to avoid impeachment. No doubt if the FBI finds semen on Monica's dress, the *Times* will insist that he provide a DNA sample.

1. This article was published on August 14, 1998, just before President Clinton's appearance before the grand jury.

It is hard to believe that anyone thinks this condition of total publicity is better for the country than the situation that prevailed a generation ago, when President Kennedy's sexual adventurism was known about but not acknowledged by the press. By 1987, when Gary Hart was staked out and exposed as an adulterer by the *Miami Herald* and expelled from politics, those habits of discretion had disappeared. From then on politicians and aspirants to high office had no rights of privacy in the United States, and every sexual irregularity became part of what the press deemed it the public's right to know about such people. Some of them survived the exposure. Clarence Thomas was appointed to the Supreme Court in 1991 in spite of credible charges of lewd and disgraceful behavior toward Anita Hill. (I regret to say that at the time, like many liberals who opposed Thomas's nomination because of his right-wing views, I hoped those charges would sink him.) Clinton himself was nominated and elected in 1992 in spite of the stories about Gennifer Flowers. But whatever their immediate effect, these forms of exposure are in themselves very damaging to public life, and the fact that they have become commonplace shows that American society has lost its grip on a fundamental value, one that cannot be enforced by law alone but without which civilization would not survive.

The distinction between what an individual exposes to public view and what he conceals or exposes only to intimates is essential to permit creatures as complex as ourselves to interact without constant social breakdown. Each of our inner lives is such a jungle of thoughts, feelings, fantasies, and impulses that civilization would be impossible if we expressed them all or if we could all read each other's minds. The formation of a civilized adult requires a learned capacity to limit expression to what is acceptable in the relevant public forum and the development of a distinct inner and private life that can be much more uninhibited, under the protection of the public surface. Sex is an important part of what must be managed in this way if a civilized human being is to be constructed on the ever-present animal foundation, but aggression, fear, envy, self-absorption, and vanity all form part of the task.

The reason for these requirements is simple. Human beings are highly complex and very diverse; the full range of what any number of them feel, want, and think would not fit into a common space without generating uncontrollable conflict and offense. The public space of interaction in which these complex individuals meet, on the other hand, is single and limited. What they introduce into it has to be likewise limited to what can be collectively faced and dealt with without generating interpersonal chaos. Of course, there are different public spaces and different levels of acceptable conflict for different groups, but all operate under some form of traffic control to accommodate multiple individuals whose potential clashes and conflicts are limitless. This is the function of the familiar forms of tact, politeness, reticence, nonacknowledgment of embarrassing lapses, and so forth—none of which are dishonest because it is generally known how these conventions operate.

Just as social life would be impossible if we expressed all our lustful, agressive, greedy, anxious, or self-obsessed feelings in ordinary public encounters, so would inner life be impossible if we tried to become wholly persons whose thoughts, feelings, and private behavior could be safely exposed to public view. The division of the self protects the limited public space from unmanageable encroachment and the unruly inner life from excessive inhibition. The boundary shifts with the company, and intimacy is the situation in which the interior of the self is most exposed; but even between spouses or lovers there are limits.

What has happened in the United States is strange. On the one hand, tolerance for variation in sexual life has increased enormously since the 1960s. We have seen a true sexual revolution, and of course the publication of explicitly sexual materials in all media is part of it. On the other hand, the loosening of inhibitions has led to the collapse of protections of privacy for any figure in whose sexual life the public might take a prurient interest. What looked initially like a growth of freedom has culminated in the reinstitution of the public pillory.

The public space of politics is designed for the pursuit and resolution of important public issues. It cannot handle the added infusion of irrelevant and incendiary private matter that results when politicians are denied the right to present a merely public face. The growth of tolerance does not make the collapse of privacy significantly less damaging. First, there are still politically important elements of American society that abhor the new sexual mores. Second, and more important, the exposure of a public figure's private life is damaging even if most people rationally judge it to be irrelevant to his qualifications for office. It tends to blot out everything else in the dirty mind of the public. And it also constitutes a gross invasion of the individual's personal life, requiring him to respond, both internally and publicly, to the world's inappropriate but relentless attention to it.

One of the truly remarkable things about Clinton is his emotional toughness, even for a politician. Most people exposed to such humiliating treatment would be corroded by rage. But we can't limit the choice of political figures to those whose peculiar inner constitution enables them to withstand outrageous exposure or those whose sexual lives are simon pure. And we can't afford to require the families of public figures to put up with this sort of humiliation. We do not and should not know what private understanding Mr. and Mrs. Clinton have about sex, but the present glare on their relations is pitiless. If these are the costs of public office, the range of available candidates will shrink drastically for reasons having nothing to do with the proper demands of public service.

The note repeated again and again in the media, about the need for Americans to trust their leaders, and the damage done to that trust by a sexual lie, is simply nauseating.

The broad acceptance of conventions of civility, which determine what may be exposed or acknowledged in what contexts and what would on the contrary be uselessly disruptive or destructive, what is essential and what irrelevant to the performance or evaluation of a social role—that is the mark of maturity in a society. Civilization is a delicate structure that allows wildly different and complex individuals to cooperate peacefully and effectively only if not too much strain is put on it by the introduction of disruptive private material, to which no collective response is necessary or possible. Americans who recognize this fact can only look on in shame at the destructive spectacle now being acted out by a group of childish and powerful figures who have never understood it.

3

Personal Rights and Public Space

I

I was once at an international seminar devoted substantially to the discussion of individual rights, their moral basis, their boundaries, and their relation to other values, moral and political—the aim being to present recent developments in American political theory to interested parties from elsewhere. The Americans in the group were much concerned over such issues as freedom of expression for racists, access to pornography, affirmative action for women and minorities, and restrictions on abortion. After listening for a while to the admirably subtle discussion of these issues, some of the other participants began to grumble. They pointed out that in the countries they came from, there were no free elections, no free press, no protection against imprisonment or execution without trial or against torture by the police, no freedom of religion—or that their countries were threatened by radical religious movements that would quickly abolish such freedoms if they came to power. Why were we not talking about those things rather than these ridiculous issues of detail that were of no concern to them?

One could certainly understand their point of view. The philosophical interest of a question of human rights is not strictly proportional to its real-life importance. Or one might go further: Perhaps the subtle refinements that worry the inhabitants of liberal democracies in which the most basic protections of the individual are taken for granted do not even belong to the same subject. Is there any meaningful sense in which freedom from torture and freedom to rent pornographic videos both raise an issue of human rights? Is there really one subject or one moral concept here at all?

31

That is the topic I want to discuss. I would like to make a case for the view that, once we recognize the most basic human rights—the ones whose violation fills the reports of Amnesty International and the various Human Rights Watch committees and makes your flesh crawl—we are committed to taking seriously the sort of highly refined and subtle issue that can easily seem unreal to those who, for want of a fortunate political and legal system, cannot take the most basic rights for granted. This means that there is a connection between being opposed to torture, political imprisonment, censorship and dictatorship in China, or to the political and civil exclusion of women in Saudi Arabia, and being concerned about the control of pornography and the regulation of racist speech in the United States. The fact that here, having secured the canonical blessings of liberty to ourselves and our posterity, we have the luxury of arguing about fine distinctions in the definition and demarcation of individual rights does not mean that we are talking about a different subject.

My focus will be on the type of rights usually called negative—forms of freedom or discretion for each individual with which others, including the state, may not forcibly interfere. I believe that if we start with the basics, the fundamental human rights that over the past fifty years have begun to make such a large international impact—however much they may be resisted by the cynical appeals to cultural relativism with which authoritarian regimes defend the cruelties they use to stay in power—we will find that a fully developed understanding of those rights makes unavoidable the kinds of questions and disagreements that occupy Western liberals today. Contrary to the suggestion of the Declaration of Independence, rights are not self-evident: They require precise argument, definition, and adjustment, which will always give rise to controversy, and there is room for substantial disagreement and development in the details of their design.

One can be against the worst abuses—torture, summary execution or imprisonment, religious or racial persecution, censorship of political criticism—for various reasons: Their wrongness is morally overdetermined. But what does it mean to object to these common horrors as violations of universal human rights? I believe it has two implications. First, it means that these are forms of treatment to which no one should be subjected—that every person, everywhere, is wronged if maltreated in these ways. Second, it means that the wrong is not a function of the balance of costs and benefits in this case—that while in some cases a right may justifiably be overridden by a sufficiently high threshhold of costs, below that threshhold its status as a right is insensitive to differences in the cost-benefit balance of respecting it in each particular case. Rights are universal protections of every individual against being justifiably used or sacrificed in certain ways for purposes worthy or unworthy.

I believe it is most accurate to think of rights as aspects of *status*—part of what is involved in being a member of the moral community. The idea of rights expresses a particular conception of the kind of place that should be occupied by individuals in a moral system—how their lives, actions, and interests should be recognized by the system of justification and authorization that constitutes a morality. Moral status, as conferred by moral rights, is formally analogous to legal status, as conferred by legal rights, except that it is not contingent on social practices. It is a universal normative condition, consisting of what is permitted to be done to persons, what persons are permitted to do, what sorts of justifications are required for preventing them from doing what they want, and so forth.

Because this normative status is possessed by all persons or none, it is nonaggregative: It is not the kind of good that can be redistributed or increased in quantity. In fact, it can't even be created, though it can be recognized. The existence of moral rights does not depend on their political recognition or enforcement but rather on the moral question whether there is a decisive justification for including these forms of inviolability in the status of every member of the moral community. The reality of moral rights is purely normative rather than institutional—though of course institutions may be designed to enforce them. That people have rights of certain kinds, which ought to be respected, is a moral claim that can be established only by moral argument.

When appeal is made to human rights in the international context, the aim is to rest one's case on features of moral status so basic that they can be invoked without having to consider in detail the broader circumstances of the situation. If someone has been tortured or shot for demonstrating peacefully or imprisoned for criticizing the government, we don't have to investigate the economic performance or popularity of the regime that has done it to decide that this was an impermissible violation of the person's rights. The particulars of the treatment are enough.

Of course, we often believe that it would be better if the regime that is using these methods to stay in power were displaced by those who are being suppressed. But that need not be the case. The real test of a belief in human rights is whether we are prepared to insist that they be respected even in the service of worthy causes—prepared to condemn their violation not only in the suppression of the democracy movement in China but also in the Peruvian campaign against the Shining Path and the Algerian campaign against the Armed Islamic Group. The recognition of rights, even if they make more difficult the achievement of a good or the prevention of an evil, expresses that aspect of morality that sees persons not only as objects of benefit and protection but also as inviolable and independent subjects, whose status as members of the moral community is not exhausted by the inclusion of their interests as part of the general good. Rights form an essential part of any morality in which equality of moral status cannot be exhaustively identified with counting everyone's interests the same as a contribution to an aggregate collective good whose advancement provides the standard of moral justification.

II

The value of rights can be defended as either intrinsic or instrumental. Although I favor the first approach, there is much to be said for the second. It is at least part of the truth that the recognition and protection of rights—by the moral sense of individuals or by institutions—serves human happiness and human interests: that the result of failing to accord to all individuals this special type of inviolability is bad in ways that can be recognized and identified without referring to the concept of rights at all. On the instrumental account, rights are morally derivative from other, more fundamental values: the goods of happiness, self-realization, knowledge, and freedom and the evils of misery, ignorance, oppression, and cruelty. Rights are of vital importance as means of fostering those goods and preventing those evils, but they are not themselves fundamental either in the structure of moral theory or in the order of moral explanation. Rather, they must be institutionally or conventionally guaranteed in order to provide individuals with the security and discretion over the conduct of their own lives necessary for them to flourish and in order to protect against the abuse of governmental and collective power.

The idea is that to promote the best results in the long run, we must develop strict inhibitions against treating any individual in certain ways, not only when the consequences in the particular case would be clearly bad, but sometimes even when we believe that doing so would in this case produce the best results in the long run. For a number of reasons, the argument runs, the alternative policy of deciding each case by reference to the general good serves the general good much less effectively than a policy that puts certain types of choice beyond the reach of such an optimizing calculation: The policy of optimizing in each case is not always the optimific policy. The arguments for this position are familiar, and I shall not rehearse them here.

Instead, I shall try to defend the distinct (but perhaps complementary) position that rights are a nonderivative and fundamental element of morality. They embody a form of recognition of the value of each individual that supplements and differs in kind from that which leads us to value the overall increase of human happiness and the eradication of misery—and this form of recognition of human value is no less important than the other. The trouble with this answer is that it has proven extremely difficult to account for such a basic, individualized value in a way that makes it morally intelligible. The theory that rights are justified instrumentally, by contrast, is perfectly clear and based on uncontroversial values.

I begin with a familiar point from recent moral philosophy. The feature of rights that makes them morally and theoretically puzzling is a logical one. If they are taken as basic, it is impossible to interpret them in terms of a straightforward positive or negative evaluation of certain things happening to people or certain things being done to them. The reason is that rights essentially set limits to what any individual may do to any other, even in the service of good ends—and those good ends include even the prevention of transgressions of those same limits by others. If there is a general right not to be murdered, for example, then it is impermissible to murder one person even to prevent the murders of two others. It is difficult to see how such a prohibition could be morally basic; in fact it seems paradoxical if it cannot be justified by its utility in the long run.

We can describe this logical property of rights in terms of the distinction between agent-neutral and agent-relative principles.[1] *Agent-neutral* values are the values of certain occurrences or states of affairs, which give everyone a reason to promote or prevent them. If murder is bad in an agent-neutral sense, for example, it means that everyone has a reason to try to minimize the overall number of murders, independent of who commits them—and this might in some circumstances mean murdering a few to prevent the murder of a larger number. But if, on the other hand, murder is wrong in an *agent-relative* sense, this means that each agent is required not to commit murder *himself*, and nothing is directly implied about what he must do to prevent murders by others. The agent-relative prohibition against murder, of course, applies to those others—in this sense the agent-relative principle is just as universal as the agent-neutral one—but it governs each agent's conduct only with respect to the murders that *he* might commit. The same applies to torture, enslavement, and various other violations. If the prohibitions against them are agent-relative, then I may not torture someone even to prevent two others from being tortured by someone else, and so forth.

The logical peculiarity of noninstrumental rights can be described by saying that they cannot be given an interpretation in terms of agent-neutral values—not even in terms of the agent-neutral value of what they protect. Rights have a different logical character: They prohibit us from *doing* certain things to anyone but do not require that we count it equally a reason for action that it will prevent those same sorts of things from *being done* to someone but not by oneself.

If murder were merely an agent-neutrally bad type of occurrence and nothing more, then the badness of one murder would be outweighed by

---

1. For a fuller discussion of this distinction and further references, see Nagel, *The View from Nowhere* (New York: Oxford University Press, 1986), pp. 152–53, 175–80.

the badness of two or three others, and one could be justified in murdering one innocent person to prevent three others from being murdered. But if there is a right not to be murdered, it does not give way when the murder of one innocent person is the only means of preventing the murder of two or three others. A right is an agent-relative, not an agent-neutral, value: Rights tell us in the first instance what not to *do* to other people rather than what to prevent from happening to them.

It is compatible with this conception of rights that they are not absolute and that there may be some threshhold, defined in consequential, agent-neutral terms, at which they give way. For example, even if there is a general right not to be tortured or murdered, perhaps there are evils great enough so that one would be justified in murdering or torturing an innocent person to prevent them. But this would not change the basic character of the right since the threshhold will be high enough so that the impermissibility of torture or murder to prevent evils below it cannot be explained in terms of the agent-neutral badness of torture or murder alone. Even if it is permissible to torture one person to save a thousand others from being tortured, this leaves unexplained why one may not torture one to save two.

It is this qualified independence of the best overall results, calculated in agent-neutral terms, that gives rights their distinctive character. Of course, if rights are instrumental—derivative from the agent-neutral value or disvalue of certain sorts of outcomes—then there is no problem because their agent-relative character is not something morally basic. But if they are not merely instrumental, then they can, as I have said, seem paradoxical; for how could it be wrong to harm one person to prevent greater harm to others? How are we to understand the value that rights assign to certain kinds of human inviolability, that makes this consequence morally intelligible?

III

This peculiar feature of rights has been the subject of extensive discussion by Robert Nozick, Judith Jarvis Thomson, and Samuel Scheffler, among others.[2] I am drawn to an answer to the question that has been proposed and developed by Frances Kamm and which was also suggested by Warren Quinn. The answer focuses on the status conferred on all human beings by the *design* of a morality which includes agent-rela-

---

2. Robert Nozick, *Anarchy, State, and Utopia* (New York: Basic Books, 1974); Judith Jarvis Thomson, *The Realm of Rights* (Cambridge, Mass.: Harvard University Press, 1990); Samuel Scheffler, *The Rejection of Consequentialism* (New York: Oxford University Press, 1982). I've written about the subject myself in *The View from Nowhere*, pp. 175–85, but what I say here contrasts with what I say there.

tive constraints of this kind. The status is that of a certain kind of *inviolability*, which we identify with the possession of rights, and the proposal is that we explain the agent-relative constraint against certain types of violations in terms of the universal but nonconsequentialist value of inviolability itself.[3]

Being inviolable is not a *condition* like being happy or free, just as being violable is not a condition, like being unhappy or oppressed. To be inviolable does not mean that one *will not be violated*. It is a moral *status*: It means that one *may not* be violated in certain ways: Such treatment is inadmissible, and if it occurs, the person has been wronged. So someone's having or lacking this status is not equivalent to anything's happening or not happening to him. If he has it, he does not lose it when his rights are violated; rather, such treatment counts as a violation of his rights precisely because he has it.

This yields a kind of answer to the "paradox" of rights. It is true that a right may sometimes forbid us to do something that would minimize its violation—as when we are forbidden to kill one innocent person even to prevent two other innocents from being killed. But the alternative possibility differs from this one not only in the numbers of innocents killed. If there is no such right and it is permissible to kill the one to save the two, that implies a profound difference in the status of everyone—not only of the one who is killed. For in the absence of such a right, no one is inviolable: Anyone may be killed if that would serve to minimize the number of killings. This difference of status holds true of everyone whether or not the situation will ever arise for him.

So even if we suppose, for the sake of argument, that in a moral world in which such rights exist and are moreover recognized and respected by most people, the chances of being killed would be higher than in a world in which there are no such rights (perhaps because the means available to control violators would be weaker than they would if utilitarian methods were employed)—still, this would not be the only difference between the two worlds. In the world with no rights and fewer killings, *no one* would be inviolable in a way in which, in the world with more rights and more killings, *everyone* would be—including the victims.[4]

3. See Frances Myrna Kamm, "Harming Some to Save Others," *Philosophical Studies*, 57 (1989), 251–56; Kamm, "Non-consequentialism, the Person as an End-in-Itself, and the Significance of Status," *Philosophy & Public Affairs*, 21 (1992), 381–89; Kamm, *Morality, Mortality*, vol. 2 (New York: Oxford University Press, 1995); and Warren S. Quinn, "Actions, Intentions and Consequences: The Doctrine of Doing and Allowing," *Philosophical Review*, 98 (1989), reprinted in Quinn's collected essays, *Morality and Action* (Cambridge: Cambridge University Press, 1993).

4. See Quinn, *Morality and Action*, p. 173: "The value that lies at the heart of my argument—the appropriateness of morality's recognizing us as independent beings—is in the first instance a virtue of the moral design *itself*. The fittingness of this recognition is not a goal of action, and therefore not something that we could be tempted to serve by violating

We may actually have an example of this sort of choice in the criminal enforcement practices of modern liberal societies. I would not be surprised if the rate of violent crime in the United States, for example, could be substantially reduced if the police and courts were free to use methods to control, arrest, and imprison criminal suspects that carried a greater risk of violating people's rights than the methods now legally permitted. Violent crimes are also violations of people's rights, so the balance might be quite favorable: The average person's chance of being mugged or murdered might decrease much more than his chance of being beaten up by the police or falsely imprisoned would increase. Yet a believer in individual rights will reject what appears to be the lesser evil in this case, preferring to maintain strict protections against maltreatment and strict standards of evidence and procedural safeguards for suspected offenders, even at the cost of a higher crime rate and a higher total rate of rights violations. I believe that such a policy is difficult to justify on rule-utilitarian grounds and that it expresses instead a recognition of the independent value of inviolability for everyone, quite apart from the value of not being violated.

This may strike you as a pretty abstract difference to hang a moral argument on. But I think it is not without weight. What actually happens to us is not the only thing we care about: What *may* be done to us is also important, quite apart from whether or not it *is* done to us, and the same is true of what we *may do* as opposed to what we actually do. In some cases the only way to minimize actual violations may be to accord no weight to inviolability as an independent value.

I have introduced two rather abstract distinctions: (1) the distinction between the agent-neutral value of human freedom from various kinds of violation and the agent-relative restriction against interfering with people's freedom in those ways, and (2) the distinction between the value of what actually happens to people or is done to them and the (noninstrumental) value of their being or not being liable to such treatment—its being or not being allowable. And we are trying to explain the moral significance of agent-relative rights by saying that not only is it an evil for a person to be harmed in certain ways, but for it to be *permissible* to harm the person in those ways is an additional and independent evil.

---

or infringing anybody's rights. It is also true, of course, that we think it good if people actually respect each other's rights. But this value depends on the goodness of the moral design that assigns these rights. It is not that we think it fitting to ascribe rights because we think it a good thing that rights be respected. Rather we think respect for rights a good thing precisely because we think people actually have them—and, if my account is correct, that they have them because it is fitting that they should. So there is no way in which the basic rationale of a system of rights rules it out that a person might have a right not to be harmed even when harming him would prevent many others from being harmed in similar ways."

Is such an explanation possible? It is not supposed to be merely an argument for *creating* or *instituting* rights through laws or conventions. In a sense the argument is supposed to show that the morality that includes rights is *already true*—that this is the morality we ought to follow independently of what the law is and to which we ought to make the law conform. The argument is that the most plausible alternative morality, which is based solely on the agent-neutral value or disvalue of the actual enjoyment or infringement of certain freedoms, and so on, fails to give any place to another very important value—the intrinsic value of inviolability itself. The argument is that we would all be worse off if there were no rights—even if we suffered the same transgressions that in that case would not count as violations of our rights—ergo, there are rights.

This is a curious type of argument, for it has the form that *P* is true because it would be better if it were true. That is not in general a cogent form of argument: One cannot use it to prove that there is an afterlife, for example. However it may have a place in ethical theory, where its conclusion is not factual but moral. It may be suitable to argue that one morality is more likely to be true than another, because the former makes for a better world than the latter—not instrumentally, but intrinsically. This would require us to be able to conceive and compare alternative moral worlds to determine which of them is actual. I will not attempt a full defense of the idea here.

One problem with any argument of this type is that it seems in danger of being circular. For what is the value that a morality without rights would fail to recognize and realize? It seems to be nothing more nor less than the existence of rights, for which "inviolability" is just another name. I do not think this is too great a cause for worry, however. Any attempt to render more intelligible a fundamental moral idea will inevitably consist in looking at the same thing in a different way, rather than in deriving it from another idea that seems at the outset completely independent. In this case, the system of agent-relative constraints embodied in rights is seen as the expression of a status whose value for individuals cannot be reduced to the value of what actually happens to them, and that is not as trivial as saying that people have rights because they have rights.

Another problem is that this explanation of rights in terms of the value of the status they confer might be thought instrumental or consequentialist after all, if not actually rule-utilitarian.[5] For what is the value of this status if not the value for the people who have it of being *recognized* as not subject to certain kinds of treatment, which gives them a sense of their own worth? It seems difficult to distinguish this argument from an instrumental argument for the institutional establishment of rights as a means for improving people's well-being.

5. I am indebted to Joseph Raz for discussion of this point.

The answer to this objection is that we cannot understand the well-being in question apart from the value of inviolability itself. What is good about the public recognition of such a status is that it gives people the sense that their inviolability is appropriately recognized. Naturally they are gratified by this, but the gratification is due to recognition of the value of the status rather than the opposite—that is, the status does not get its value from the gratification it produces. (This is analogous to the question of whether guilt is the reason to avoid wrongdoing, or whether on the contrary an independent recognition of the reasons not to do wrong is the explanation of guilt.) It may be that we get the full value of inviolability only if we are aware of it and it is recognized by others, but the awareness and the recognition must be of something real.

Kamm's approach enables us to understand rights as a kind of generally disseminated intrinsic good.[6] As she says, we can regard inviolability as having a value for everyone, which would be defeated by a moral system that endorsed the violation of *anyone* for the greater good. We can distinguish the desirability of not being tortured from the desirability of its being impermissible to torture us; we can distinguish the desirability of not being murdered from the desirability of our murder's being impermissible; we can distinguish the desirability of not being coerced from the desirability of its being impermissible to coerce us. These are distinct subjects, and they have distinct values. To be tortured would be terrible; but to be tortured and also to be someone it was not wrong to torture would be even worse.[7]

IV

But even supposing we admit its intrinsic value, what is to be included in this core of inviolability? That is the question that links the fundamentals of international human rights policy with the refinements of American civil liberties debates. The further we get from the fundamentals, the more difficult it is to answer and the more plausible it seems that the answer can legitimately vary from culture to culture.

Within limits, I am prepared to be a relativist about the ways in which equality of moral status is expressed, not only by the legal systems of different societies but also in the moral systems of different cultures. That is, I believe individuals can be accorded an adequate form of inviolability by various alternative allocations of individual discretion, privacy, and freedom from interference, provided certain basics are in-

6. A bit like a public good, complete with its own version of a free-rider problem: Even people who don't recognize the rights of others have them.

7. The argument of this and the previous section derives from my essay "La Valeur de l'Inviolabilité," *Revue de Métaphysique et de Morale*, no. 2 (1994).

cluded in the package. Circumstances may have a big effect on what kind of space for personal autonomy and discretion ought to be left protected by individual rights—circumstances ranging from economic development to population crowding to racial, religious, and ethnic conflict. But the issue, when determining the scope of individual rights in the light of the circumstances, is always the same: What kind of force may be used against people and for what reasons? The limits always represent a balance between collective goods and individual independence, but every morality should accord to each individual some substantial space of personal independence, immune from coercion by the will of others.

The value of inviolability has been described so far in very general terms—too general to permit the derivation of specific results. The rights that give substance to this value must be explained category by category, and the best I can do is to try to describe some of the contested forms of immunity from interference in a way that makes their intrinsic (noninstrumental) importance evident. The aim is to make it credible that these rights merit a degree of respect and protection beyond what could be justified by the balance of costs and benefits generated by their protection.

One can make a rough division between two domains in which the issue arises, the public and the private. Of course, any issue of individual rights depends on there being, at least in the offing, a contention that something or other is the public's business and subject to public control; but the contested conduct itself may be more or less evidently part of public life. In this sense, the public segment of the issue of rights concerns the form of independence from external control that people must be allowed to retain when they enter explicitly into relations or transactions with others that give rise to competition and conflict—notably political and economic relations. Freedom of expression and association in political matters is the core right in this domain, but I would also include some form of economic freedom.

The private domain includes the realm of choices of personal pleasures, sexual fantasy, nonpolitical self-expression, and the search for cosmic or religious meaning. But, of course, the privacy of these matters is precisely what is at issue: It is only because some individuals' personal choices can seem to others to encroach or impinge on the public space that we have the issues of individual rights in these areas that we do. The idea of rights exempts a core of individual discretion from the authority of others—removes it from the category of conduct that *might* be regulated if good public reasons so indicated.

Those who hold political power are usually inclined to use it to push people around. This can take more or less outrageous forms. Shooting demonstrators in Tienanmen Square is not in the same category as outlawing marijuana or making it illegal to deny that the Holocaust took place. Still, these exercises of force by the state all destroy individual freedom under the authority of some misguided idea of legitimacy. We shouldn't be asked to trade in our autonomy completely in exchange for the benefits of political society: It is not, contrary to what Hobbes thought, necessary.

One of the things that prompts this discussion is a wish to account for the level of indignation provoked (at least in me) by exercises of state power that don't have terribly harmful effects. My objection to the censorship of pornography or Holocaust denial is quite out of proportion to the actual harm done by such prohibitions. It's like the reaction when someone cheats you out of a sum that, in itself, you can easily afford to lose. A sense of wrong disproportionate to the resulting loss is a good sign that a sentiment of justice, fairness, or right has been aroused. I am aware that life without pornography is perfectly livable and that the prosecution in Europe of negationists or sellers of Nazi memorabilia is merely ridiculous. But that is just the point. It isn't the consequences but the idea that state power *may* be legitimately used in such ways that seems grossly wrong; instances of such use seem like serious injustices however modest their actual costs or even if there is a net gain. They simply have no right to control people in that way. In advancing this conception of inviolability, I shall concentrate on freedom of expression and sexual freedom.

V

The purely instrumental justification for basic rights of free expression is very strong. Freedom of the press and of public dissent protect everyone against abuses of power and official harm and neglect of all kinds. In instrumental value they are comparable in importance to democracy and the rule of law, and their personal value to writers and intellectuals, as Joseph Raz has observed, is dwarfed by comparison.[8] However, since I believe that the justification of rights in terms of their beneficial effects is not the whole story, I want to concentrate on the value of the form of inviolability that freedom of expression confers on everyone, not as an effect but in itself—in virtue of its normative essence, so to speak. This becomes important if we wish to extend the justification of free expression

8. See Raz, "Rights and Individual Well-Being," in *Ethics in the Public Domain* (New York: Oxford University Press, 1994): "If I were to choose between living in a society which enjoys freedom of expression, but not having the right myself, or enjoying the right in a society which does not have it, I would have no hesitation in judging that my own personal interest is better served by the first option. I think that the same is true for most people" (p. 39).

substantially beyond the domain of political advocacy, where its instrumental value is clearest.

That the expression of what one thinks and feels should be overwhelmingly one's own business, subject to restriction only when clearly necessary to prevent serious harms distinct from the expression itself, is a condition of being an independent thinking being. It is a form of moral recognition that you have a mind of your own: Even if you never want to say anything to which others would object, the idea that they could stop you if they did object is in itself a violation of your integrity.

As an aspect of status, freedom of expression is inseparable from freedom of thought. To stifle communication is to stifle an essential aspect of the process by which free thought operates, because we function, in thinking, as members of a collective enterprise. The sovereignty of each person's reason over his own beliefs and values requires that he be permitted to express them, expose them to the reactions of others, and defend them against objections. It also requires that he not be protected against exposure to views or arguments that might influence him in ways others deem pernicious, but that he have the responsibility to make up his own mind about whether to accept or reject them. Mental autonomy is restricted by shutting down both inputs and outputs—it is a status that can only be possessed collectively. (A dictator who controlled the speech of all his subjects would not himself be free.)

This is close to the argument Scanlon offers for his principle of free expression, except that his argument goes through the conditions of legitimacy in the exercise of state power, and its conclusion is a limit on legal restrictions of expression rather than a general moral right. "An autonomous person," says Scanlon, "cannot accept without independent consideration the judgment of others as to what he should believe or what he should do. He may rely on the judgment of others, but when he does so he must be prepared to advance independent reasons for thinking their judgment likely to be correct, and to weigh the evidential value of their opinion against contrary evidence."[9]

Worst, of course, is the suppression of dissenting opinion because of the danger that it may persuade people, thus depriving the reigning orthodoxy of support. Apart from its epistemological stupidity, this is the ultimate insult not only to the dissenters but also to the rest of us, their potential audience, who are not trusted to make up our own minds. But while this kind of thought control is an element in the repressive impulses to be found in modern liberal societies, it is not the main one. Most civilized threats to individual autonomy are motivated by the desire to prevent offense, insult, or social discomfort or to insure a moral environment of one kind or another. The greater the ambitions of those

9. T. M. Scanlon, "A Theory of Freedom of Expression," *Philosophy & Public Affairs*, 1 no. 2 (Winter 1972), 216.

who hold power to supply a certain kind of harmonious social environment, the greater will be the pressures on individuality and against variations in divisive individual expression. Prominent among the targets of
such control are expressions of racial, religious, or sexual bigotry—so-
called hate speech.

Because of the Bill of Rights, such regulations have been generally
limited to the private, nonlegal sphere in the United States, but even this
can be a substantial form of restriction. In Europe, Britain, and Canada,
government is under no such inhibitions, and laws against the expression of racial or religious bigotry are common. Now it would be easy to
criticize such laws on the ground that they lend themselves much too
readily to abuse, catching the wrong people. For example, the eminent
scholar Bernard Lewis was taken to court in France for having expressed
doubt in an interview with *Le Monde* that the mass slaughter of Armeni-
ans during World War I qualified as an example of genocide—the doubt
being about the motives of their Turkish killers.[10]

But I don't want to make the case on those grounds, for I think it is already sufficiently inexcusable that anyone should be jailed or fined for
denying that the Holocaust took place or selling books that deny it or for
conducting a mail order business in Nazi medallions, small busts of
Hitler, and so forth. Those restrictions are deeply offensive in themselves, and I believe they are damaging to the situation of Jews in those
societies that enforce them. They carry the message that the reality of the
Holocaust and the evil of Nazism are propositions that cannot stand up
on their own—that they are so vulnerable to denial that they need to be
given the status of dogma, protected against criticism and held as articles of faith rather than reason. To claim the need for such protection of
one's beliefs invites only contempt. Willingness to permit the expression
of bigotry and stupidity, and to denounce or ignore it without censoring
it, is the only appropriate expression of the enlightened conviction that
the proper ground of belief is reason and evidence rather than dogmatic
acceptance.

I find it a personal affront to be protected from the expression of such
claims by others—thinking as a person with a mind of my own. But it is
also an affront that the state should have the power to silence anyone—
and therefore to silence me if I were to start spouting equally con-
temptible nonsense. The censorship of a fanatical bigot is an offense to
us all.

10. It is a criminal charge, but it was brought by a private party—an Armenian organization in France. The charge was eventually dismissed on the ground that the crime of *né-
gationnisme* referred only to denials of the Nazi genocide. The Forum des associations ar-
méniennes and the Ligue internationale contre le racisme et l'antisemitisme reacted by
bringing a civil suit against Lewis. They won their case, and Lewis was assessed one franc
in damages. See *Le Monde*, May 19, 1995, and June 23, 1995.

The same can be said about the pressures to control racially offensive and sexist expression in the United States. And here again I am talking not just about the more ridiculous excesses of political correctness but also about the prohibition of hard-core, intentional expressions of hostility. The situation in which those who hold such opinions or attitudes are prevented from expressing them publicly seems to me extremely unhealthy, with its suggestion that the opposite, right-thinking view is a dogma that cannot survive challenge and cannot be justified on ordinary rational and evidential grounds. The status of blacks and women can only be damaged by this kind of protection.

Even if this were not the case, however—even if such restrictions did some social good, on balance—the offense would remain. That is because it is not just the burden imposed by actual restrictions that counts against them but, more important, the assumption that such restrictions are subject to that kind of justification. The existence of a morally protected sphere of mental autonomy depends on the rejection of that assumption. The autonomy we value is defined not just by how we are treated but also by how we may be treated. To admit the right of the community to restrict the expressions of convictions or attitudes on the basis of their content alone is to rob everyone of authority over his own mental life. It makes us all, equally, less free.

I don't deny that direct personal insult, if it is offensive enough and not a part of public political commentary and debate, can legitimately be considered a form of assault liable to legal action. But that should be true whatever the content of the insult, not only when it has to do with membership in a politically sensitive group. It is bad to be nasty and wounding, and while the law is not a very effective instrument for the imposition of civilized standards of discourse, perhaps it can be used in extreme cases—provided, again, that this does not serve as an excuse to stifle political polemic or the criticism of public actors.

VI

My final topic is sexual control. American political culture is in a condition of generalized adolescent panic with regard to sex, brought on by a sudden overthrow of puritanism without a concomitant development of worldliness. This is manifest in the constant intrusions of sexual prurience into electoral politics. When the *Miami Herald* staked out Gary Hart and the rest of the press and television promptly joined in hooting him off the political stage, I could hardly believe it. If every American citizen who had ever committed adultery had sent him a dollar, he would have been the best-financed politician in the country. Since then things have only gotten worse, and we are subjected to a chronic fever of journalistic hypocrisy that shows no sign of slowing down.

However, my concern is with the broader problem of the conflict between individual sexual expression and the sexual character of the common culture. What about the range of cases in which sexual expression offends or does harm, from unorthodox sexual practices to private consumption of pornography to the display of nude photos in the workplace to sexual harassment? Here my views are determined by a strong conviction of the personal importance and great variety of sexual feeling and sexual fantasy and of their expression. Sex is the source of the most intense pleasure of which humans are capable and one of the few sources of human ecstasy. It is also the realm of adult life in which the defining and inhibiting structures of civilization are permitted to dissolve and our deepest presocial, animal, and infantile natures can be fully released and expressed, offering a form of physical and emotional completion that is not available elsewhere. The case for toleration and an area of protected privacy in this domain is exceptionally strong. Relations between the sexes form an important aspect of the public space in which we all live, but their roots in individual sexuality are so deep that the protection of individual freedom within the public sexual space is an overwhelmingly important aspect of the design of a system of individual rights.

Having made great progress in the past few decades, we are now threatened with a reactionary movement that is probably inevitable, given the size of the recent changes. The effort to recapture some of the domain of sexuality recently lost to public control is not limited to abortion but extends to the impingement of private sexual fantasy and impulse on public awareness. The reduction of censorship and the decriminalization of many kinds of nonmarital sex have made unavoidable a spreading consciousness of things that some people find disturbing and an affront to their own sexual feelings. Yet in this respect, as with differences of religion, it is essential that we learn to live together without trying to stifle one another's deepest feelings.

A common public understanding of sexual life is very difficult to achieve, because each of us has such a limited supply of information. The sexual republic is a huge population of individuals with different, often incompatible fantasies and imaginations, and each of them has full-scale sexual relations with a very small proportion of his or her fellow citizens. We are all dependent on our own sexual experience and the sexual experience of our sexual partners and perhaps their sexual partners for whatever we really know about the subject. Even this source is problematic, since intimate sexual relations do not automatically overcome the barrier of imaginatively noncongruent sexual feelings and fantasies. People who sleep together don't know everything that's going on, and often they know very little. In any case, the selection of partners is hardly a random sample of the electorate.

The literary and cinematic culture doesn't do much to foster a less private understanding of sexual reality. Sex is one of the most difficult subjects to treat artistically, and what appears in the public domain is largely dominated by conventions that change over time but are not very reliable guides to the truth. Sex tends to be treated for the most part from a safe distance, however explicitly. Occasionally a brilliant writer like Henry Miller will get closer, but it doesn't happen often.

The result is that when a political or legal issue forces us to argue with one another on the basis of our sexual feelings, we find that what come to the surface, to be expressed in the public arena, are profound and sometimes alarming differences in the way people see the world and one another. We do not inhabit a common sexual world in the sense— limited, to be sure—in which we inhabit a common natural, or economic, or medical, or military, or educational, or even artistic world. When we try to discuss sex publicly for policy reasons, what usually results is a great clash of expression of private sexual feelings and fantasies, generalized without warrant into conflicting conceptions of universal sexual reality. All this is stoked with the heat that always infuses the subject, and the result is a type of political argument like no other. The beginning of wisdom is to recognize this fact and not to confound sexual fantasies with objective reality.

The area in which we have seen the most important progress, I believe, is the treatment of homosexuality. There has recently developed in our culture a fairly widespread (though still far from dominant) attitude of toleration that is remarkable because it is not based on general sympathy or understanding. (Of course that's why "toleration" is the word for it.) My guess is that many of the heterosexuals who have come in recent years to oppose laws against homosexual conduct or discrimination against homosexuals are still, viscerally, homophobic. The imagination of homosexual feelings and relations alarms or disturbs them; they hope their children won't be homosexual; their own sexuality shrinks from the full appreciation of this alternative form and finds it threatening. We can see from the arguments over admission of homosexuals to the military that one of the most threatening prospects for the heterosexual man in the street is having to imagine that he is an object of the homosexual fantasies and desires of others with whom he is in personal contact. (This is not an element in male heterosexual attitudes toward lesbianism—an important fact, since it has made the persecution of lesbians less virulent than that of male homosexuals, which in turn has helped the campaign for a general lifting of restrictions.)

But even without imaginative sympathy, there has been gradual recognition of the obvious fact that the role of sexual relations is as central and fundamental in the lives of homosexuals as in those of heterosexuals and that it therefore demands the kind of protection that can be provided only by rights of personal discretion, choice, and privacy. This is simply a consequence of the removal of homosexuals from their former official role as monstrous fictional characters at the boundaries of the sexual fantasies of heterosexuals and their reconstitution as people with lives and sexual imaginations of their own and claims to be treated as members of the public moral community. It has resulted, importantly, from the courageous refusal of homosexuals to keep quiet any longer.

All this has required the end of control over the public sexual space by forces, particularly religious forces, that would prefer that people whose primary desires are homosexual should feel guilty and abnormal and should try to deny themselves sexual expression and gratification or, failing that, pursue their pleasures in secret. There is no doubt that many people would be more comfortable in such a world. But if we take the idea of moral equality that is at the root of human rights seriously at all, this seems like an exceptionally clear case for exempting a central area of individual choice from public control in the interest of communitarian values. Acknowledgment of the failure of understanding and of the dangers of projective illusion is in this area the primary insight. People are finally beginning to realize that they cannot understand one another's inner lives by consulting their own emotional reactions to what other people do.

VII

If this seems obvious, I emphasize it because I believe it bears directly on another set of vexed contemporary issues, the relation of sexual life to the moral equality of women. Here, too, there are conflicts between individual autonomy and features of the public space that many would find desirable, so the issue of the scope of individual rights inevitably arises. Here, also, the clash of private sexual fantasies, illegitimately generalized and spilling out into the open, tends to generate obstacles to a fair accommodation.

The status of women in any society—all women, not only those engaged in a heterosexual life—is strongly affected by the public norms of heterosexual relations, because these resonate throughout the social structure and are also intimately connected with the family and the division of labor within it, which is the dominant influence on general expectations and opportunities for women. There is a great deal to be said about how the resulting economic and social inequalities between men and women might be attacked directly, but that is not my subject here. I want rather to discuss the perceived and actual conflicts between equality of status for women and the form of sexual life itself.

The most important advance in this area has been the extension to many, perhaps most, American women of a degree of sexual freedom close to that of men—the abolition of the ancient double standard, with the help of easily available contraception and finally abortion. Although the old dichotomy between sluts and virgins is not really dead, it has certainly weakened its hold on the public imagination, as we can observe both in popular culture and in real life. This is an immense liberation for both sexes, and the more it is confirmed and extended to all social classes the better it will be.

But something else is now happening, also in the name of equality, that seems to me unhealthy, both politically and sexually—an attempt from some quarters to take over greater control of the sexual atmosphere and environment by restricting the expression of forms of sexuality that feel threatening, at least to many women, and whose unrestricted indulgence is perceived as creating a generalized status injury to women who have to live in a society that permits it.

Now I am quite aware that plenty of heterosexual men hate and fear women and regard them at an instinctive level as less than fully human, and that these attitudes are often woven into their sexual desires and sexual fantasies. I'm talking now not only about rapists and wife beaters but about large numbers of ordinary slobs who aren't about to attack anyone. And there is something else, which is in its way even worse: the insidious and nearly subliminal idea that it is *in itself better* to be a man than a woman. I believe that it is a very deep and essentially inevitable result of the long-standing inferior social and economic and interpersonal status of women in our culture, as in every other, that simply *being a woman* is instinctively felt to be a worse thing than being a man—a kind of misfortune that afflicts half of the human race, a less valuable form of existence, and one whose interests matter less. This is the most profound form of status injury, caused by the psychologically natural association, at a level beneath thought, of good or bad fortune with a corresponding valuation of any other defining property consistently and pervasively associated with it. And the victims are as susceptible to this miserable evaluative reflex as those on top. It accompanies all status hierarchies—of aristocracy, of class, of race, of sex—and helps to perpetuate them.

So I don't think the situation of women, even in modern secular liberal cultures, is just fine. But the wish to improve it by the device of interfering with the sexual fantasy life and sexual expression of heterosexual men, so long as they do not directly harm specific women, is unwise and morally obtuse. I think the level of society's tolerance for offense in this domain should be quite high, nearly as high as it should be for political and religious expression.

My reason is that the impulse to control some people's sexuality on the ground that it makes others feel threatened comes from a misguided desire to treat the riot of overlapping and radically incompatible sexual fantasies among which we live as if it were part of the public environment and to subject it to the kind of control and accommodation that is suitable for the public space. But this is completely ridiculous. We all have to live surrounded by sexual fantasies, of which we are sometimes the object and which are often potentially extremely disturbing or alarming in virtue of their relations of incompatibility or resonance with our own sexual imaginations. No one is polymorphously perverse enough to be able to enter with imaginative sympathy into the sexuality of all his fellow citizens. Any attempt to treat this psychic jungle of private worlds like a public space is much too likely to be an expression of one's own sexual fantasies, rather than being based on an accurate appreciation of the meaning of the sexuality of others.

Reactions to pornography vary enormously. Many women like heterosexual pornography and are aroused by it. But it is clear that some women find it extremely disturbing and think it reveals a world around them that is overwhelmingly hostile and dangerous to a paralyzing degree. I believe this itself has to be seen as a reaction of the sexual imagination. The offending images arouse disturbingly violent sexual fantasies or fantasies of threatening degradation, which clash with the sexual feelings that the viewer can accept. The violence is then projected onto those who derive sexual pleasure from pornography. (In extreme cases I have the impression that a quite generally violent sexual fantasy life is at work behind the projections—in the interpretation of all heterosexual relations as charged with aggression and rape, for example.) But the fact that a pornographic film evokes unacceptable feelings in someone who would not choose it as a source of sexual stimulation is no indication of what it means to someone who watches it for that purpose. The blind clash of sexual fantasies in this case is directly analogous to what happens when a homophobic heterosexual projects his own horror of homosexual feelings onto the actual sexual relations between men, so that they are seen as unnatural and revolting in themselves.

I would say the same about sadistic and masochistic fantasies, about which I don't know much but which can be extremely disturbing to those who don't share them. To take these things at face value, as equivalent to real threats, seems to me laughably naive about the way in which the sexual imagination works. I don't want to see films depicting torture and mutilation, but I take it as obvious that they do something completely different for those who are sexually gratified by them; it's not that they are delighted by *the same thing* that revolts me; it's something else that I don't understand, because it does not fit into the particular configuration of my sexual imagination—something having to do with the sense of one's body and the bodies of others, release of shame, disinhibition of physical control, transgression, and surrender—but I'm guessing.

Life is hard enough without trying to impose a sexual grid of the normal and civilized on the wildly various sexual inner lives that result from the complex and imperfect individual histories that have formed each of us. We live in a world of separate erotic subjects and we are all surrounded by sexual fantasies all the time. Who knows what unspeakable acts you are performing in the imagination of the mortgage officer as he explains to you the relative advantages of fixed and variable interest rates, or the policewoman who is giving you a traffic ticket, or the butcher who is wrapping your pork chops? If some men get their kicks by watching movies of women with big breasts engaged in fellatio and if others get theirs by watching depictions of gang rape or flogging or mutilation, this really shouldn't give rise to a claim on anyone's part not to be surrounded by, or even included in, such fantasies. We have no right to be free of the fantasies of others, however much we may dislike them. If the division between the public and the private means anything, sexual fantasies and means of sexual gratification belong firmly in the private domain. An awareness that things go on there that might disturb, disgust, or frighten you, together with an unwillingness to regard this as providing any ground for interference whatever, should be a fundamental aspect of the kind of recognition of inviolability that makes up a commitment to human rights. And crude male sexuality is as deserving of protection against public repression as any other kind.

I'll comment very briefly on the issues of public display and sexual harassment. The same respect for the privacy of sexual imagination that demands tolerance also opposes the involuntary imposition of disturbing sexual images on others. Inevitably the regulation of what can be displayed on billboards or newsstands will depend on a rough empirical judgment of what significant numbers of the public will find genuinely upsetting. The same goes for pinups in the workplace. The problem is to distinguish genuine revulsion from mere disapproval.

Regarding harassment, I believe real care is needed to stay with the original meaning of the term. That does not include the expression of sexual interest, even if unwanted, unless it persists beyond reason or is backed up by an abuse of authority. Nor does it include sexual compliments or evident sexual appreciation. The toleration of sexual feelings should include a certain margin of freedom for their expression, even if it sometimes gives offense and even though it will often impose the unpleasant task of rejection on its target. Adults should be able to take care of themselves.

The radical communitarian view that nothing in personal life is beyond the legitimate control of the community if its dominant values are at stake is the main contemporary threat to human rights. Often, of course, it is invoked in bad faith by ruling minorities who claim to speak on behalf of the community. But not always. Sometimes the values and even the majorities are real, and then the only defense against them is an appeal to the form of moral equality that accords to each person a limited sovereignty over the core of his personal and expressive life. My contention has been that this sovereignty or inviolability is in itself, and not just for its consequences, the most distinctive value expressed by a morality of human rights.

4

Chastity

When she was nine, Wendy Shalit's parents arranged that during sex education classes at her school, she would be permitted to go to the library instead of hearing about masturbation. When she was fourteen, she went to pursue an argument about political economy with her twenty-four-year-old counselor at debate camp, in his room, at one in the morning, but fled when he began to stroke her hair—the impulse of chastity following hard upon the first stirrings of sexual arousal. A few years later she went to Williams College and was disgusted to find that she had to use unisex bathrooms in the coed dorms. She wrote an article about it for *Reader's Digest*, and after she graduated in 1997 the college changed the policy. Now she offers herself as the prophet of a sexual counterrevolution.

Her book, *A Return to Modesty*,[1] is low-octane social analysis framed as autobiography, the autobiography of a ludicrously self-satisfied young woman who reports on the moral decay by which she is surrounded and from which she has managed to escape. It is inflated with hundreds of quotations from articles and letters in women's magazines like *Cosmopolitan* and *Mademoiselle*, from other books about the current sexual and emotional scene, and from various people she has interviewed. There is a lot about anorexia, bulimia, self-mutilation, Prozac, divorce, rapists, stalkers, adolescent promiscuity, condoms given out in grade schools, and girls having sex under pressure. Then there is the other side of the coin: extracts from old etiquette manuals; anecdotes about the sexual happiness and family stability of orthodox Jews who

1. Wendy Shalit, *A Return to Modesty: Discovering the Lost Virtue* (New York: Free Press, 1999).

don't touch before marriage and are forbidden contact for ten days a month during marriage; evocations of the devotion of Shalit's own grandparents, stemming from the fact that when they were dating she wouldn't let him so much as hold her hand at the movies; and even some edifying quotes from Islamic women about the virtues of covering up.

Sexual life is so various and complicated that anecdotes and samples of testimony prove very little. Under almost any cultural dispensation, there will be people who are happy and people who are miserable, and adolescence has presumably never been easy in this respect, whatever the social rules. But Shalit poses the excellent question of whether the sexual revolution has produced a result better than what it replaced, and she concludes that the reverse is true: We would be better off on balance, women in particular, if modesty (in the sense of chastity) became again an important virtue, governing the instincts, judgments, and behavior of girls, their suitors, their parents, and their teachers. The fear of pregnancy, the jealousy of reputation, and the preservation of virginity for a single romantic love that would be a woman's only occasion for sex were and are, in her view, essential conditions for the possibility of what most women naturally want and need. The enforcement costs are worth it.

Women have been sold a bill of goods, she says, in being offered sexual freedom on a par with men. The significant result is an expansion of male sexual opportunity because of the greater availability of women. Far from being free, young women have been deprived of the old reasons for refusing sex they don't want; they are now ashamed to admit to sexual inexperience and are taunted if they do. "To pretend that the female sexual drama is exactly the same as the male sexual drama is a sick-making lie," says Shalit, and she describes the postrevolutionary culture as misogynist because it imposes a taboo on the romantic hopes and desires that are natural to women. Not only that, but the disappearance of modesty has taken the thrill and mystery out of sex for everyone, as if we all lived in a huge nudist colony.

Being almost forty years older than Shalit, I was an adolescent when things were closer to her ideal, and it is strange to hear the taboos and attendant hypocrisy of that era celebrated. Although I believe her when she says that she is speaking for many women of her generation, it would take more than her anecdotal method to make it plausible that the great change in sexual norms and the easy availability of contraception have done women more harm than good. But she is right to say that the changes cannot be defended on the ground that they merely leave everyone free to follow the path that suits them, so that no one who values chastity has been in any way constrained:

Modesty simply cannot be "just" a private virtue—a "personal choice"—in a culture where there is such a high survival value placed on immodesty. The choices some women make restrict the choices open to other women. Perhaps this is where liberalism failed, because it claimed society could be simply neutral about individuals' choices, and it never can. The direction of social pressure cannot be discounted. (p. 228)

This is a familiar conservative misrepresentation of liberalism, but the main point is sound: When social inhibitions are removed, forms of life that were supported by those inhibitions will become difficult or impossible, even if they are not prohibited by law. Opening up some possibilities closes off others; the pressure of what is publicly accepted in sexual life is particularly constraining, since it shapes each person's hopes and expectations and those of his or her potential partners. That is why strict religious communities try to restrict the contact of their young people with the wider liberal culture. And that is why Shalit wants to establish a new "cartel of virtue."

Hume explained the virtue of chastity in women on utilitarian grounds, saying it was needed to assure men of their paternity, so that they would accept the burdens of supporting a family. Citing Rousseau, Shalit suggests that to defend modesty in instrumental utilitarian terms alone is "just one step away from seeking its extinction." Her preference is to defend it as a part of women's nature, as well as a necessary condition for bringing men and women together in a type of relation that will be better for both than the impersonal promiscuous sex that she believes is the consequence of its eclipse.

There was bound to be a reactionary response to the sexual revolution. Perhaps Shalit's book will help people who feel as she does to find each other, but I hope it is a fantasy to imagine that the old rules can be brought back into force. From what I have seen, the emotional power of sex and the importance of love in the lives of both sexes have not been destroyed by the decline of modesty. It is true that we are still searching collectively for a way to combine the gains in opportunity for women with a realistic respect for the distinctiveness of their sexual, familial, and emotional lives. Shalit is right that this effort is not helped by the dogmatic insistence that most differences between men and women are culturally imposed. But if we are lucky, we should be able to deal with those differences without relying on the kind of shame that was inseparable from the conventions she admires. Sex, let us hope, will retain its vital transgressive character whatever happens.

5

Nussbaum on Sexual Injustice

Any society concerned with fairness must try to decide what general structures or modes of treatment, applied to persons who differ greatly one from another, will qualify morally as a form of equal treatment, or at least not egregiously unequal treatment. In some cases, such as the vote, identical treatment will do. In other cases, such as taxation or maternity leave, it clearly will not. Sex is one of the most important dimensions in which people differ. They come in two sexes and a variety of sexual roles and orientations. Apart from being one of the most important things in life, sex is at the heart of the structure of families and responsibility for children, and therefore at the heart of everyone's socioeconomic status. So it is hard to tell what laws, practices, and institutions would come closest to meeting the conditions of normative equality or equal consideration of persons against the background of such deep differences and inequalities.

In the face of such a problem, there almost inevitably develops an opposition between liberal and radical approaches. Liberals attempt to discover a way of taking the differences into account in the design of fair institutions without hoping to transcend the differences themselves, because they are considered part of that human complexity and diversity that cannot be abolished without tyranny. Radicals are more optimistic about eliminating the source of the problem, root and branch, persuaded that differences that many find natural or inevitable are really the social product of temporary conditions, to be transformed by a revolution in conventions, mores, or human self-understanding. The conflict within feminism between liberals and radicals is an example of this classic problem.

Martha Nussbaum presents a broadly liberal outlook in *Sex and Social Justice,*[1] a collection of essays about feminism, homosexuality, the subjection of women in the Third World, and the social, historical, and religious variations in sexual consciousness. The political theory she relies on derives from John Rawls, Susan Okin, and Amartya Sen and contains no surprises. It is an egalitarian but individualistic liberalism that aims to secure for everyone the basic capacities, opportunities, and freedoms that will allow them to pursue a good life. What is of interest is the application of this idea to the complexities of sex and their wide variation across cultures. Nussbaum considers important issues about the degree to which sexual desire and sexual norms are socially shaped and about the relation between liberal tolerance of religious and cultural differences and liberal concern for equality of status and treatment, and she engages with radical feminists, cultural relativists, and antigay conservatives. On most of these topics she is a voice of good sense and good will and a reminder, for those who need it, that sex is the scene of some of the worst injustices in the world.

Her most sobering chapters are those that deal with the situation faced by women in parts of Asia and Africa, where cultural and religious traditions of crushing subordination and restriction are pervasive and powerful. In this era of international recognition of human rights, the oppression of women deserves equal status with racial or religious persecution and police state methods as a target of protest. This oppression may be imposed by the state, as in Afghanistan, but it is often privately enforced. Nussbaum describes a widow in India who is subject to beatings by her in-laws if she breaks the ban, applicable to women of her caste, on leaving the house, even to work the plot of land that provides the only food for herself and her children. In Pakistan, Nussbaum reports, conviction for rape requires four male witnesses, and an unsuccessful accusation of rape constitutes a confession to fornication, an offense punishable by whipping. There is a grim chapter on female genital mutilation, widespread in Africa, and designed to make sexual pleasure a male monopoly, so that women can be trusted to leave the house and work in the fields without being led astray by uncontrollable lust. Think about the diabolical genius who invented those procedures of cutting off the clitoris and labia. And think about the sexuality of men who prefer to take their pleasure with a numb partner.

Another chapter documents the important point that often, though not always, the disabilities of women are imposed with the authority of religion, particularly Islam; but there are very serious Hindu examples as well, and a few milder Jewish and Christian ones. Nussbaum discusses the dilemma this poses for liberalism, which is committed to both religious toleration and individual rights. India and Bangladesh,

---

1. New York: Oxford University Press, 1999.

though they have liberal democratic constitutions, allow religious law to govern certain aspects of private life. (To a degree, the same is true of Israel.) This can result in severe disadvantages to women in regard to marriage, divorce, property, child custody, and so forth. Toleration of religious pluralism can overshadow concern for equal treatment of individuals. She also observes that, when it comes to international response to the maltreatment of women, "these violations do not always receive the intense public concern and condemnation that other systematic atrocities against groups often receive—and there is reason to think that liberal respect for religious difference is involved in this neglect."

As she astutely notes, the 1972 Supreme Court decision in *Wisconsin v. Yoder*, permitting the Amish on religious grounds to withdraw their children from school after the eighth grade, provides an American example of the link between respect for religion and sexual inequality. It did more damage to the freedom of girls than of boys since the boys learn marketable skills like carpentry that make it easy for them to leave the community later if they choose—a further reason why it was a bad decision.

In the worst cases, like Afghanistan, Iran, and Sudan, religious law is imposed by a tyrannical state, so there is no question of defending it out of respect for religious pluralism. But elsewhere the attitude toward religion poses a real problem for liberalism—a problem of the limits of toleration. It is a difficult question of priorities. Right now, in the United States, most religions teach that homosexuality is sinful, promoting torments of guilt, concealment, and self-denial among their members who discover after puberty that their primary sexual attraction is to members of their own sex. Given its effect on individuals, how much toleration should liberals want to accord to groups that form the lives and minds of children as well as adults?

The anticlerical impulse is a real test for the liberal inhibition against imposing one's own values across the board. The French prohibit girls from wearing the Islamic head scarf to school, which would be unimaginable here, but the motivation is understandable. Nussbaum's horror stories show that there is a hard question about where to draw the line between respect for religious communities and protection of individual autonomy. And she takes a fairly tough line, which seems right.

Her position starts from the principle that "the fundamental bearer of rights is the individual human being." This means that the state should not enforce religious rules about marriage, divorce, and education and that it should not discriminate between the sexes, even if it does so in a system that treats all religions symmetrically. But active state interference is a trickier matter. Nussbaum would not allow antidiscrimination law to require the Catholic Church to admit women to the priesthood; but she thinks that conduct by a religion that does not lie within what she calls "the core of worship" should be subject to review for violation of equal rights. One might add that it is essential that anyone should be free to leave a religion and that policies that affect nonmembers should be much more vulnerable to public scrutiny than policies that do not.

The inferior status of women in America and other Western democratic societies pales by comparison with much of the world, but in spite of recent progress, it displays a stubborn persistence. This raises the question of how deep beneath the surface of legal and institutional structures it is necessary or possible to extend a movement of social reconstruction. Institutional change is essential, of course, to overcome political, legal, and above all economic inequality between men and women. And much remains to be done: Even if conditions of employment, child care, child support, and divorce can be improved by governmental action, the most basic institution, the family, will alter its division of labor and power only by the transformation of habits and conventions over generations. Progress in all these respects is under way and widely regarded as a good thing. What is more controversial is the question of transformations in sex itself—in sexual life, feelings, conduct, and the understanding people have of their sexuality.

The controversy is connected with the issue of how much sexual desire is socially shaped, or "constructed." Nussbaum is far more sympathetic to the radicalism represented by Catharine MacKinnon and Andrea Dworkin than most liberals are. She credits them with having exposed deep-seated attitudes that support the inequality of power between men and women while concealing those inequalities from view, particularly in the treatment of rape, domestic violence, and sexual harassment, but not only there. Fortunately, we are getting rid of the idea that it is the role of men to try to impose themselves sexually on women, the role of virtuous women to resist until marriage and then to submit, and a mark of general lasciviousness in a woman, and a forfeiture of protection against being forced, if she ever willingly has sex outside of marriage. This conception was responsible for the requirement of active resistance, even at the risk of physical injury, to sustain a charge of rape; for the admission of evidence about the sexual history of the victim in rape trials; for the nonrecognition of marital rape; and for the indifference to sexual harassment as a serious offense in the workplace or other institutional settings. The blend of excitement, fascination, and contempt aroused in unreconstructed males by female desire is one of the ugliest elements of this syndrome.

Even if radical feminists have contributed to the decline of these attitudes, it is part of a wider sexual revolution in which others have been just as important. But Nussbaum expresses particular sympathy with the claim that social injustice invades and shapes sexual feelings themselves. Just how far she is prepared to go with MacKinnon and Dworkin is not clear. She says at one point, "Certainly we may agree with Mac-Kinnon and Dworkin that sexual intercourse is, in crucial respects, a meeting of socially constructed fantasies and role enactments more than it is of uninterpreted bodies," but this is too vague to count as a significant agreement.

In another essay, however, she says that Dworkin should have been "more circumspect" in her rhetoric to avoid giving the impression that she thinks all heterosexual intercourse is rape:

> Examining her rhetoric with care, one may discern a far more plausible and interesting thesis: that the sexualization of dominance and submission, and the perpetuation of these structures through unequal laws (such as the failure to criminalize marital rape or to prosecute domestic violence effectively), have so pervasively infected the development of desire in our society that "you cannot separate the so-called abuses of women from the so-called normal uses of women." This sentence certainly does not say that all acts of intercourse are abuses. It does say that the dominant paradigms of the normal are themselves culpable, so we can't simply write off the acts of rapists and batterers by saying that they are "abnormal." Gendered violence is too deep in our entire culture. (p. 245)

It is not perfectly clear what Nussbaum is saying, but she seems to be endorsing the claim that rape and battery are just fuller and franker expressions of the feelings present at the core of most heterosexual relations in our society.

MacKinnon and Dworkin have gotten a lot of mileage out of this charge, and they have been helped along by the discreditable thrill too many men feel at being portrayed as dangerous rapists—they all want to hear about how terrible they are. I think it is nonsense, though without looking into the souls of my fellow Americans, I can't prove it. Anyone who does not flee from self-awareness knows that the inner life is a jungle, most of it never expressed. Apparently some women and some men are aroused by fantasies of rape and degradation, and there is pornography addressed to such fantasies, but it is simple-minded to regard this as a matter for societal concern.

The socially important features of sexual consciousness are more mainstream and closer to the surface, and these have responded to criticism: It is now impossible not to cringe at even the best movies from the 1950s, with their thoughtless assumption that women would be passive, unprincipled, and subjected to hilarious humiliation at the hands of men. (The same is true of the portrayal of blacks as childish and ridiculous.) The fact that these conventions, which were once second nature, now seem benighted shows that things can improve. But to overcome the maltreatment of women and the refusal to take them seriously it shouldn't be necessary to attack all asymmetries in the sexual relation as infections of "dominance."

Nussbaum has a lengthy discussion of the charge of "objectification," in which she comes down finally in favor of D. H. Lawrence's way of seeing women as sex objects and against *Playboy*'s: "One cannot even imagine Mellors boasting in the locker room of the 'hot number' he had the previous night, or regarding the tits and ass or the sexual behavior of Connie as items of display in the male world." This is rather high-minded, and uncharitable to the readers of *Playboy*, whose drooling over the centerfold need not be incompatible with treating women with respect and, even more important, with regarding the sexual desire and sexual behavior of women without contempt. Women's bodies are great erotic vessels, and there is nothing wrong with erotic art that displays them as such and arouses the physical imagination.

We all speak inevitably out of our own experience in discussing these matters. Being a man and not a woman and inhabiting a relatively feminized corner of this society, I may underrate both the sexual solipsism of most American males and the sense of violation on the part of most American women on receiving their gross attentions. Certainly the appeal to many women of Dworkin's and MacKinnon's violent images reveals something—if only that there is a great deal of sexual unhappiness out there. But as Nussbaum observes, one kind of sexual objectification, the surrender of autonomy and control during sex, can be personally and sexually fulfilling for women. Sexual dismantlement drives us all, men and women alike, deeper into our bodies and thereby reunifies the multiple layers from most to least civilized.

The mere fact that sexual desire and sexual relations are socially shaped does not mean that they have to be infected with injustice. Other natural appetites, for food and drink, are subject to elaborate, socially created forms of expression and fulfillment without carrying much of a message, except when they become vehicles for conspicuous consumption. Of course, sex is a relation between people and more likely to be entangled with their other relations. Yet sexual feelings are powerful enough to determine a good deal in their own right, whatever the social setting. It is not a mere convention that men and women are anatomically and sexually different and that in sexual intercourse these differences are imaginatively and physically expressed and acted out. Social structures can reach deep into the core of the self, but they usually do not replace it—certainly not in the case of anything as fundamental and powerful as sexuality.

It is almost impossible to get reliable information about this subject because the motives and opportunities for concealment of what really goes on in the minds and bodies of people in bed are nearly unlimited. What is revealed will be strongly influenced by whatever social norm holds public sway. But the datum that convinces me that social construction is relatively powerless over sexual desire is the unquenchable survival of homosexuality in the face of the most severe repression and public obloquy. Nussbaum is sensibly skeptical about the social explanation of basic sexual orientation, invoking "the feeling of determination and constraint that is such a common feature of self-reports concerning homosexuality in our society." We must distinguish, she rightly says, between the social explanation of norms and the social explanation of desires. One of her essays offers a heartfelt defense of gay and lesbian rights. It seems to me that the much-maligned desires of horny heterosexual males deserve comparable understanding.

6

Bertrand Russell: A Public Life

I

Bertrand Russell was born in 1872 and died in 1970. The second volume of Ray Monk's historically authoritative biography[1] begins exactly halfway through the life, in 1921. It has the curious property of transcending the emotional and sympathetic limitations of its author: Russell's greatness and indomitable force of life shine through the scrupulously researched narrative in spite of the relentless contempt and distaste with which Monk presents it. To his credit, Monk acknowledges in the preface that his attitude toward Russell may have distorted the account; but equally to his credit, I found that even with Monk's emphases, the facts presented did not support his attitude.

This is another of those painful biographies of a major creative figure that exposes personal failings and sexual agonies to the kind of intimate scrutiny that none of us could withstand. Those who read Monk's first volume may have felt, as I did, the indecency of being exposed to the depths of Russell's misery and the expression of his sexual passions. Why does a great philosopher, or a great artist or a great scientist, forfeit his privacy forever, so that we all get to read his love letters and sneer at his weaknesses? What such people create is always something far finer than they are. It is extracted from a flawed and messy self so that it can float free, detached from the imperfect life that produced it.

Granted, in Russell's case there is more excuse than usual for comprehensive attention since he himself went public about so much. He

---

1. Ray Monk, *Bertrand Russell: The Ghost of Madness, 1921–1970* (New York: Free Press, 2001).

published an autobiography that was at least an attempt at self-expo-sure, and he wrote a great deal about life, sex, and the pursuit of happi-ness. He had the self-assurance of an aristocrat and the independence of mind of a great intellect, and perhaps he would not have cared what we know about him.

Certainly he was not consumed by shame and by the desire to hide, like Wittgenstein, the subject of an equally excruciating and informative biography by Monk. In that book it is clear that Wittgenstein has Monk's profound sympathy, yet he comes across as an insufferably selfish and heartless human being. Russell comes across as a basically decent and generous man with personal flaws, who led a life of stupendous energy and achievement in which he attempted to have some good effect on the world in his murderous and creative epoch. The life was also shot through with personal disasters, and Monk does what he can to blame Russell for these. He castigates Russell for vanity, egotism, and personal coldness, and he heaps scorn on the reams of popular journalism that Russell produced to make a living and to care for others after he had given away his inheritance, mainly to support T. S. Eliot and the London School of Economics.

Russell also did not share, to put it mildly, Wittgenstein's reluctance to publish or his conviction that philosophers should stay out of the world. When Wittgenstein in the 1920s rebuked Russell for his activities in favor of peace and freedom, Russell asked whether it would be preferable to establish a World Organization for War and Slavery. Wittgenstein replied, of course, "Yes, rather that, rather that!"

Though it is popularly and journalistically thought to be central to the job description of a philosopher to discover how we should live and then to reveal the secret to the rest of us, it is in fact rare for philosophers to set themselves this audacious task. Most of the major philosophers of the past have concentrated their efforts on trying to understand the na-ture of reality, truth, and knowledge. Although this includes ethical the-ory, that is not the same thing as knowing how to live, since one cannot live merely by not doing what is wrong. This tradition of the abstract and theoretical character of philosophy continues unbroken for the most part, and analytic philosophers belong to it.

Russell is the great exception. He was a figure of towering originality, one of the founders of mathematical logic, analytic philosophy, and the philosophy of language, and a logicometaphysical visionary of the type of Leibniz, with a brilliant command of the mathematics and the science of his day. But he spent a large proportion of his time and energy in try-ing to communicate to his fellow human beings a set of ideas about sex, love, happiness, religion, social organization, public responsibility, edu-cation, war, and peace—an effort that increasingly dominated the sec-ond half of his life, though it had already been prominent in the first—and he did so with a wit reminiscent of Voltaire. He was fearless, outspoken, and eloquent, and although his judgment was sometimes egregiously wrong, for someone who spoke out continually on so many subjects he had a pretty good record.

He was a believer in reason, and it is easy to deride him for this, given the dark forces at work in the world against whose evils he fought. Monk quotes Keynes's remark that Russell held the inconsistent beliefs that all the world's ills were due to irrationality and that the solution to them was simply that we should conduct ourselves rationally. Keynes had a point, because the explanation of irrationality is not in most cases a failure of understanding, so it will not be put right by patient instruction. Yet Russell's unstinting effort to be the voice of reason was an honorable course. Whatever other forces may be at work, it is a contribution to progress to try to say as clearly as possible what makes sense and what does not; at least it applies pressure in the right direction and indicates the path to be followed when people are ready to listen to reason.

Monk is particularly dismissive of Russell's rationalistic claim that romanticism as an intellectual movement was partly responsible for fascism because of its denigration of reason and of the idea of objective truth, by comparison with feeling and instinct. "Rationality," wrote Russell, "in the sense of an appeal to a universal and impersonal standard of truth, is of supreme importance to the well-being of the human species, not only in ages in which it easily prevails but also, and even more, in those less fortunate times in which it is despised and rejected as the vain dream of men who lack the virility to kill where they cannot agree." It is, of course, equally possible to murder millions of people in the name of objective truth, as Stalin did, and we cannot for that reason blame the Gulag on the Enlightenment. But I think that Monk underrates the power of ideas to infuse and give shape to fanaticism that depends also on other causes. The rejection of reason and objectivity was fundamental to the character of Nazism and quite explicitly so, and the strength of philosophical romanticism in Germany probably weakened resistance to it. (Less lethal political fallout from debased forms of the view that there is no such thing as objective truth is still with us, in the excesses of multiculturalism.)

II

Russell's most famous popular book was *Marriage and Morals*, which appeared in 1929. So much of what he called for in that volume has been achieved by the sexual revolution and the feminist movement that I suppose no one reads it any more. Its rationality and its good sense exist in painful counterpoint with the unraveling of his second marriage, to Dora Black, which was happening when he wrote it. The book is not a defense of free love, but it offers an argument that adultery should not in general lead to divorce because it is so important to keep families with children together:

> A marriage that begins with passionate love and leads to children who are desired and loved ought to produce so deep a tie between a man and a woman that they will feel something infinitely precious in their companionship even after sexual passion has decayed, and even if either or both of them feels sexual passion for someone else. This mellowing of marriage has been prevented by jealousy, but jealousy, though it is an instinctive emotion, is one which can be controlled if it is recognized as bad, and not supposed to be the expression of a just moral indignation.[2]

It would be easier and healthier, Russell thought, to suppress jealousy than to suppress errant sexual attraction, but here reason proved not to be a good guide, at least in his own life. He had underrated the power of sex. In his autobiography he said that he had been "blinded by theory."

At the age of forty-nine he was overjoyed at the arrival of his first child, John, and two years later there was a daughter, Kate; but after seven years of marriage he became impotent with his wife. Dora was half his age and much more radical, politically and personally. She had always believed in complete sexual freedom, and during one of Russell's lecture tours to the United States she became pregnant by one of her lovers, Griffin Barry. She wrote to ask Russell if he wanted her to terminate the pregnancy; Russell said no, and the child, Harriet, was registered legally as his, though after the marriage broke up he expended a major effort to get her name removed from *Burke's Peerage* and *Debrett's*.

Russell himself took up with someone else, and all four adults and three children more or less cohabited off and on for a period of time, under severe emotional strain. Eventually Dora and Griffin Barry had a second child. Throughout this period Russell and Dora were also running the progressive school that they had founded to implement their theories of education, unfortunately influenced by the American behaviorist John B. Watson. This involved a partial abandonment of the close individual relation that they had earlier had to their children, who became instead ordinary members of the student body and were treated somewhat impersonally.

Everything went to pieces in a protracted and bitter divorce, followed by Russell's marriage in 1936 to his lover and secretary, Patricia Spence, a woman in her twenties, and the birth to her of his second son, Conrad. Russell and Dora fell into constant conflict over the children. John began to show signs of disturbance as a young adult and was eventually diagnosed as schizophrenic, after having married the daughter of the poet

2. Bertrand Russell, *Marriage and Morals* (London: Unwin, 1929), pp. 73–74.

Vachel Lindsay, herself mentally unbalanced, and had two daughters, both of whom also became schizophrenic. One of them committed suicide by burning herself to death at the age of twenty-six. The other son, Conrad, was forbidden by his mother from any contact with Russell after their divorce in 1950, and when he did take up relations with his father as an adult, shortly before the end of Russell's life, his mother kept her word and has not spoken to him since.

Russell—frightened and repelled by John's madness and wanting to take over the care of the granddaughters—tried to have John committed, but Dora kept him with her and he managed to survive in her care and even to attend the House of Lords occasionally, having inherited the earldom without regaining his sanity. Monk suggests that the strains to which John was subjected by Russell's mismanaged personal life contributed to his illness, but this is causally naive. Russell had always been afraid of hereditary madness in the family line, and he was evidently right. Fortunately his relations with his daughter Kate were always good, and his fourth marriage, at the age of eighty, to Edith Finch, an American woman a mere twenty-nine years younger than himself, was happy and stable. Monk's relentless censoriousness about Russell's personal troubles seems uncalled for; things can go badly wrong in any family, even that of a tireless social commentator.

III

Russell wrote books called *How to be Free and Happy*, *Why I Am not a Christian*, *The Conquest of Happiness*, and *In Praise of Idleness*—a kind of popular antidevotional literature, calling for the abandonment of conventional religious and moral taboos and their replacement by freedom, kindness, and a fearless openness to knowledge. He also defended socialism and stood twice for Parliament as a Labour candidate in a safe Conservative district. Monk quotes approvingly Beatrice Webb's dismissals of Russell as lazy and flippant in his social and political commentary, but at least Russell, unlike Webb, was never enraptured by the Soviet Union; he understood and condemned it from the start.

His polemical style was always ironical and mocking rather than dour or enraged, but he had a solid core of decency and common sense that usually kept him on the right track. His popular writings are light, fluent, and full of amusing sound bites: "Children were idealized by Wordsworth and un-idealized by Freud. Marx was the Wordsworth of the proletariat; its Freud is still to come." It is perhaps Monk's lack of humor, an unfortunate quality in a biographer of Russell, that makes him immune to Russell's charm.

Russell also produced excellent books of popular science—*The ABC of Atoms*, and *The ABC of Relativity*—and was absorbed by both the promise and the menace of science. It is a sphere where reason and objectivity reign, and it offers the possibility of eventually making the world a material paradise; but it also puts into the hands of irrational and power-mad political leaders technologically advanced means of destruction that could eventually destroy civilization. Russell sounded this warning long before the invention of nuclear weapons, and the danger he saw from coupling advanced science with barbaric politics is still acutely real.

His powerful concern with war and peace led to some of his finest moments, and also to some of his most foolish moments. He was sent to prison and fired from Trinity College, Cambridge for advocating resistance to conscription during World War I. He was not a pacifist on principle, but he regarded it as monstrous that two nations as civilized as Britain and Germany could go to war with one another. Who can disagree with him? He favored world government as a basis for peace but thought that it could be achieved only by forceful domination of the world by one overwhelming power, and he had some hope that the United States might play this role.

Russell's hatred of war led him to favor British neutrality in the 1930s, and in 1936 it resulted in what was probably his most ridiculous publication, *Which Way to Peace?* It argued that, if Britain simply disbanded its own armed forces, the continued military posturing of the Nazis would come to seem ridiculous, and they would be laughed out of power by their own compatriots. It was only when the war started that he finally acknowledged the necessity of a military response to Hitler.

The advent of nuclear weapons at the end of the war fulfilled Russell's long-standing fears of the technological threat to the survival of civilization. During the brief period when these weapons were an American monopoly, he urged that the Soviet Union be forced by the threat of their use to submit to a world government whose dominant power would be the United States. He had for a long time been fiercely anti-Soviet. He believed Stalin was bent on world domination, and he maintained in private correspondence the ruthless position that even an actual nuclear war against the Russians would be worthwhile if it prevented Soviet domination of Europe and Soviet acquisition of the bomb.

Once the American nuclear monopoly ended, however, Russell's overwhelming concern became the prevention of a nuclear war in which the two sides would destroy each other and take with them the populations of many countries that had no nuclear weapons. He favored the unilateral abandonment of the bomb by Britain, not in the unrealistic hope that it would lead the United States and the Soviet Union to follow suit, but in the hope that it would enable Britain to play a role in getting the two superpowers to cooperate in preventing any further nuclear proliferation—which he regarded as posing the greatest danger to the survival of civilization.

The threat of proliferation is still present, but it is getting hard to remember the threat of global annihilation that formed a basso continuo to our lives for decades. The United States and the Soviet Union were fully prepared to destroy each other and much of the rest of the world completely, under certain conditions. Perhaps it was unrealistic to hope that this threat could be eliminated without the disappearance of the absolute political conflict over the future of mankind that lay behind it, which is what finally happened. Yet in the absence of this resolution, some effort seemed called for in the face of the greatest danger that humanity had ever faced.

Russell did not regard the abolition of nuclear weapons as possible, and he even recognized their value as a deterrent; but he worked tirelessly to give effect to the common interest in reducing the threat of nuclear war. He was instrumental in setting up the regular meetings of scientists from both sides of the Iron Curtain, known as the Pugwash Conferences, and he campaigned for the suspension of nuclear tests, which was a realistic goal. He published *Common Sense and Nuclear Warfare* in 1959 and served as president of the British Campaign for Nuclear Disarmament. This involvement led to the entry into his life of Ralph Schoenman, an American radical and former Princeton philosophy student who was twenty-four when he met Russell, then eighty-eight, in 1960.

Schoenman persuaded Russell to lead a movement of civil disobedience against the bomb and, in 1962, to set up the Bertrand Russell Peace Foundation, which attracted substantial monetary contributions, including large sums from Russell himself, that were used to further Schoenman's agenda. Schoenman was virulently anti-American and pro-Cuban, and as the Vietnam War developed into a major American commitment, Russell was drawn into Schoenman's Guevarist position, favoring "many Vietnams" as the way to bring down American imperialism. Statements and letters began to appear over Russell's signature whose heavy style showed that they had not been composed by him (as both he and Schoenman eventually admitted): "The message that Cuba has for the peoples of the world is one of utter determination in struggling against great odds for liberation from brutal foreign domination and rapacious economic exploitation." Russell even sent a telegram to Alexei Kosygin, urging him "to place part of the air force of the Soviet Union at the disposal of the Vietnamese." Monk finds no reason to believe that Russell did not understand or approve of what he signed, but the issue is hardly straightforward. Russell had evidently lost his independence of mind. It is true that he repeatedly declared that Schoenman was his authorized representative; but given that he was in his mid-nineties and in deteriorating health, it seems both uncharitable and unrealistic to construe this as an example of fully informed consent.

There were attempted interventions in the Sino-Indian border dispute, the Cuban missile crisis, the Bolivian trial of Regis Debray, and of course the Vietnam War again through the war crimes tribunal run by Sartre and Vladimir Dedijer, of which Russell was honorary president, though he did not attend the sessions. It was only in 1968 that Russell, with the support of his wife, Edith, detached himself from Schoenman, dismissed him as director of the Peace Foundation, and wrote him out of his will. In 1966, Russell had written a will that bequeathed almost everything he owned, including the copyright of his books, to the foundation and that made Schoenman his executor and trustee. The foundation had absorbed the large advance that Russell received for his autobiography and the proceeds from the sale of his papers to McMaster University. Russell's infatuation with a manipulative disciple and his abdication of judgment near the end of his life was tragic and absurd. Monk's detailed account of Schoenman's activities is highly absorbing, but the spectacle was painful to witness at the time for those who admired Russell as a lifelong champion of reason.

Monk has not written an intellectual biography; he comments only briefly on the abstract philosophical works that Russell produced during the second half of his life, which included a second edition of *Principia Mathematica*, the great logical classic; *The Analysis of Mind*; *The Analysis of Matter*; *An Inquiry into Meaning and Truth*; and *Human Knowledge, Its Scope and Limits*. The best intellectual biography of Russell is his own, *My Philosophical Development*, published in 1959.

A creature of his time, Monk gives the back of his hand to Russell's views on epistemology and the mind-body problem: "Most philosophers regarded, and still regard, Russell's view that what we *see* is an event in our heads as bizarre, an unfortunate legacy from the British empiricism of the eighteenth century." This is a narrow-minded response; Russell's monistic theory of mind and world and his attempts to explain how knowledge of the external world is possible deserve to be taken seriously. But he lived long enough to become a distant historical figure while he was still energetically publishing books. A philosophical climate came to dominate Britain that was hostile to the kinds of metaphysical and epistemological ambitions that motivated Russell and most philosophers before him.

This new climate was the outlook derived from Wittgenstein's later work, which flourished in Cambridge, and in Oxford took a somewhat different form, as ordinary language philosophy—the view being that the traditional questions of philosophy are confusions based on misunderstandings of how language functions and that, in asking and trying to answer those questions, we violate the conditions of meaning of the words by which they are posed. Like all theories that claim to bring philosophy finally to an end, this one failed to achieve its aim. The Wittgensteinian hope that philosophical problems could be dissolved by the examination of language has very few adherents today, and the ambition to construct large and substantive philosophical theories of the world has again come to dominate the field.

Wittgenstein was a great philosopher, and Russell was always proud of having encouraged him in youth—but Russell, too, was a great philosopher, though not as deep or as obscure. In the present philosophical climate, depth is unfashionable, and systematic, scientifically based theories of knowledge, thought, and reality are again pursued without embarrassment by analytic philosophers much more in the mold of Russell than of Wittgenstein. (Indeed, the idea that the problems of philosophy can be solved by the methods of science has been taken by some philosophers much further than Russell would have contemplated.) Things will certainly change again, but in Russell's technical virtuosity, his distrust of obscurity, and his vast appetite for a comprehensive understanding of the universe, he has left his imprint on our time.

Russell was an extraordinarily fully expressed figure: His popular writings even won him the Nobel Prize for Literature in 1950. No doubt vanity and self-love were part of what drove him, and he may have been hard to like, but surely this is trivial by comparison with the result, warts and all. He gave incomparably more to the world than he took from it, and he did little harm. Aristotle advised us to call no man happy until he is dead. Even though Russell's long, embattled, and densely crowded life included much personal misery and public failure, we can now call him happy.

PART II

Right and Wrong

7

The Writings of John Rawls

I

Major works of philosophy are not easy to read. Try curling up with Kant's *Critique of Pure Reason* or Aristotle's *Metaphysics* some evening. Political philosophy, with its combination of theoretical and worldly ambitions, often aims to be more accessible, and it has produced rhetorical masterpieces in the writings of Hobbes, Hume, and Rousseau. But the writings of John Rawls, whom it is now safe to describe as the most important political philosopher of the twentieth century, are very different. They owe their influence to the fact that their depth and insight repay the close attention that their uncompromising theoretical weight and erudition demand.

Rawls is the most unworldly of social and political philosophers. His life has been devoted to reflection, teaching, and writing about the problem of how human beings whose interests and values put them into potential conflict can inhabit with decency a common world. There is never a breath of personal information in his published work, except for generous expressions of thanks to students and colleagues for their intellectual contributions. But those who know him are aware of the personal significance of his dominant concerns, which have always been the injustices associated with race, class, religion, and war.

He is an upper-class Southerner by origin, whose heroes are Abraham Lincoln and Immanuel Kant, figures he has studied all his life. His own life has been much more like Kant's than Lincoln's, but Lincoln serves as his point of reference for the engagement between the hope of justice and the nearly overwhelming obstacles of the real world. Black slavery is his paradigm of injustice, and it is a test for moral theories that

75

they must explain its injustice in the right way—not merely, for example, by pointing out that its benefit to the slaveholders is outweighed by its cost to the slaves. Injustice is not mere inefficiency, not even extreme inefficiency.

Rawls's concern with social and economic inequality is not unusual in a contemporary political philosopher, though he is far more egalitarian than most. But his concern with religion, born of a vivid sense of the importance of religion in human life and of the historical crimes committed in its name, sets him apart. Though his work is entirely secular, he has, I believe, a religious temperament and an understanding of both the power and danger of the aspiration of transcendence, with its capacity to overwhelm worldly constraints.

Rawls was an infantryman in the Pacific during World War II, and his sense of the world is strongly marked by having seen in his time the deadly fanaticism of the Japanese military, the murderous romanticism of the Nazis (he startlingly describes Hitler's worldview as "in some perverse sense, religious"), and the calculated massacre of civilians by the allies in Tokyo, Hiroshima, Nagaski, and Dresden. The continuing capacity of human beings to be led to prodigies of cruelty and destruction for which they are prepared to offer justifications—from the Inquisition to the Holocaust—is always in the background of his thought about the conditions of liberal civilization. He is not a pessimist, but his hopes for peace and justice are not based on blindness to the darkest possibilities of human nature:

> The evils of the Inquisition and the Holocaust are not unrelated. Indeed, it seems clear that without Christian anti-semitism over many centuries—especially harsh in Russia and Eastern Europe—the Holocaust would not have happened. That Hitler's "redemptive anti-semitism" strikes us as demonic madness—how could anyone believe such fantasies—doesn't change this fact.
>
>   Yet we must not allow these great evils of the past and present to undermine our hope for the future of our society as belonging to a society of liberal and decent peoples around the world. Otherwise, the wrongful, evil, and demonic conduct of others destroys us too and seals their victory.[1]

In 1995 Rawls had the first of several strokes, but by a determined effort he managed by 1998 to complete the final, expanded version of his essay "The Law of Peoples," which contains some of his strongest published expressions of feeling, and also to revise the accompanying essay on public reason, his closing statement on the central concept of political

---

1. John Rawls, *The Law of Peoples, with "The Idea of Public Reason Revisited"* (Cambridge, Mass.: Harvard University Press, 1999), p. 22.

liberalism. These are the final products of a remarkably pure and concentrated career, which can now be surveyed.[2]

II

As is always the case with philosophy, Rawls's direct influence is almost entirely intellectual. Even political philosophy has an impact on the world, when it does, only indirectly, through the gradual penetration, usually over generations, of questions and arguments from abstruse theoretical writings into the consciousness and habits of thought of educated persons, from there into political and legal argument, and eventually into the structure of alternatives among which political and practical choices are actually made.

Rawls is read by economists, political scientists, and legal academics, as well as by philosophers, and he is a staple of the undergraduate curriculum, but this is still the world of ideas and not the world of practice. In any case he is self-consciously ahead of his time, engaged in what he calls "realistic utopianism"—the imagination of human possibilities that when properly described will give us something to aim at.

He has influenced the world for which he writes as much through the opposition his thought has aroused as through the converts it has made. The positions he has developed and defended and the problems he has posed define a large area of controversy that was relatively barren before he occupied it. All those who now take it for granted that it is possible to engage in rational argument over issues of right and wrong, justice and injustice, are in his debt for having imbued those topics with a substantiality and structure that they had lost in the first half of this century, through the combined influences of Marxism and logical positivism, both of which in different ways were skeptical about the reality of moral questions.

The course of Rawls's career can be followed clearly in the *Collected Papers*, whose twenty-seven chapters span forty-eight years. It is striking how slowly and deliberately he began. Rawls was born in 1921, and his first article was published in 1951, his second in 1955, and his third in 1958. That 1958 publication, "Justice as Fairness," presents the basic idea of his contractualist theory; in the next decade came six more essays, working out the conception that would finally appear in 1971 as *A Theory of Justice*.

---

2. In addition to *The Law of Peoples*, I shall discuss *A Theory of Justice* (Cambridge, Mass.: Harvard University Press, 1971; rev. ed. 1999); *Collected Papers*, Samuel Freeman, ed. (Cambridge, Mass.: Harvard University Press, 1999); and *Political Liberalism* (New York: Columbia University Press, 1993). Since this essay was written, two further books by Rawls have appeared: *Lectures on the History of Moral Philosophy*, Barbara Herman, ed. (Cambridge, Mass.: Harvard University Press, 2000), and *Justice as Fairness: A Restatement*, Erin Kelly, ed. (Cambridge, Mass.: Harvard University Press, 2001).

One of the most important elements of Rawls's outlook, his moral realism, is expressed in his first publication, "Outline of a Decision Procedure for Ethics." Moral realism is the conviction that moral questions at least sometimes have objectively correct answers, even if it is difficult to discover them. Rawls seems always to have been convinced that, whatever the difficulties of providing a semantic account of moral language or a metaphysical account of moral truth, morality was a real subject that we could think about and discuss without having to settle those intractable metaethical questions.

He takes our moral convictions about particular cases to manifest deeper principles of which we may not be explicitly conscious but which can be uncovered through investigation of a recognizably philosophical kind. Those principles must be tested against our considered convictions. Abstract principles, whatever their a priori plausibility, must not be permitted to sweep away concrete moral judgments too easily. He has always proceeded on the assumption that the reality of moral value does not depend on its reduction to anything else—something more scientifically respectable, for example—and that we should not disregard the pretheoretical voice of conscience unless good reasons can be offered that are themselves firmly based in the deliverances of moral sensibility. This position is more fully expressed in "The Independence of Moral Theory," written in 1975.

But Rawls's main subject has been not moral epistemology, but social justice, and he has given the topic the form it has in contemporary discussion. The problem is this: Each person's prospects and opportunities in life are strongly influenced by the position into which he is born through no choice of his own—by his place in a political, social, and economic structure defined by the basic institutions of his society. This introduces a tremendous amount of luck into human life, but it is luck determined by institutions that are to some extent under human control. Being born the child of slaves or the child of slave owners, the child of unskilled laborers or the child of wealthy entrepreneurs, is in a sense a matter of pure luck, but the institutions of slavery or capitalism are human creations, and we can ask ourselves, as members of a society (and ultimately of a world order), whether the conditions for life-governing good and bad luck that our institutions create are morally acceptable.

Rawls believes that we have to ask ourselves this question, and have to try to achieve a society whose deep structural inequalities are morally justifiable, in order to be able to look each other in the face. Some inequalities of social status, economic resources, and political power are inevitable in any functioning, articulated society, but they have to be justified. Rawls's view of what it takes to justify a deep social inequality is severe, though this is not immediately apparent from the initial statement of his position in "Justice as Fairness":

First, each person participating in a practice, or affected by it, has an equal right to the most extensive liberty compatible with a like liberty for all; and second, inequalities are arbitrary unless it is reasonable to expect that they will work out for everyone's advantage, and provided the positions and offices to which they attach, or from which they may be gained, are open to all.[3]

Most of his work has been devoted to the elaboration and defense of these two principles of justice. As stated here, their meaning is indeterminate, for two main reasons. First, it isn't clear what is to be included in "liberty." If it includes unrestricted economic liberty, the result would be extreme economic laissez-faire; but that is not what Rawls has in mind. The equal liberties he thinks justice requires are personal and civil liberties and basic political rights; they do not include unrestricted freedom of contract and disposition of property or freedom from taxation for redistributive purposes.

Second, it is not clear what is meant by saying that inequalities must work out to everyone's advantage. The obvious question is, By comparison to what? Almost any social system, however unequal, will be to everyone's advantage compared to a Hobbesian state of nature with no social institutions or government at all. Yet no social system, whatever its degree of equality or inequality, will be to everyone's advantage compared to every other possible social system. A strongly egalitarian system may be to the advantage of the have-nots compared to a less egalitarian system, but it will not be to the advantage of the haves and similarly, mutatis mutandis, for an inegalitarian system.

Rawls answers this question with what is probably his most disputed substantive doctrine: the difference principle. In place of the indeterminate requirement that socioeconomic inequalities should be to everyone's advantage, he proposes that they are acceptable only if they cannot be eliminated without making the worst-off class even worse off: "The basic structure is perfectly just when the prospects of the least fortunate are as great as they can be."[4]

This solution first appears in "Distributive Justice," an article written in 1967, but it is prefigured by a remark in "Justice as Fairness": In describing the reasoning by which he believes we would arrive at principles of justice, he says, "The restrictions which would so arise might be thought of as those a person would keep in mind if he were designing a practice in which his enemy were to assign him his place."[5] This conception of the foundations of justice is highly distinctive and of the first importance in understanding Rawls's outlook.

3. *Collected Papers*, p. 48.
4. *Collected Papers*, p. 138.
5. *Collected Papers*, p. 54.

It is in stark opposition to another conception, superficially similar, which might also claim the title of fairness: namely, that the requirements of social justice are those a person would keep in mind if he were designing a practice in which his place was going to be assigned to him at random, so that he had an equal chance, so to speak, of being anybody. This thought experiment, unlike the one Rawls proposes, would not encourage such strong priority to avoiding the worst that could happen to you (the so-called maximin principle of choice) and might favor instead a principle of maximizing the average welfare, balancing disadvantages to some against greater advantages to others, wherever they fall in the distribution of fortune.

By giving strict priority to improving the situation of the least fortunate, Rawls opts for a radically egalitarian standard of social justice. This puts him sharply to the left of center. At the same time, however, his insistence in the first principle on equal basic liberties that may not be infringed even for the purpose of promoting socioeconomic equality marks him clearly as belonging to the liberal tradition, in its social democratic form.

III

The idea that principles of justice should be the product of an imaginary prior agreement, by persons deprived of knowledge of their actual social position, is a prominent part of Rawls's theory and is regarded by him as its foundation, though in my view it is much shakier than the substantive moral conception it is supposed to support. Rawls's hypothetical social contract construction, which he calls the original position, asks what self-interested people would agree to as the standard for evaluation of the basic structure of society if they knew nothing about where they would end up in the social order. (The combination of self-interest and ignorance requires them to consider the interests of everyone.) He concludes that they would give priority to protecting themselves against the worst possibilities and that this would result in the choice of his two principles rather than a utilitarian standard that would maximize average expectations, perhaps at the cost of allowing a bigger spread from least to most fortunate.

There has been endless discussion of whether a person in the original position would be rational to choose as if his enemy were going to assign him his place in the resulting society. In my view it doesn't really matter because if Rawls is wrong, and the rational thing would be to choose as if one were going to be assigned one's place by a giant roulette wheel, that only shows that the original position doesn't accurately express Rawls's moral conception.

The heart of that conception is the priority given to basic liberties, political and legal equality, decent material conditions of life, and bases of self-respect. Providing these things for everyone, including the least fortunate and the least competitive, takes strict priority in his theory over raising the general prosperity or the average welfare. Inequalities can be justified under such a system, but they cannot be justified because the advantages to the better off outweigh the disadvantages to the worse off: They have to be optimal for the worst off.

Rawls's defense of this view has generated a fundamental debate in moral theory about how conflicts among the interests of different people should be resolved. His position is a direct challenge to the utilitarian answer and its modern version, cost-benefit analysis—according to which we should add up the pluses and minuses and try to choose policies that produce the maximum amount of total benefit, aggregated from the advantages and disadvantages to all persons affected. This method, he famously said, does not take seriously the distinction between persons. Tradeoffs across lives should be avoided and replaced by a system of priorities for the most serious needs and interests, even if this means improving the condition of a less fortunate minority before that of a more fortunate majority.

Rawls believes that deep inequalities built into a social and economic structure that is sustained by the power of the state present the greatest potential for unfairness. While people retain some control over their lives through the choices they make against the background of this structure, the influence of the structure itself dominates Rawls's moral conception: It offers people very different possibilities, depending on their sex, their race, their religion, the class of their parents, and their ability or inability to acquire skills that command desirable rewards. People are not responsible for these facts about themselves, and Rawls's ideal of justice would minimize the disadvantage to members of a society caused through the social structure by factors that are not their fault.

The most controversial implication of his outlook is that differences in ability, to the extent that they have genetic sources, do not in themselves justify differences in reward. We may need differential rewards for the talented and productive to provide incentives on which the system runs, but that is their only justification. They may be justified, that is, because the less gifted would be worse off under a more leveling type of regime since productivity and efficiency would drop.

Rawls's conception of a just society is one of exceptional solidarity, in which the more fortunate are entitled to gain from the system only to the extent that this benefits the less fortunate. There is nothing intrinsically fair about the fact that people with scarce productive skills can command higher salaries than unskilled laborers who are a dime a dozen. His view is diametrically opposed to the common idea that people have a moral entitlement to what they can earn in a free market, so redistributive taxation is taking away from them what is rightfully theirs.

IV

When these views were set out at length in *A Theory of Justice*, the book was immediately given the full attention of an academic world hungry for serious, morally based political theory. Through students and younger colleagues, Rawls had already had an influence in the direction of substantive moral thought, also provoked by the Vietnam War and domestic controversies over affirmative action, sexual freedom, and legalized abortion. His contribution was a large, intellectually rich theory—above all a theory that had strong and highly contestable consequences. By showing that disagreements about how society should be ordered could be traced to differences in fundamental moral conceptions, he illuminated not only the views of those who agreed with him but also those of his opponents.

Oddly, the revised version was completed in 1975 for the German translation but makes its first appearance in English only now. There are some changes to the discussion of the principle of equal liberty, to clarify what it covers and why it has the priority it does, and many small changes to the writing throughout, but there are no significant changes of doctrine. What struck me were a few places where Rawls pulled down some rhetorical red flags that had attracted strong adverse reaction. Several examples occur in the section called "The Tendency to Equality."[6]

- The first edition says, "We see then that the difference principle represents, in effect, an agreement to regard the distribution of natural talents as a common asset and to share in the benefits of this distribution whatever it turns out to be." This becomes in the revised edition, "The difference principle represents, in effect, an agreement to regard the distribution of natural talents as in some respects a common asset and to share in the greater social and economic benefits made possible by the complementarities of this distribution." There is less of a handle here for the charge that Rawls thinks we all own each other.
- The first edition says, "No one deserves his greater natural capacity nor merits a more favorable starting place in society. But it does not follow that one should eliminate these distinctions. There is another way to deal with them." Rawls was evidently stung by Robert Nozick's retort, "And if there were not 'another

6. Theory of Justice, pp. 100–8 in 1st ed.; pp. 86–93 in the rev. ed.

way to deal with them'?"[7] The revised edition has, in place of the last two sentences, "But, of course, this is no reason to ignore, much less to eliminate these distinctions."

- The first edition says, "Thus the more advantaged representative man cannot say that he deserves and therefore has a right to a scheme of cooperation in which he is permitted to acquire benefits in ways that do not contribute to the welfare of others." In the revised edition this is replaced by, "To be sure, the more advantaged have a right to their natural assets, as does everyone else; this right is covered by the first principle under the basic liberty protecting the integrity of the person. And so the more advantaged are entitled to whatever they can acquire in accordance with the rules of a fair system of social cooperation. Our problem is how this scheme, the basic structure of society, is to be designed."

These changes forestall misinterpretation, but I will miss the more incautious originals.

V

A great deal of the critical response to the book focused not on equality but on the foundations of liberal toleration and freedom. This depends on an issue at the heart of liberal theory for whose form Rawls is largely responsible—namely, the relation between political and more comprehensive values. Rawls places great weight on the fact that pluralism with regard to ultimate values is inevitable—religious disagreement being historically the most important form—and that the attempt to impose a single comprehensive value system on a society inevitably results in oppression. He believes that justice requires fairness not only in the distribution of material and social advantages but also toward different conceptions of the good. So the contractors in the original position are deprived of information about their full conception of the good life and must choose principles in light of the possibility that they might be anything from religious ascetics to atheistic libertines.

The result is a regime of toleration, with strong protections for the freedom of individuals and groups to pursue different ends in life. This is not, according to Rawls, a mere modus vivendi; it is a requirement of mutual respect. The sense of justice should lead us not to want to impose our own conception of the human good on others against their will, even if we have the political power to do it. We should want, instead, to base the justification of state coercion on a narrower set of

---

7. Robert Nozick, *Anarchy, State, and Utopia* (New York: Basic Books, 1974), p. 229.

purely political values, leaving the comprehensive values of religion and ultimate ends of life to voluntary communal and personal pursuit.

This liberal position, according to which certain principles of right are prior to the good, has provoked the so-called communitarian objection, associated with Alasdair MacIntyre and Michael Sandel, according to which only a shared conception of the human good can justify a social order, and the kind of mutual respect based on fairness that Rawls proposes is not adequate to keep in check more comprehensive values, should they conflict. Whether such critics, with their nostalgia for a mythical past of harmonious communities, would be prepared to accept the coercive imposition of religious orthodoxy by a dominant majority is not always clear. But they do not think it makes sense to expect adherents of a religion to accept a restriction on the use of state power simply because they would have agreed to it if they did not know what their religious convictions were.

Much of Rawls's writing after *A Theory of Justice*, including *Political Liberalism*, has been about the special grounds needed for political justification against a background of value pluralism. The distinction between political values and comprehensive values is fundamental to Rawls's conception of pluralistic liberalism. It is not the distinction between values on which everyone agrees and others about which they disagree. Disagreements about justice are just as fierce and intractable as disagreements about religion. Rather, Rawls is making a distinction between disagreements that have to be fought out in determining the basic structure of society and the use of political power and other disagreements that can be left unsettled. The way to draw this boundary will itself be one of the most fundamental political disagreements of all.

The extent to which political power can be insulated from religion, for example, has been one of the most important questions of political theory since the seventeenth century and continues to be hard fought to this day, especially outside the liberal West. Rawls believes that following the terrible wars of religion in Europe, the liberal tradition developed a conception of toleration that may have begun as a mere modus vivendi but eventually expanded into an ideal of public reason, by which the collective use of political power was to be justified in a way that respected pluralism in ultimate beliefs about the ends of life.

Political values and public reason, according to Rawls, form a subpart of the total domain of values. Although that subpart contains plenty of disagreement, it is a space in which we are obliged to argue with and to try to convince one another—a space of attempted mutual justification —that implies toleration and pluralism outside it.

Rawls thinks the respect for others as free and equal members of one's society—an idea of the right rather than the good—is a motive strong enough to hold more comprehensive values in check and to limit them to the personal and voluntary associative sphere. This is not to be confused with the absurd notion that liberalism requires neutrality about values. On the contrary, Rawls's liberalism requires a strong commitment to the controversial claim that certain political values of freedom and equality take precedence over divergent conceptions of the human good and that these conceptions should not be allowed to overthrow the political fundamentals. That is not value neutrality; it is a non-neutral claim about the correct hierarchy among values for the purpose of determining the basic structure of society. All this is discussed in a number of essays after *A Theory of Justice* and set out with particular clarity in "The Idea of Public Reason Revisited."

VI

In *The Law of Peoples*, Rawls takes an analogous approach to international relations—not, as one might expect, by applying his principles for justice among individuals to the world as a whole, but by seeking the analogue of freedom, equality, and mutual respect for entire societies in their relations to one another. This entails, in his interpretation, a degree of intersocietal toleration for differences in conceptions of justice, including some "decent" nonliberal conceptions.

The tolerance has limits, and it does not extend to outlaw societies that violate the most basic human rights of their subjects or engage in aggression against their neighbors; but apart from that it implies respect for sovereignty, standard requirements of customary international law, and laws of war that include protection for civilians. Although it requires some aid to peoples in especially unfavorable conditions, it does not include an international analogue of the difference principle, because that kind of economic justice, Rawls believes, can be collectively chosen and pursued only through political institutions with much fuller authority over the social and economic life of individuals than can or should exist internationally.

Because of the difference in its effect on interpersonal relations, Rawls is much less concerned about economic inequality between societies than within any given society. This has been a point of contention between him and some of his liberal critics, notably Charles Beitz and Thomas Pogge, who argue with some plausibility that individuals rather than peoples should be the morally relevant units when we think about global justice.[8]

Rawls believes that hope for the future of humanity resides in the spread of liberal democratic societies, which have so far fulfilled Kant's

8. Charles Beitz, *Political Theory and International Relations* (Princeton, N.J.: Princeton University Press, 1979); Thomas Pogge, *Realizing Rawls* (Ithaca, N.Y.: Cornell University Press, 1990).

remarkable prediction that they will not go to war with one another and have left behind the worst forms of domestic oppression. But it will have to happen gradually. The forcible imposition of liberal democracy, or of any one form of liberalism, is not in his view appropriate as an international goal, any more than the imposition of one comprehensive conception of the good, however reasonable, is appropriate as a national goal. "Enlightenment about the limits of liberalism," he says, "recommends trying to conceive a reasonably just Law of Peoples that liberal and non-liberal peoples could together endorse."[9] This is the global analogue of a public political conception of justice. He believes such an international order is the best hope for the evolution of the world in the direction of liberalism. But I find this degree of intersocietal toleration more plausible as a modus vivendi than as a moral ideal—otherwise it goes too far in subordinating the value of justice among individuals to the value of equal respect among societies.

Rawls says that two ideas motivate the law of peoples: "The first is that the great evils of human history—unjust war, oppression, religious persecution, slavery, and the rest—result from political injustice, with its cruelties and callousness. The second is that once political injustice has been eliminated . . . these great evils will eventually disappear."[10] He calls such a world a "realistic utopia" and regards its description as important quite apart from its foreseeable realization:

> I believe that the very possibility of such a social order can itself reconcile us to the social world. The possibility is not a mere logical possibility, but one that connects with the deep tendencies and inclinations of the social world. For so long as we believe for good reasons that a self-sustaining and reasonably just political and social order both at home and abroad is possible, we can reasonably hope that we or others will someday, somewhere, achieve it.[11]

Some may find these sentiments too noble to bear, but they give the spirit in which Rawls's life work has been carried out.

9. *The Law of Peoples*, p. 78.
10. *The Law of Peoples*, p. 126.
11. *The Law of Peoples*, p. 128.

8

Rawls and Liberalism

I

"Liberalism" means different things to different people. The term is currently used in Europe by the Left to castigate the Right for blind faith in the value of an unfettered market economy and insufficient attention to the importance of state action in realizing the values of equality and social justice. (Sometimes this usage is marked by the variants "neoliberalism" or "ultraliberalism.") In the United States, on the other hand, the term is used by the Right to castigate the Left for unrealistic attachment to the values of social and economic equality and the too ready use of government power to pursue those ends at the cost of individual freedom and initiative. Thus American Republicans who condemn the Democrats as bleeding-heart liberals are precisely the sort of people who are condemned as heartless liberals by French Socialists.

Both of these radically opposed pejorative uses have some basis in the broad tradition of liberalism as a group of political movements and political ideas, sharing certain convictions and disagreeing about others. It is a significant fact about our age that most political argument in the Western world now goes on between different branches of that tradition. Its great historical figures are Locke, Rousseau, Constant, Kant, and Mill, and in our century its intellectual representatives have included Dewey, Orwell, Hayek, Aron, Hart, Berlin, and many others. With the recent spread of democracy, it has become politically important in countries throughout the world.

John Rawls occupies a special place in this tradition. He has explored and developed its philosophical foundations to an unprecedented depth, and thereby transformed the subject of political theory in our

time; and he has defended a distinctive, strongly egalitarian view that is
at odds with many others in the liberal camp, though he sees it as following the basic ideas of liberalism to their logical conclusion.

One indication of the importance of a political theory is the vehe-
mence with which it is attacked and the need its opponents feel to explain their disgreements and situate themselves in relation to it. Rawls
has been attacked relentlessly, and from many directions, because his
theory of justice has the kind of real substance that arouses strong disagreement. Though the style of presentation is always accommodating
rather than challenging, the views themselves are highly controversial.
They do not, for example, represent the main stream of liberal opinion in
the United States today.

In brief, what Rawls has done is to combine the very strong principles
of social and economic equality associated with European socialism
with the equally strong principles of pluralistic toleration and personal
freedom associated with American liberalism, and he has done so in a
theory that traces them to a common foundation. The result is closer in
spirit to European social democracy than to any mainstream American
political movement.

Rawls's theory is the latest stage in a long evolution in the content of
liberalism that starts from a narrower notion, exemplified by Locke,
which focused on personal freedom and political equality. The evolution has been due above all to recognition of the importance of social
and economic structures, equally with political and legal institutions, in
shaping people's lives and a gradual acceptance of social responsibility
for their effects. When the same moral attention was turned on these as
had earlier been focused on strictly political institutions and uses of political power, the result was an expansion of the liberal social ideal and a
broadened conception of justice. Indeed, the use of the terms "just" and
"unjust" to characterize not only individual actions and laws but also
entire societies and social or economic systems is a relatively recent
manifestation of this change of outlook. Rawls's liberalism is the fullest
realization we have so far of this conception of the justice of a society
taken as a whole, whereby all institutions that form part of the basic
structure of society have to be assessed by a common standard.

The original impulse of the liberal tradition, found in Locke and
Kant, is the idea of the moral sovereignty of each individual. It implies
limitations on the ways in which the state can legitimately restrict the
liberty of individuals, even though it must be granted a monopoly of
force in order to serve their collective interests and preserve the peace
among them. Freedom of religion, of speech, of association, and of the
conduct of private life and the use of private property form the core of
the protected liberties. Mill gave a different, rule-utilitarian justification
to these limits on the authority of the state over the individual. They
have remained central to liberalism through continuing arguments

both about their moral foundation and about their proper scope and interpretation.

The other great moral impulse of liberalism, a hostility to the imposition by the state of inequalities of status, overlaps at its point of origin with the protection of liberty, since both of them mean that slavery, serfdom, and caste are ruled out. But opposition to inequality extends gradually to more positive requirements, such as equal citizenship for all groups, universal suffrage, the right to hold office, and the abolition of hereditary political authority—in short, political and legal equality as a general feature of public institutions.

What has led to the development of modern forms of egalitarian liberalism, of the kind that Rawls defends, is the recognition that a society may impose inequalities of status on its members in many other ways than by making them legally explicit. The entire system of social and economic institutions—partly made possible by laws, such as the laws of contract and property, but really shaped by conventions and patterns that are the sum of countless transactions and choices by individuals acting in this framework over time—offers very unequal life chances and opportunities to different persons, depending on where they are situated in it by fate.

Consciousness of the hereditary inequalities of class led, of course, to other political movements besides liberalism, but it expanded the concerns of liberalism through a natural extension of the opposition to inequality, from inequality that was deliberately imposed to inequality that was foreseeable and preventable, but tolerated. This has led to a great expansion of what liberalism can demand of the state because it is not just a prohibition but a positive requirement—the requirement that the state use its power to prevent certain severe social inequalities from arising, or from having their worst effects.

But the egalitarian impulse in liberalism, as opposed to movements further to the left, has always been strictly tied to the limits on state power imposed by each individual's sovereignty over himself. However much is required of the state in a positive direction to curb the development of deep institutional and structural inequalities, it may not violate the basic rights to liberty of individual citizens when carrying out this charge. Putting these impulses together in a coherent theory is not always easy, and the task has resulted in familiar disagreements within the liberal camp.

Rawls's theory is remarkable for the distance to which he has followed both of these moral impulses and for the way in which he connects them. Rawls interprets both the protection of pluralism and individual rights and the promotion of socioeconomic equality as expressions of a single value, that of equality in the relations between people through their common political and social institutions. When the basic structure of society deviates from this ideal of equality, we have societally imposed unfairness, hence the name "justice as fairness." A society fails to treat some of its members as equals whether it restricts their freedom of expression or permits them to grow up in poverty.

It is the very strong interpretation he gives to the requirements of justice for all of the basic institutions of society that makes Rawls's liberalism so controversial. It is very different from the liberalism of Mill, with its dominant insistence on limits to government action. Mill was aware of the egalitarian appeal of socialism, and he responded to it in his posthumously published "Chapters on Socialism."[1] His doubts about the economic and psychological viability of a system of that type were of the kind that have persisted and have proven valid. But the egalitarian impulse also persisted, and it eventually had its effect on the development of the liberalism of the welfare state. How extensive that effect will be remains uncertain; the question is very much under current political debate in all broadly liberal regimes.

The other big difference from Mill is that Rawls's account of the individual rights central to liberalism is not instrumental. He does not think they are good because of the results they will bring about; he thinks they are good in themselves. Or rather, he holds that they are principles of right and that the right is prior to the good. The protection of certain mutual relations among free and equal persons, giving each of them a kind of inviolability, is a condition of a just society that cannot, in Rawls's view, be explained by its tendency to promote the general welfare. It is a basic, underived requirement. This noninstrumental conception of individual rights is also supported by Rawls's rejection of the utilitarian method of aggregating advantages and disadvantages across persons and choosing the system that maximizes the total. The importance for morality of the distinctness of persons also accounts for the special form he gives to the social contract as a foundation for political theory. But the details would take us too far from the topic of this essay.

II

The relation of Rawls's theory to other views will show up clearly if we examine his two principles of justice in detail. We will then see how his choices among alternatives express a specific moral position and what other positions would have been expressed by other choices. The two principles, in their latest formulation in *Political Liberalism*, are as follows:

---

1. John Stuart Mill, "Chapters on Socialism," S. Collini, ed., *On Liberty and Other Writings* (Cambridge: Cambridge University Press, 1989).

a. Each person has an equal claim to a fully adequate scheme of equal basic rights and liberties, which scheme is compatible with the same scheme for all; and in this scheme the equal political liberties, and only those liberties, are to be guaranteed their fair value.

b. Social and economic inequalities are to satisfy two conditions: first, they are to be attached to positions and offices open to all under conditions of fair equality of opportunity; and second, they are to be to the greatest benefit of the least advantaged members of society.[2]

The first principle (equal rights and liberties) has priority over the second, and the first part of the second principle (fair equality of opportunity) has priority over the second part (the difference principle).

Note that the first principle is a principle of strict equality, and the second a principle of permissible inequality. The first applies roughly to the constitutional structures and guarantees of the political and legal systems, and the second to the operation of the social and economic systems, particularly insofar as they can be affected by tax policies and various approaches to social security, employment, disability compensation, child support, education, medical care, and so forth. The strict priority of individul rights and liberties over the reduction of social and economic inequalities is the true core of liberalism, and it has attracted the scorn of the radical Left over a long period. This ideological battle is not over, as we see from the denigration of "Western values" by the latest generation of non-Western despots.

However, the issue of what to include in the required scheme of rights and liberties marks an important division among liberals. There are those who believe that the core rights are connected with the protection of the democratic process and the prevention of political oppression—such rights as freedom of speech, freedom of association, due process of law, the right to vote and hold office, and freedom of religion. On this view, purely personal and cultural liberties, such as those involved in disputes over the legal enforcement of sexual morality or the legality of abortion, do not have the same status. On these issues Rawls's interpretation of the scope of basic rights tends to be broader, for reasons having to do with the foundations of those rights and with the ways in which a just society must accept pluralism, reasons that will be discussed below.

On the other hand, there is one significant kind of right that Rawls excludes from the full protection of the first principle, namely, property rights. Those who give significant moral weight to property rights—not just to the right to possess some personal property, which Rawls

2. John Rawls, *Political Liberalism* (New York: Columbia University Press, 1993), pp. 5–6.

includes, but significant rights to accumulation and disposition of private property—belong to the libertarian branch of liberalism. Even if strict libertarians are rare, the high valuation of economic freedom is a significant element in the outlook of those who retain a Lockean sympathy for the natural right of individuals to enjoy the fruits of their labor and their gains from other uncoerced economic transactions.

Rawls will have none of this. Entitlement to what one has earned or otherwise legally acquired has a completely different status in his theory from free speech, freedom of worship, or freedom to choose one's employment. Economically significant property rights are valued not as an essential part of individual liberty but as indispensible features of the economic system, without which the reliable expectations and security that are essential for long-term planning, investment, production, and capital accumulation would not be possible. Reliance on contracts, salary agreements, the payment of dividends, and so forth is economically essential, and it is only the justification of the whole system that provides the moral support for an individual's entitlement to what he earns or otherwise acquires through the actions he and others take in accordance with its rules. What he is entitled to is determined by the rules, and what the rules should be, including the rules of taxation and redistribution, is determined by which overall system would be most just in its results, taken as a whole. In Rawls's theory, individual property rights are the consequence, and not the foundation, of the justice of economic institutions. In theories of a libertarian tendency, the reverse is the case.

This rejection of economic freedom as a value in itself is one feature of Rawls's view that has attracted opposition, along with the closely related rejection of individual desert as a fundamental political value. For the purposes of political theory, at least, Rawls holds that people deserve the product of their efforts only in the sense that if they are entitled to it under the rules of a just system, then they have a legitimate expectation that they will get it. This view is I think more uncompromising than would be accepted even by most of those who would describe themselves as liberals. There are certainly those who would maintain that even preinstitutionally, people deserve what they gain by their own efforts, and that this should be allowed to have some effect on the form of a just economic system. That might be expressed by some modification in the interpretation of Rawls's first principle to admit a measure of economic freedom as a protected right.

If we move now to the second principle, the first thing to observe is that the inclusion of any such principle at all—limiting the inequalities that can be permitted by a just state to arise through the free choices of individuals who are acting under a regime of adequate and fully protected individual rights and liberties—marks the difference between laissez-faire liberalism and welfare state liberalism. It expresses the recognition that class stratification and the resulting inequality of chances in life are social evils, bearing on the justice of a society.

To begin with the first part of the second principle: Equal opportunity has come to be a central tenet of most liberal positions, but it is open to two very different interpretations, negative and positive. Negative equality of opportunity means the absence of barriers to competition for places in the social and economic hierarchy, so that anyone can rise to a position for which he is qualified. This is what Rawls calls the principle of "careers open to talents." Positive equality of opportunity, or what Rawls calls "fair equality of opportunity," requires more: It requires that everyone, whatever his starting place in life, have the same opportunity to develop his natural talents to the level of which he is capable so that he can compete for a position, when the time comes, without handicaps that are due to a deprived background. The second interpretation, enabling everyone to realize his potentialities, demands much more state action than the first, making sure the doors are open to anyone who qualifies.

Attachment to negative equality of opportunity—condemning the deliberate exclusion of anyone on grounds of race, class, sex, or religion from an equal chance to compete—is now nearly uncontroversial.[3] And to some degree, the value of fair or positive equality of opportunity, or equality of chances, is more and more widely recognized. The obligation of an affluent society to insure access to education through university to all who are willing and able to benefit from it, and some obligation to see that children receive adequate nourishment and medical care, however poor their parents may be, is accepted by most segments of the political spectrum in broadly liberal societies. The disagreements are over the degree to which inequalities of opportunity ought to be evened out.

They cannot be eliminated entirely, because differences between families have a big effect on children that state action cannot completely override. But there is room for disagreement over how much has to be done. Some of that disagreement may be due to differences of opinion about how powerful the effect of class is on people's options, some parties claiming that anyone can succeed by hard work, others pointing out how much more difficult it is if you start at the bottom than if you start at the top. But most of the disagreement, I suspect, is due to a difference of moral focus. Those who are inclined to regard the competitive advantages children get from the luck of having been born to prosperous

---

3. It has been breached by the policy of affirmative action, which is, of course, highly controversial in liberal societies, but is probably best understood in Rawlsian terms as an attempt at corrective justice—an attempt to rectify the residual consequences of a particularly gross violation in the past of the first principle of equal rights and liberties. Affirmative action therefore doesn't form a part of what Rawls would call "strict compliance theory" or ideal theory, which is what the two principles of justice are supposed to describe. See Rawls, *A Theory of Justice*, rev. ed. (Cambridge, Mass.: Harvard University Press, 1999), p. 8.

parents as unobjectionable probably focus on the fact that they result from normal and irreproachable family affection. Others, who think those advantages, and the corresponding disadvantages of those born poor, are unfair probably focus on the fact that their recipients have done nothing to deserve them.

Still, the debate over the proper form of equal opportunity is much less divisive than that over whether a just society should go beyond this to strive for equality of results. That brings us finally to the second part of the second principle—the difference principle—which is Rawls's most strikingly egalitarian requirement and one of his most contested claims. It says, to repeat, that social and economic inequalities "are to be to the greatest benefit of the least advantaged members of society." One can conceive of an even more egalitarian principle, one that favored greater equality even if it would lower everyone's level of welfare, including that of the worst off. But this doesn't hold much appeal outside the tradition of utopian socialism and is in any case probably the reflection of something else—the idea that strict equality of possessions would promote a universal level of self-esteem and mutual respect that is impossible in a socially and economically stratified society. That is the appeal of the perennial fantasy of the abolition of all hierarchy. But Rawls's difference principle is still very egalitarian, and it can be contrasted with several alternatives that command support within the spectrum of liberal views.

First there is the view that the only equality required for justice is equality of opportunity and that since the inequalities that arise under a regime of equal opportunity are the result of what people make of their opportunities, they are not unjust. Second, and somewhat more egalitarian, is the view that certain forms of misfortune, including disability, serious illness, and particularly low earning capacity due to lack of skills or overwhelming parental responsibilities, should not be allowed to render their victims helpless and destitute. The provision of some kind of social safety net is widely favored to deal with such cases, though there is disagreement over how high the net should be—what level of social minimum it should guarantee. This view is perhaps best interpreted not as a fundamentally egalitarian one but rather as the consequence of something else, the judgment that certain absolute forms of deprivation are particularly bad and no decent society should tolerate them if it has the resources to prevent them.

A third view that has egalitarian consequences, although it is not fundamentally egalitarian, is utilitarianism, the position that the maximization of total welfare should be a social goal. Destitution seriously brings down the total, and the diminishing marginal utility of resources means that transferring some of them from the rich to the poor, if it can be done without too much loss, will increase the total welfare. It seems likely that most support for moderate policies of assistance to the disadvantaged is due to moral positions like these rather than to the much more deeply rooted egalitarianism that Rawls defends.

Rawls's difference principle is based on the intuitively appealing moral judgment that all inequalities in life prospects that are dealt out to people by the basic structure of society and for which they are not responsible are prima facie unfair, and that they can be justified only if the institutions that make up that structure are the most effective available in achieving an egalitarian purpose—that of making the worst-off group in the society as well off as possible. It is an egalitarian aim because it blocks the pursuit of further equality only if that would make everyone worse off.

This may be a radical position, but it should be kept in mind that it applies only to deep structural inequalities that affect statistically large numbers of people in the different social categories. It does not apply to the countless inequalities among individuals that will inevitably arise as people make choices and interact, and succeed or fail in their efforts, in the context of any socioeconomic structure, however just. If the broad structure of society satisfies the principles of justice in its large-scale statistical effects on the life prospects of different groups, then, according to Rawls, any individual inequalities that emerge from its operation will be ipso facto just. That is what he means by calling it a system of pure procedural justice: The broad design of the system confers legitimacy on the specific outcomes, whatever they are.

Nevertheless, the difference principle means that the broad design of the system is supposed to be evaluated by its success in eliminating those inequalities that are not needed to provide maximum benefit to the worst off. And this imperative depends on the moral claim that it is unfair if people suffer or benefit differentially because of differences between them that are not their fault. A society that does not try to reduce such differentials is not just, and that applies whether the differences in question are racial, sexual, or religious or differences in the fortunes of birth, such as being born rich or poor or being born with or without unusual natural abilities.

It is this last point, the unfairness of society's systematically rewarding or penalizing people on the basis of their draw in the natural or genetic lottery, that underpins the difference principle. Even under ideal conditions of fair equality of opportunity, such inequalities will arise from the normal operation of a competitive market economy in which there is bidding for scarce productive skills. According to Rawls, those inequalities are unjust unless supplemental policies insure that the system works to the maximum benefit of the worst off. People do not deserve their place in the natural lottery any more than they deserve their birthplace in the class structure, and they therefore do not automatically deserve what "naturally" flows from either of those differences.

One other point about the second principle deserves attention: the priority of the first of its conditions over the second. Rawls holds that fair equality of opportunity may not be sacrificed even if this would benefit the worst-off group in a society. It may be difficult to imagine how that might be so, but I mentioned above the deviation from equality of opportunity represented by affirmative action, and it is perhaps possible that, even in the absence of the historical legacy of slavery or a caste system, someone might favor an ongoing program of preference in the assignment of desirable positions to the less talented, or perhaps some randomization of assignment, in order to prevent the development of a hereditary meritocracy. That kind of reversal of priority between equality of opportunity and equality of results would represent a more radically egalitarian position than Rawls's, as well as one that was in a sense more anti-individualistic.

This brief survey of the alternatives shows that in putting forward his two principles of justice, Rawls has not only expressed a distinctive position but also provided a framework for identifying the morally crucial differences among a whole range of views on the main questions of social justice. I now want to go more deeply into the justifications for the most controversial features of his view—its pluralism and its egalitarianism.

III

An important element in Rawls's conception of liberty is the requirement that a just state refrain, so far as possible, from trying to impose on its members a single conception of the ends and meaning of life. This is most straightforward in the requirement of freedom of religion, and Rawls assigns great importance to the historical descent of ideas of toleration from the seventeenth-century wars of religion and their aftermath. But he applies the principle much more widely, to cover all deep differences in fundamental conceptions of the good. Toward these, he believes a just society should adopt an attitude of toleration and the expectation of pluralism, and that it should leave people free to pursue their ultimate aims provided they do not interfere with the other requirements of justice.

What this position opposes, in particular, is one or another form of perfectionism, based on commitment to a particular contested idea of the ends of life, and insistence that it is the proper role of a political community to guide its members in that direction, by coercion, education, the exclusion of other options, and control of the cultural environment.

Rawls opposes perfectionism not merely because the contest for religious or cultural hegemony has divisive results and is potentially dangerous for all parties. That would be to accept pluralism and toleration as a mere modus vivendi, necessary for practical reasons though falling short of the ideal. Rawls believes, on the contrary, that pluralism and toleration with regard to ultimate ends are conditions of mutual respect between citizens that our sense of justice should lead us to value intrinsically and not instrumentally. In the original position, this ideal receives formal expression through the fact that parties to the hypothetical contract are supposed not to know their own full conception of the good—so they have to choose principles of justice based on a thin, purely formal conception that they know would be consistent with any of the thicker conceptions that might be their actual one. This feature of the veil of ignorance, like not knowing one's race or class background, is required because Rawls holds that equal treatment by the social and political systems of those with different comprehensive values is an important form of fairness.

The distinction between comprehensive values and more narrowly political values is discussed extensively in *Political Liberalism*, and Rawls suggests that in *A Theory of Justice* he failed adequately to attend to this difference.[4] This is a rather subtle matter. I myself think that the aim of making the theory of justice independent of any particularly comprehensive view was already implicitly present in the earlier book, though the later discussion is very important in working out how Rawls believes this can coherently be accomplished. In any case, the questions of whether it is possible and, if so, whether it is desirable have generated a great deal of attention. Rawls himself points to others in the liberal tradition, such as Kant and Mill, who take it for granted that political liberalism should be derived from a comprehensive moral conception. That outlook has many adherents still. And since Rawls has raised the issue, a number of skeptics have argued that it is impossible to ground a political theory of justice on a much narrower base, as he wishes to do—that the kind of neutrality or abstinence that he requires of us when thinking about justice is unavailable and incapable of sustaining the moral commitment to principles of tolerance and antiperfectionism.[5]

This corresponds to a heated dispute that arises again and again in public debate over whether typical liberal demands for tolerance and individual liberty with respect to religion, sexual conduct, pornography, abortion, assisted suicide, and so forth really depend on the requirement of state impartiality toward deep and contested personal convictions or whether they are in reality based on the quite specific, contested convictions of those very liberals, convictions that they think it politically inadvisable to invoke directly—religious skepticism, sexual libertinism, and moral endorsement of abortion and assisted suicide. Alternatively, the

4. See the introduction to *Political Liberalism*, pp. xvii–xx.
5. See, for example, Joseph Raz, "Facing Diversity: The Case of Epistemic Abstinence," *Philosophy & Public Affairs*, 19 (1990).

charge may be that the true basis of all liberal positions is a comprehensive belief that the best thing for each person is to live his life in accordance with his own autonomous choices, whatever they are, and that that is what a just society should make possible, so far as it can be managed for people with widely varying preferences and commitments. This is an important issue both theoretically and substantively; the appropriate form of liberal toleration turns on it.

It is true that with respect to any issue of individual rights, such as homosexuality, two very different arguments can be offered on the side of liberty. The first is that there is nothing wrong with homosexuality, so it should not be prohibited. The second is that whether or not homosexuality is morally wrong, sex is one of those highly personal matters that should not be controlled by a society on the basis of the convictions of a majority of its members. It is also true that many of the people who would be willing to offer the second argument would also endorse the first, and perhaps not many who would reject the first would be persuaded by the second. Still, there is an important point to the appeal by some liberals, in the style of Rawls, to the second, higher order argument, which belongs specifically to political rather than overall moral theory. Whether or not it actually commands wide acceptance, the second-order argument tries to appeal to a value that all members of a pluralistic liberal society could reasonably accept, even if they disagree fundamentally in their beliefs about sexual morality. It is not the overriding value of individual personal autonomy, which may be rejected by many religious and other comprehensive views. It is the value of mutual respect, which limits the grounds on which we may call on the collective power of the state to force those who do not share our convictions to submit to the will of the majority.

All government, all society, requires that the state must have such power; the issue concerns only its extent and the admissible grounds of its exercise. The way in which it defines those limits is one of the most important features of any liberal position—what makes it a liberal theory of democracy rather than mere majoritarianism. As we know from the case of Mill, strict limits on both the extent and the admissible direct grounds for the exercise of state power can be defended directly by appeal to the comprehensive value of happiness and individual human flourishing, without relying on any principle of second-order impartiality among comprehensive views. *On Liberty* is a powerful rule-utilitarian defense of liberal principles.

But Rawls wants something else, something that is in a way more difficult, and perhaps less likely to persuade in real political argument. He wants a justification for liberty and pluralism that does not rely on the individualistic system of values that so many liberals share. Political liberalism should be compatible with religious orthodoxy. Rawls wants this because, when it comes to constitutional essentials, it is insufficiently respectful toward those many members of a liberally governed society who do not share those comprehensively individualistic values to justify the institutions under which we all must live, and the rights that those institutions guarantee, by reference to grounds those individuals cannot be reasonably expected to accept. The reach of a justification for constitutional guarantees of individual freedom must be wider than that, even if this means its grip will be more precarious.

Rawls identifies the type of argument he has in mind in his extensive discussions of what he calls "public reason" and its relation to the fact of reasonable pluralism. These concepts are very important in *Political Liberalism* and receive their most developed treatment in a still later essay of 1997.[6] The greatest difficulty in defining such a view is to distinguish between those conflicts of value that belong within the domain of public reason and those that do not. Disagreements outside of the public domain, religious disagreements being the clearest example, should be so far as possible avoided when justifying the design of basic social and political institutions. But disagreements within the domain of public reason can be just as fundamental, yet Rawls believes that those who hold the balance of political power need not hesitate to exercise it on the basis of their views on such questions or to impose the result on those with opposite views. This happens all the time in political debate over issues of war and peace, economic policy, taxation, welfare, or environmental protection, for example. So what is the difference?

Rawls emphasizes that public reason is not to be thought of as an effective decision procedure, guaranteed to produce agreement, but rather as a special kind of disagreement, argument, and counterargument, which tries to use mutually recognized methods of evaluation and evidence, whether these produce consensus or not. Even if we are not convinced by an opponent's arguments about distributive justice, for example, we can recognize them as offering grounds that he thinks it would be reasonable for us to accept, simply in virtue of the reasoning capacity that we all share. The same cannot be said for appeals to faith or revelation.

Whether an argument constitutes an appeal to public reason is itself likely to be a contested issue (think of the question of the permissibility of abortion). But the concept of public reason is not put forward by Rawls as a mechanical test for the admissibility of arguments, but rather as a characterization of what we should be looking for in an admissible ground for the design of basic institutions. In applying the concept, there will be higher-order disagreements, just as there are conflicting arguments within the domain of public reason. But the sense of justice should lead us to try, in good faith, to offer to our fellow citizens grounds

6. Rawls, "The Idea of Public Reason Revisited," *University of Chicago Law Review*, 64 (1997), 765–807.

for the exercise of collective power that we believe they from their point of view as fellow reasoners have reason to accept—even if they do not actually do so. To invoke only our private convictions is, according to Rawls, a violation of the requirement of reciprocity that applies to members of a just society.

In addition to these problems of definition there is the big problem of justification. How can we put aside some of our deepest convictions—convictions about the ultimate ends of life—in deciding how our society should be arranged? It can seem like a betrayal of our values to deliberately refuse, if we have the power, to put everyone on what we believe to be the true religious path to salvation or, on the contrary, the true secular path of individual autonomy and self-realization through the design of the political, social, and educational systems. To base political values on something less than our most comprehensive transcendent values can seem both morally wrong and psychologically incoherent. For how can these narrower political values have the leverage to hold in check transcendent religious values, for example—particularly when the latter are concerned not just with my own interests but with what I take to be the most important interests of everyone, and therefore of my fellow citizens, whatever their own convictions may be? The same question arises about individualistic secular values, which would seem to justify political opposition to orthodox religion.

This is a difficult question of moral theory, lying at the foundation of the idea of individual rights and therefore at the foundation of a liberalism based on rights. The central issue is whether a requirement of mutual respect, operating in the context of the exercise of collective power over the individual members of a society, is strong enough to hold in check not only the unlimited pursuit of the self-interest of the majority at the expense of the minority but also the unlimited pursuit of the ostensibly transcendent values of the majority against the will of the minority who do not share them. Skeptics answer that to base our principles of political right and wrong on something less than our full system of values is to accord those values only superficial importance, by comparison with an abstract, almost contentless universality.

Rawls's attempt to answer this question by grounding liberal toleration and freedom on principles of right that are prior to conceptions of the good is one of his most significant contributions. The difficulty of the task is considerable, and the suspicion remains on the part of many critics that such views are a kind of liberal camouflage for much more partisan arguments—that the proposed ecumenical appeal of liberalism is hollow. Some of these critics are themselves liberals, who believe it is better to defend liberal ideals by appealing to an explicitly liberal conception of the human good.

But I believe Rawls's alternative is a moral idea of the first importance and that it represents a political ideal worth striving for. Even if it is much harder to explain and defend than a liberalism based straightfor-wardly on individualistic and utilitarian values, a Rawlsian political lib-eralism that could be justified even to those of orthodox religious belief who do not share those values would be preferable as a ground for de-termining the legitimacy of the exercise of power by a state over all its citizens. Rawls has tried to describe a form of liberalism that can claim the allegiance not only of secular individualists, and not only as a modus vivendi or second best. I believe he has identified a source of moral conviction and motivation that does not depend on religious skepticism or an ethic of individual autonomy, and that has an impor-tant role to play in the justification of liberal democratic institutions.

IV

The other great source of controversy in Rawls's moral outlook is his strong egalitarianism, exemplified by the difference principle. Not only the principle itself but also many of the claims offered in its support have aroused substantial opposition. He qualifies its status somewhat in *Political Liberalism*, saying that it is part of basic justice but not a constitu-tional essential and that it is much more difficult to ascertain whether it has been realized than is true of the basic liberties; but it remains a very important part of his overall view.

Rawls defends the difference principle most fully in chapter 2 of *A Theory of Justice*, arguing that it follows intuitively by a kind of analogy from other principles of equality that are less controversial. His main point is that we cannot be content with equality of opportunity. Even the principle of negative equality of opportunity, which excludes deliberate discrimination, depends on the belief that the social system should not assign benefits or disadvantages solely on the basis of differences be-tween people for which they are not responsible and which they have done nothing to deserve. To exclude qualified candidates from a profes-sion because of their race or sex is to penalize them on grounds that are arbitrary in the worst sense, and a society that permits such a thing is unjust.

This is only a first step, however, because people are no more respon-sible for the socioeconomic status of the family into which they are born than they are for their race or sex. Yet a system that guarantees only neg-ative equality of opportunity permits class inequalities to develop and accumulate, without doing anything to counteract the enormous differ-ences they generate in the opportunities for individuals to acquire the training and background needed to develop their abilities, and so to compete for formally open positions. Negative equality of opportunity is therefore not full equality of opportunity. It must be supplemented by positive provision of the resources that will permit each potential competitor to develop his natural abilities and therefore to be in a position to take advantage of his opportunities. That is what Rawls means by fair equality of opportunity.

The same reasoning leads him further. Even under a regime of fair equality of opportunity, undeserved inequalities would continue to arise. Fair equality of opportunity, to the extent that it can be realized, guarantees only that persons of equal natural ability will have roughly equal chances to prosper. But people are not equal in natural ability, and their natural or genetic differences will continue to affect the benefits they gain from interaction with the social and economic order. Yet this, too, is morally arbitrary, for people are no more responsible for their genetic endowment than for their race or for the economic status of their parents. Consequently a just society will counter these undeserved differences in benefit to the extent that it can do so without hurting the very people whose arbitrary penalization it is most concerned to rectify, namely, those who come in last in the socioeconomic race—hence, the difference principle.

Despite the persuasiveness of these analogies, not everyone is convinced that there is anything unfair about people's benefiting differentially from the employment of their own natural abilities, even though they have done nothing to deserve those abilities. Even if they have done nothing to deserve it, their genetic makeup is part of their identity, and it can seem like an assault on the independence of persons to say that they have no right to the benefits that flow from that identity, except insofar as this also benefits others. Such reactions have seized on Rawls's striking remark that "the difference principle represents, in effect, an agreement to regard the distribution of natural talents as a common asset and to share in the benefits of this distribution whatever it turns out to be."[7]

The issue identifies a fundamental cleavage in the liberal tradition, between those who identify justice with the fight against any kind of undeserved inequalities that the design of the social system can ameliorate and those who believe that the scope of justice is narrower—that society is exempt from responsibility for certain forms of "natural" difference, even if they are in a nonpolitical sense unfair. In this more limited conception, a just society should provide a framework, with fair equality of opportunity and a decent social minimum, in which people can rise by their own efforts to the level to which their natural abilities and efforts are able to take them.

The moral significance of the choice between this vision and Rawls's is quite difficult to characterize. Both are interpretations of the vague idea of relations of mutual respect and cooperation among the separate,

---

7. Rawls, *A Theory of Justice*, 1st ed. (Cambridge, Mass.: Harvard University Press, 1971), p. 101.

autonomous individuals that make up a society. We do not own one another and we want to interact on equal or reciprocal terms, in some sense. But in Rawls's conception, we should not want the collectively sustained system of which we are all equally members to allow us to reap benefits on the basis of lucky accidents of fate, which we do not deserve, at the expense of others less fortunate, who also do not deserve their fate. The fact that one's draw in the natural lottery is undeserved communicates itself morally to what flows from it through the operation of the economy. As Rawls says in another memorable formulation, "In justice as fairness, men agree to share one another's fate."[8]

The opposite view is that we retain more independence than this of the claims of others when we enter a society, and we don't even metaphorically hand ourselves over to it. Just as basic personal freedom remains protected by liberal equality, so does the right to benefit from one's efforts and one's talents. Our responsibility for one another, as fellow members of a society, is substantial but nevertheless definitely limited by our continued independence.

The moral key to Rawls's more expansive position is in the idea that, because of the essential role of the state, the law, and the conventions of property in making possible the extraordinary productivity and accumulations of a modern economy, we bear collective responsibility for the general shape of what results from the sum of individual choices within that framework. We are therefore responsible for large-scale inequalities that would not have arisen in an alternative framework, and if they are morally arbitrary, we have reason to want to alter the system to reduce them. There is simply something repellent about a joint enterprise in which rewards are apportioned in accordance with genetic endowment—unless there is some further, instrumental justification for this apportionment, as there is when an inequality satisfies the difference principle.

Among those who would agree with Rawls in accepting society's responsibility for all outcomes that it permits, and not only for those that it produces deliberately, there is still room for disagreement with the strong egalitarianism of the difference principle. The strict priority given to improvements in the situation of the worst off, in preference even to greater individual and aggregate improvements to the situation of those better off, seems unreasonable, particularly to those drawn to utilitarianism. Utilitarians might agree that social inequalities require justification but hold that they may be justified because they contribute to the general welfare, not just to the benefit of the worst off.

Even those who would admit some priority to the needs of the worse off over the better off—after all, the better off already have what the

8. *A Theory of Justice*, 1st ed., p. 102.

worse off need—may think the difference principle too absolute. It seems to devaluate the interests of the middle class unreasonably to say that a socioeconomic order will always be more just if it sacrifices them to the interests of the lower class. Such doubts are also voiced at the level of the hypothetical contract: It is often questioned whether the parties in the original position would be rational to adopt the maximin strategy of choice, which leads to the choice of the difference principle, as a way of ensuring that the worst possible outcome will be as good as possible. Rawls's strong egalitarianism displays an exceptionally strong aversion to the generation by social institutions of what he regards as undeserved differences.

In addition to the familiar opposition from his Right, on the grounds that the difference principle is too egalitarian, there is an interesting criticism from the Left, to the effect that Rawls is too ready to countenance economic inequalities under the difference principle even if they are the result of acquisitive motives on the part of members of society, motives diametrically opposed to the ideal of equality.[9] The point is that in a market economy, it is assumed that inequalities in income and wealth will arise as a result of the wage and profit incentives that drive economic activity. The claim that these inequalities are necessary for the benefit of the worst off depends on the assumption that individuals will not be adequately motivated in their roles as participants in the economy without personal incentives that appeal to the purely individualistic desire to accumulate resources for the discretionary use of oneself and one's family. But the question then arises: Can a society be truly just if there is such a gulf between the egalitarianism that determines the design of its institutions and the individualism that motivates its members when they act in the context of those institutions?

The fact that Rawls accepts this division is a mark of his unqualified attachment to the liberal tradition, in spite of his strong institutional egalitarianism. Political theory is one thing; personal morality is another. Justice is conceived as a specifically political virtue, leaving individuals free to live their lives in pursuit of their own aims and commitments, be these hedonistic or puritanical, libertine or devoutly religious. The special demands of equal respect for the interests of all that justice imposes apply to the sphere of collectively sustained institutions, not to personal life. So liberalism involves a division of the moral territory and leaves individuals free to instantiate a great plurality of forms of life, some of them highly self-absorbed, so long as they are compatible with a just, basic structure of cooperation.

9. See G. A. Cohen, "Incentives, Inequality, and Community," in Grethe B. Peterson, ed., *The Tanner Lectures on Human Values*, vol. 13 (Salt Lake City: University of Utah Press, 1992); and Cohen, *If You're an Egalitarian, How Come You're So Rich?* (Cambridge, Mass.: Harvard University Press, 2000).

V

This division between the personal and the political, and the assignment of justice firmly to the political category, has come to prominence in Rawls's writings after *A Theory of Justice*, culminating in *Political Liberalism*. He has emphasized that justice as fairness is a freestanding political conception, partly in response to criticisms of *A Theory of Justice* that alleged that it relied on a conception of the self as an autonomous, unconstrained subject of choice, whose good consisted in forming its own preferences and pursuing their satisfaction, whatever they were. Although most of those criticisms depended on misinterpretation, including the gross misinterpretation of attributing to Rawls the view that actual persons were like the stripped-down characters in the original position, they also threw into relief the difficult question of the coherence of a position that makes political values independent of comprehensive values and capable of dominating them in the political sphere, even if they are concerned with the most important things in life, such as salvation and self-realization.

One of the important points Rawls has made is that the alternative, of deriving the political order from a particular comprehensive value system, is often supported by nostalgia for a communitarian past that never existed, in which all the members of a society were united in devotion to their common conception of the good—the Christian world of the middle ages, in fantasy. Rawls points out that the maintenance of orthodoxy of that kind has always required oppression because harmonious agreement over fundamental values does not maintain itself naturally. The Inquisition was no accident; the persecution of heretics and apostates is an inevitable part of the attempt to maintain comprehensive unity and to prevent the outbreak of conspicuous dissent. Pluralism, on the contrary, is the natural result of a regime of basic individual rights and freedoms.

It follows that support for the core of liberalism, the guarantee of basic rights, must be compatible with pluralism. Now admittedly, it would be possible to argue for such rights purely instrumentally, on the ground that each party in the plurality of comprehensive views has more to lose from the danger of becoming an oppressed minority than it has to gain from the chance of being the controlling majority. Then liberalism would be adopted as a modus vivendi among parties each of which would prefer, if only it were possible, to impose its comprehensive conception on the others. But Rawls favors the more demanding standard that the equal respect for others expressed by recognition of their rights should be valued for itself and that this should be the highest value in the sphere of political institutions, though not in the conduct of personal life.

The importance of liberal rights depends precisely on the fact that there are things people care about more than the political order, but with respect to which a plurality of beliefs and commitments is inevitable. The only way to live together on terms of equality with others with whom we disagree fundamentally about the ends of life, in a framework that imposes its basic shape on all our lives, is to adopt principles for the evaluation of the framework that can be accepted by as many of us as possible. Their basis must therefore be compatible with a wide range of reasonable but mutually incompatible comprehensive views.

That means that some comprehensive views are not reasonable, because they do not permit their own subordination to the requirement of reciprocity—that is, to the aim of seeking a collectively acceptable basis of cooperation. Fanatical movements that subordinate the individual to the community depend on comprehensive values that are unreasonable in this sense. But Rawls believes that each of a wide range of views, forming the plurality typical of a free society, is reasonable and can support the common institutional framework. That is what he means by an "overlapping consensus." Overlapping consensus does not mean the derivability of common principles of justice from all the comprehensive views in the pluralistic bouquet, but rather the *compatibility* of each of those comprehensive views with a freestanding political conception that will permit them all to coexist.

There are many forms of liberalism, and there will continue to be. And while the liberal tradition is now in the ascendant politically in economically advanced countries and is making considerable inroads elsewhere, it continues to be the object of attack not only from apologists for tyranny and fanaticism but also from many others who cannot accept its severe restraints on the legitimate use of government power—its insistence that the end, however worthy, does not justify the means. Rawls's advocacy of a specific liberal position and his deep exploration of its foundations in ethical and political theory constitute an enduring contribution to this tradition.

9

Cohen on Inequality

If You're an Egalitarian, How Come You're So Rich?[1] is an unusual book, a remarkably successful blend of autobiography, intellectual history, and moral philosophy that reflects the author's distinctive outlook and background. It is the published result of the Gifford Lectures delivered in 1996 by G. A. Cohen, a lapsed Marxist who is Chichele Professor of Social and Political Theory at Oxford. Cohen's historically self-conscious reflection on the ideal of social and economic equality—and on the form in which that ideal can survive once its Marxist version is recognized to be morally, politically, and economically bankrupt—presents, I believe, the most important contemporary challenge to the egalitarian form of liberalism found in the work of John Rawls and others. The questions he asks are the ones we should all be worrying about.

Cohen finds liberal egalitarianism morally incoherent, for reasons expressed in his title: the sharp distinction between the pursuit of equality that it assigns to public institutions and the competitive pursuit of individual aims that it assumes will govern the private choices of individuals who are leading their lives within those institutions. This idea, which appears in some form in the thought of most left-of-center liberals, gets its most famous theoretical expression in Rawls's difference principle. According to that principle, against a background of protected personal and political liberties and measures like public education that provide rough equality of opportunity, the standard of distributive justice is that social and economic inequalities are warranted if the system that generates them helps the poorest members of society at least as much as any alternative system would. The theory does not

1. G. A. Cohen (Cambridge, Mass.: Harvard University Press, 2000).

favor reduction of inequality as an end in itself but only as a means to benefit the worst off.

If, for example, a market economy that permits large returns to capital and large wage differentials creates incentives to work, innovate, and invest that result in high productivity, low unemployment, and substantial tax revenues that can be used for social services, and if confiscatory marginal tax rates would reduce those incentives, with adverse effects on the welfare of the poor, then there is nothing wrong with the large inequalities of income and wealth that such an economy generates. In fact, it would be wrong to reduce the inequalities by higher taxes on the rich if that would leave the poor worse off.

Cohen's objection is not that we ought to level down, even if it will make the poor still poorer. His objection is that a society in which it is impossible to optimize the condition of the poor without permitting large inequalities is not a just society. It is unjust because what makes these inequalities "necessary" is the distinctly nonegalitarian motivation of the individuals whose pursuit of personal gain drives the economy. If high earners were willing to work just as hard and be just as inventive and productively competitive for a much lower reward, the economy could generate just as much employment while the government took out much more in taxes—taxes that could be used to raise the condition of the poor through public provision or direct transfers.

This ethos of nonacquisitive industriousness does not exist in modern liberal democracies, so, as a matter of sociological fact, the difference principle cannot be satisfied unless substantial inequalities are permitted. But Cohen finds the standard liberal attitude to this fact unacceptable. He believes that egalitarian institutions alone do not make a society just if their consequences are radically unequal because individual conduct is exempt from the egalitarian values that shape the institutions. And he believes that the many well-to-do people who endorse egalitarian political values but do not conduct their private economic lives with a view to benefiting the poor are being morally inconsistent.

That is the meaning of the book's title. Actually Cohen's question applies in two ways. First, it could be asked of someone living in what he thinks is a just, egalitarian society—one that satisfies the difference principle, for example—who feels that he pays his dues through the tax system and is morally entitled to try to maximize his disposable income and personal wealth within the rules of that system by charging whatever the market will bear for his services as an executive or a professional. Second, it could be asked of a well-to-do egalitarian living (as nearly all do) in a society whose institutions do not meet his standards of justice. In that case the question is why he does not feel obliged, through personal contribution, to try to benefit the worst off in the way that he believes a just social order would. How can he ignore in his personal choices the values of distributive justice that he condemns the state for disregarding?

Cohen includes himself in the class to which these questions are addressed. Though he is not rich as academics go, he is better off than most people in Britain. And he is certainly correct to observe that prominent philosophical defenders of liberal egalitarianism are, on average, much wealthier than other people are. He suggests gently that this may be no accident. Self-interest is a wonderful stimulus to moral inconsistency and rationalization. I do not want to dispute the suggestion, but I do think it is worth seeing what can be said for the moral division between egalitarian institutions and nonegalitarian private choices that is at the heart of the liberal conception.

But first let me say something about the historical background of Cohen's critique, which is of exceptional interest. The first half of the book is largely about Marxism and Cohen's relation to it. He was born in 1941 into a working-class (antireligious) Jewish communist family in Montreal, took on the egalitarian ideals and historical certainties of the movement completely, and was active in communist youth organizations. The community began to fray after Khrushchev's secret anti-Stalin speech in 1956, but he remained basically pro-Soviet until visits to eastern Europe in 1962 and 1964 and the invasion of Czechoslovakia in 1968 thoroughly disillusioned him. Cohen is a wonderful raconteur, and his account of his early life and the texture of this world is priceless. He attended Morris Winchewsky School, which was run by the United Jewish People's Order. "Our report cards were folded down the middle, with English subjects on the left side and Yiddish on the right, because of the different directions in which the two languages are written. One of the Yiddish subjects was 'Geschichte fun Klassen Kamf' (History of Class Struggle), at which, I am pleased to note, I scored a straight *aleph* in 1949."

This early distinction no doubt contributed to the understanding he now offers us. His chapters on Hegel and Marx, on the dialectical conception of history, on what he calls the *obstetric* conception of political practice in Marxism, and on the place of equality in the communist ideal are superb expositions of one of the most compelling and disastrous intellectual creations of all time.

Its most disastrous aspect was the conviction that capitalism was pregnant with the system that would replace it and resolve its contradictions, so that revolutionaries had only to serve as midwives, assisting in the destruction of the old order and the emergence of the new; they did not have to plan ahead or think about how a just society should be organized. They didn't worry about either morality or politics because they knew the solution was contained in the problem and would appear in due course through the inevitable process of dialectical transformation. Midwives do not have to design the babies they deliver.

Questions about equality and distributive justice, in particular, had
no place in the theory because Marx believed that industrial forms of
production, once freed of their connection with capitalism, would yield
such abundance that everyone would have everything they wanted,
and conflicts of interest would vanish along with scarcity of goods:

> Under conditions of scarcity, so traditional Marxism maintains,
> class society is inescapable, its property structures settle questions
> of distribution, and discussion of the nature of justice, in general
> terms, is therefore futile, for a political movement whose task must
> be to overturn class society, rather than to decide which of the
> many criteria by which it comes out unjust is the right one to use to
> condemn it. (114)

The earlier utopian socialists had offered a moral criticism of capitalism under the illusion that the intellectual construction of an ideal of social justice could move us toward its realization; but scientific socialists
were able to see the historical necessity of the coming transformation
and to understand that the sense of injustice was merely a sign, and
could not be a cause, of its impending occurrence. But none of this is
true, and we know what resulted when those who believed it came to
power. What remains of his Marxist heritage, for Cohen, is the repressed
moral demand for equality that was part of its appeal and that now
needs to find expression in a positive theory of distributive justice under
conditions of scarcity, of the kind that Marx scorned.

Egalitarian liberalism is not that theory because it evaluates the justice of a society only by its institutional arrangements and does not extend the same egalitarian values to individual conduct. It therefore accepts some class stratification as the inevitable result of blameless
partiality by individuals, however just their institutions may be. Cohen
now believes, contrary to both Marxism and liberalism, that the equality that justice requires cannot be produced by transformed institutions alone but requires a revolution in the human soul. In that respect
his attitude is more like a Christian one than like either of the others.
The Gifford Lectures are supposed to have some bearing on religion,
and Cohen's lectures meet that condition handsomely, with serious attention to Judaism, Christianity, Hegel's conception of God, and
Marx's thesis that religion is the opium of the people. The quasi-reli-
gious transformation Cohen seeks, a revival of the utopian tradition,
would make justice not a political value but one that pervades all
of life.

Rawls maintains that the principles of justice apply to the basic institutional structure of society, and that if the structure is correctly designed, whatever results from the actions of private individuals who are
living within that structure will be just, even if they themselves act only

from private motives. As I have said, Cohen believes that this division makes no sense, because the same values that support egalitarian institutions like redistributive taxation are frustrated by acquisitive private motives. Those motives mean that the poor cannot be best provided for unless others are permitted to be rich. In a truly just society, Cohen believes, an ethos of equality would permeate individual conduct, as well as institutions, and the same level of production would be possible with much higher levels of taxation and redistribution.

In response to this critique, three arguments might be offered by the defender of liberalism—two practical and one moral. The first is that the tendency to favor ourselves and our families in private choices is part of human nature, and it is useless to hope for its abolition. In response, Cohen can reply that the transformation he has in mind is not the abolition of self-interest and partiality but just an extension of egalitarian values to the types of economic choices that, taken together, have a large effect on social and economic stratification. It is a question not of asking people to abandon the special interest they have in their own lives but of shrinking the boundaries within which it is seen as appropriate to pursue those interests at the expense of others. This is not an unthinkable remaking of human nature.

The second (and in my view most telling) response would be that we cannot envision how, without the profit motive, a market economy would work to generate the level of innovation, risky but potentially creative investment, intense competition, long hours, and concentrated work by entrepreneurs, managers, and professionals that is responsible for the quantity and quality of production in the most effective capitalist economies. Something else would have to replace the hope of economic gain and the fear of failure in guiding people's choices, and even if it could be found, it would almost certainly have different results. It is, of course, true that in some fields (philosophy, for instance) people are motivated to work hard by the desire for recognition, or even for pure understanding, but such motives will not help run an essentially decentralized and prodigiously prolific consumer-oriented economy. Without the profit motive, I suspect we would still be producing multiple drafts on typewriters and eating only root vegetables in the winter. There are worse fates, and maybe a true egalitarian wouldn't mind, but it's a real question how we are to imagine this world working and whether the poor would be better off in it.

The third response is what Cohen is really after: an account of why the institutional-private division in liberalism is morally justified, rather than being a mere concession to the intractable demands of human psychology or economic efficiency. He rejects a number of possible responses, including the one most liberals would probably appeal to—"that each person has the right to a private space into which social duty does not intrude."

His reply is that he does not favor the elimination of such a private space:

> In a society with a state-imposed egalitarian income distribution, there is plenty for everyone to decide without regard to social duty about the shape of their own lives, and the same goes for prodigious donors in an unequal society . . . private spaces exist, but, because the egalitarian principle is fulfilled, they are more similar in size than they otherwise would be, and some are bigger than they would otherwise be. (167–68)

I have to admit that, although I am an adherent of the liberal conception, I don't have an answer to Cohen's charge of moral incoherence. It is hard to render consistent the exemption of private choice from the motives that support redistributive public policies. I could sign a standing banker's order to give away everything I earn above the national average, for example, and it wouldn't kill me. I could even try to increase my income at the same time, knowing the excess would go to people who needed it more than I did. I'm not about to do anything of the kind, but the equality-friendly justifications I can think of for not doing so all strike me as rationalizations. (An exception mentioned by Cohen applies only to the superrich: that in an unequal society their status gives them influence and power with which they may be able to do more to help the poor than they could by giving all their wealth away.) One person to whom I presented Cohen's question replied, "I guess I'm not an egalitarian."

That may be the right answer, and the discomfort induced by the question may be a form of false consciousness. But then what morally coherent position do we hold, those of us who confine the responsibility for distributive justice to public institutions? Those institutions represent us and act in our name, so why aren't we prepared to put our money where our vote is? Can a fundamental moral distinction be made between what we owe one another collectively and what we owe one another as individuals—even where the summing of individual choice has substantial collective consequences? I don't know, and that is why Cohen's simple question seems to me one of the hardest for contemporary political theory.

10

Justice and Nature

I

Justice plays a special role in political argument: To appeal to it is to claim priority over other values. Injustice is not just another cost; it is something that must be avoided, if not at all costs, then at any rate without counting the costs too carefully. If a form of inequity in social arrangements is unjust, it should not be tolerated, even if that means giving up things that may be very valuable in other ways.

So the *scope* of justice is very important. How much of the structure of social institutions it covers will determine how much elbow room is left in a just society for the legitimate pursuit of other values. The more comprehensive the requirements of justice are—the more they expand to fill the space of social possibilities—the less room there will be for the pursuit of other social goals, and the more restricted will be the means available.

I am going to describe and, tentatively, defend a position that limits the scope of justice and by implication leaves the range of legitimate social arrangements more open, by giving greater scope to the social pursuit of ends that have nothing to do with justice and that are not mandatory in the same way. But this is still an account of justice considered as a strict requirement, not to be overridden merely on the basis of cost-benefit calculations. And the type of account I shall be concerned with is a *deontological* one, specifically concerned with the avoidance of arbitrary social inequality. Let me explain what I mean.

Disputes about justice are disputes about which determinants of political, social, and economic status are admissible and which are not.

Formally, all the leading candidates for an answer to the question are theories of *procedural* justice—theories according to which the legitimacy of any particular allocation of advantages and disadvantages depends on whether the *system* in which it arose is just. But there are two different types of standards for evaluating those systems—consequentialist standards and deontological standards—and they correspond to two very different conceptions of what makes an inequality unjust.

Consequentialist standards evaluate each system on the basis of the kinds of results it tends reliably to produce—results for equality, welfare, freedom, opportunity, and so forth. The procedures that confer legitimacy on any particular allocation are themselves evaluated by reference to those results, even though the allocation itself is not. Deontological standards, on the other hand, evaluate each system on the basis of the intrinsic character of the procedures themselves—what kinds of causes they permit to determine social outcomes, whether they discriminate between individuals on grounds that are unfair, whether they fail to treat people as they deserve, whether they penalize people for things that are not their fault, and so forth—the aim being to describe conditions of *pure* procedural justice.

These two types of standards may be combined in the evaluation of a system, but they are distinct. Deontological principles of justice are supposed to limit the means by which a society may pursue other aims, and in this discussion I shall be concerned with a problem in the interpretation of deontological standards of justice, though I'll also have something to say about the choice between deontological and consequentialist approaches.

The question I want to ask is this: What must be the causal responsibility of society for an inequality in order for it to be unjust? And paired with this question is another: When does the causal responsibility of nature for an inequality save it from being unjust? What, in other words, is the relation between natural unfairness and social injustice? It is clear that, even though these questions are very crudely put, different answers to them will yield different conceptions of the scope of justice—of the amount of social space that is taken up by the requirements of justice. In view of its connection with equality, justice is potentially omnivorous, so the question is how its reach may reasonably be limited.

The problem arises in the controversial type of case in which a natural difference between people interacts with social mechanisms in such a way that it gives rise to differential advantages or disadvantages—even though the mechanisms do not specifically aim to produce any such correlation. Deliberately imposed inequalities—like the systematic exclusion of blacks from all but menial employment—are uncontroversially unjust. But what about inequalities of access to public facilities and public transport for the disabled? To what extent does justice (as opposed to utility or plain decency) require a society to eliminate or reduce the differences in social opportunity that result from blindness, deafness, or confinement to a wheelchair?

Virtually every expansion of social opportunities will bring with it such differences. But the problem does not stop with physical disabilities. It applies to at least some of the inequalities that arise between men and women, between persons differently favored by what Rawls calls the natural lottery, or between those who are more and less energetic or enterprising—through the operation of a system of social and economic relations that is not designed to produce those results but that produces them nonetheless.

The reason that these cases give rise to controversy is obvious. On the one hand, the involvement of social mechanisms in generating the results, once it is understood, implies some responsibility on the part of society for the creation of inequalities that may seem arbitrary, even though they are not deliberately imposed. On the other hand, since the interpersonal differences that produce the inequalities are not socially created but natural, the responsibility of society for avoiding such results is not clear. Every society is in the business of transcending the state of nature, but how far it is obliged to resist the differential impact of fate and natural variety is a difficult question. One can think of it as a question about what belongs among the background or baseline conditions from which issues of social justice begin and what belongs in the foreground as part of the subject matter of social justice. The more one regards nature as a given, the less one will regard society as accountable for those inequalities in whose generation nature plays a central role. Then the judgment will seem possible that certain misfortunes are simply bad luck and that society can legitimately ask whether the benefit of alleviating them is worth the cost.

Another element has to be included in this picture: the responsibility of individuals for what happens to them. I have described the contrast between the responsibility of society and the workings of nature or fate. But there is also a contrast between both of those and the responsibility of each individual for what he makes of his life, against the background of what he is dealt by nature and the social system in which he finds himself. The allocation of responsibility among these three elements in the actual circumstances of human life, where they interact inextricably to yield complex patterns of benefit and disadvantage, is an uneasy moral task. The scope of society's responsibility, and therefore of the claims of social justice, is determined by how far the (nonmoral) responsibility of nature and the (moral) responsibility of individuals encroach on it, in light of their common agency.

I am going to explore the relation among these factors in the deontological theory of justice, with special reference to the significance of nature. Things look very different if one takes a consequentialist approach, based on the equity of outcomes rather than on the intrinsic legitimacy of causes. From that perspective nature has no special significance: The fact that a misfortune is due to nature is no reason whatever for society to accept less responsibility for relieving it. I shall not ignore this alternative. In fact, I shall suggest that it may be better suited to handle inequalities due to nature than a deontological approach. But my main concern will be with the significance of naturally caused inequality as a problem for a deontological conception of pure procedural justice.

The influence of nature can be seen in two directly opposed ways: as a factor for which *individuals* are not responsible, and whose inequities society must therefore correct, or as a factor for which *society* is not responsible, and whose unequal results it can therefore accept. I myself have always been sympathetic to the liberal-egalitarian tendency to expand the scope of social responsibility and correspondingly to diminish the scope both of nature and of individual responsibility in justifying inequality. But I am beginning to have my doubts, and I want to investigate the resistance this expansive tendency encounters from a more limited conception of justice—one that centers on equal treatment rather than on the avoidance of inequality in the broadest terms. Even a position of this kind will require that society consider all the results of public policies and institutions—those that are permitted, as well as those that are actively produced—but it will assign the special priority associated with justice only to those results that are produced in certain ways. My main aim is to describe the issue accurately.

II

I shall begin my discussion with John Rawls, whose application of a particular standard of fairness to every aspect of social institutions is the most prominent contemporary refusal to accept either the verdict of nature or the demands of individual responsibility as limits on the scope of justice. As he strikingly puts it, "In justice as fairness men agree to share one another's fate."[1]

Rawls's approach is theoretically deontological in foundation, though its development leads in a consequentialist (but nonutilitarian) direction. On the one hand, he argues that certain causes of social inequality are unjust because they are morally arbitrary. On the other hand, he moves toward the position that all social inequalities are unjust unless they work to the benefit of the worst off. Such a general egalitarianism does not require reference to certain types of causes, since it could

---

1. *A Theory of Justice* (Cambridge, Mass.: Harvard University Press, 1971), p. 102. This sentence has been eliminated from the rev. ed. (Cambridge, Mass.: Harvard University Press, 1999).

reflect a pure assignment of priority to the interests of the worst off.[2] This is the natural result of his method of identifying the principles of justice as those that would be chosen in the original position, under the veil of ignorance.

Persons choosing in the original position—all of them identical in motivation and information—are concerned primarily with the effects on themselves of social institutions, and only secondarily and instrumentally with the procedures by which those effects are produced; the original position is designed to focus attention on each of the lives in the society as if it were one's only life, and thereby to motivate the contracting parties to give priority to averting the worst possible outcomes for anyone before going on to the next worst, and so forth—avoiding trade-offs based on aggregation across lives. (I set aside the long-standing controversy over whether Rawls is right to claim that it would be rational for parties so situated to choose in that way.) This individualized priority method for dealing with conflicts of interest is an important alternative to the aggregative–maximizing method of utilitarianism, and sometimes its results may correspond to those of procedural fairness, but they are not the same idea. It is true that the original position is itself supposed to be an example of pure procedural justice—a hypothetical choice under conditions that are fair—but that claim raises further questions that I want to postpone.

Setting the original position aside, we can see the deontological idea of fairness at work in Rawls's principles of justice themselves and the intuitive support he offers for them, particularly in his interpretation of the second principle in section 12 of *A Theory of Justice* and his discussion of the tendency to equality in section 17.

The two principles of justice are really three principles, to be applied in order of priority:

1. Maximum equal basic liberty
2a. Fair equality of opportunity
2b. The difference principle

The first is a principle of strict equality in certain basic personal and political rights and freedoms—such as the right to vote and hold office, freedom of expression and association, freedom of religion, and due process of law—but not including any kind of broad economic liberty. The two-part second principle is one of permissible *in*equality. It distinguishes admissible from inadmissible causes of socioeconomic inequality, and is therefore particularly expressive of a conception of fairness.

2. See Derek Parfit, *Equality or Priority?* Lindley Lecture (Lawrence: University of Kansas Press, 1995).

Holding the first principle fixed, Rawls considers three possible two-part principles of distributive justice, in order of increasing egalitarianism:

1. Natural liberty: negative equality of opportunity (careers open to talents) plus efficiency (otherwise known as Pareto optimality)—in other words a more or less laissez-faire socioeconomic system against the background of a political and legal system of equal rights, which also prohibits discrimination in employment and contract.

2. Liberal equality: positive (or fair) equality of opportunity plus efficiency—in other words a system that guarantees a level playing field so that people of equal natural talent have equal access, regardless of wealth, to the educational and other resources that will permit them to develop their potential qualifications for competitive positions. Beyond that, the economy is not geared to redistributive purposes, and the chips are allowed to fall where they may.

3. Democratic equality: positive equality of opportunity plus the difference principle—whereby not only do people of equal talent have equal chances of success but also the range of variation of success available in the society is that which will allow the least successful, irrespective of their talent, that is, the bottom of the range, to fare as well as possible.

Rawls's strategy is to argue that liberal equality is fairer than natural liberty and that when we think about the reasons for this, we see that by a parallel argument democratic equality is fairer than liberal equality.

There is already an important element of fairness in the system of natural liberty. The principle of negative equality of opportunity—which is opposed to nepotism; exclusion on the basis of race, class, sex, or religion; and other forms of bias that displace merit as the basis of appointment or promotion—is one of the fundamental rules of fairness. It eliminates from the social system certain sources of inequality in the allocation of advantageous positions that clearly fail to justify their results. By opening the doors to competition and eliminating private bias and discrimination, it blocks an important type of unfairness not covered by the equal basic liberties of the first principle. Once those conditions are met, the results of free interactions between individuals through a market system are claimed by the defender of natural liberty to be fair, because they will not be influenced by morally irrelevant factors. As Rawls says, the model of natural liberty, like all conceptions of fairness, including his own, is one of pure procedural justice, since the fairness of the outcomes, whatever they are, depends only on the background conditions and procedures that give rise to them.

But Rawls objects that under the system of natural liberty other morally irrelevant factors will still be operative, notably the competitive advantages and disadvantages in the starting point that people inherit from the socioeconomic fortune of their ancestors:

> The existing distribution of income and wealth, say, is the cumulative effect of prior distributions of natural assets—that is, natural talents and abilities—as these have been developed or left unrealized, and their use favored or disfavored over time by social circumstances and such chance contingencies as accident and good fortune. Intuitively, the most obvious injustice of the system of natural liberty is that it permits distributive shares to be improperly influenced by these factors so arbitrary from a moral point of view.[3]

Here we have a more controversial judgment of unfairness, for it adds to the category of unfair causes of inequality the unequal effects on present generations of inequalities of success that arose in the past. It is held to be unfair that a person should be socially rewarded or punished simply because of the success or failure of his ancestors, however fair that success or failure may have been in itself. Note that the objection is on *historical* rather than *end-state* grounds (to invoke, for a purpose contrary to his, the distinction drawn by Robert Nozick in *Anarchy, State, and Utopia*.)[4] The trouble with natural liberty is that it permits outcomes to be determined by a historical process that does not confer just entitlement on the result.

We are now very used to the idea that hereditary class advantages are unfair, particularly when they interfere with equal opportunity. The step from natural liberty to liberal equality is a familiar one. As Rawls says, the provision of fair, as opposed to purely formal, equality of opportunity is an attempt to create the social conditions under which those with similar abilities and skills have similar life chances, whatever class they are born into.

But Rawls finds this ideal insufficient for two reasons. First, as a practical matter it is unattainable: So long as the family exists, social class will inevitably have a substantial effect on the probability of competitive success through its influence on training, connections, and motivation,[5] however much may be done in the public domain by public education and social programs to level the playing field. Second, liberal equality

3. *A Theory of Justice*, rev. ed., pp. 62–63.
4. (New York: Basic Books, 1974).
5. That is the point of this statement: "Even the willingness to make an effort, to try, and so to be deserving in the ordinary sense is itself dependent upon happy family and social circumstances" (*A Theory of Justice*, rev. ed., p. 64)

leaves untouched an enormous source of inequality in social advantage
that Rawls also thinks unfair namely, the natural lottery of talent. This is
the most radical of Rawls's claims. He finds that from a moral standpoint the influence of either social contingencies or natural chance on
the determination of distributive shares seems equally arbitrary. What
can be said of being born with a silver spoon in your mouth also goes for
being born with golden genes.

Clearly there are differences among the three causes of inequality
here identified as unfair. Discriminatory exclusion is practiced inten-
tionally by individuals and firms; class is a predictable effect of the operation of the social system; natural talent is biological. Someone might resist Rawls's claim of equal arbitrariness, from a moral point of view, on
the ground that a person's development and employment of his own
abilities, whatever they may be, is an entirely legitimate determinant of
his fate. But Rawls believes that the implication of the social system in
the process by which natural ability is translated into unequal social and
economic advantage means that this is another form of unfairness, unless (as under the difference principle) the process is harnessed for essentially egalitarian ends.

It would be difficult to dispute Rawls's claim that "No one deserves
his greater natural capacity nor merits a more favorable starting place in
society,"[6] except perhaps by appealing to a theory of the transmigration
of souls. Rawls's principle of fairness seems to be that inequalities of social advantage that are substantially caused by differences over which
people have no control and which they can't be said to deserve are arbitrary from a moral point of view, and can be saved from unfairness only
if they are justified by an aim that is not arbitrary from a moral point of
view. That gives society the task of resisting all social inequalities partly
caused by nature, even when they are also partly caused by individual
choices and by useful institutions.

One source of resistance to this claim comes from the idea that deontological importance attaches to individual responsibility. Any system
that reduces the variation in outcome due to factors over which people
have no control is likely also to affect the variation that can be influenced
by choices, decisions, and effort. For example, a system that satisfies the
difference principle will raise the lowest level to which someone can fall
as a result of sheer laziness, and probably also lower the highest level to
which any given person can rise through the energetic development and
application of his abilities. So if there is a positive value, from the point
of view of justice, in a process through which results are determined by
choice and effort, there is a potential conflict between limiting the influence of the natural lottery and preserving the influence of choice.

6. *A Theory of Justice*, rev. ed., p. 87.

The doubts I want to investigate, however, have to do with the naturalness of the natural lottery itself. Rawls regards the social consequences for individuals who differ in natural endowment as in themselves prima facie unfair, and it is important to distinguish this reason for the difference principle from one (also offered by Rawls) that emphasizes the adverse effects on fair equality of opportunity for those, whatever their natural endowment, who are born into the lower classes of a socially and economically stratified society. I believe that considerations of class in fact provide a stronger argument for favoring the worst off than does the arbitrariness of the natural lottery. It is the effect of differential rewards correlated with the natural lottery on the *next generation*—the adverse effect on their fair equality of opportunity—that provides the best deontological argument for the justice of raising the social minimum as high as possible. The idea is that injustice and social responsibility are clearer when involuntary *social* differences cause inequality than when involuntary natural differences do.

There are even elements of this idea in Rawls's theory, in spite of its tendency toward a general egalitarianism. Rawls clearly believes that some causes of inequality are more unjust than others. Consider the priority of equal opportunity, for example. Rawls argues convincingly for fair or positive equality of opportunity, but the issue arises even earlier, with respect to negative equal opportunity, or careers open to talents. Why should the prohibition of exclusionary discrimination in employment take priority over the difference principle, which is designed to combat the unequal effects of the natural lottery? Discrimination in some cases hurts those who are among the economically worst off, but not always. Quite often there is discrimination against *successful* racial, religious, or ethnic minorities. Yet even when it doesn't harm the worst off, this cause of inequality seems worse than the economic consequences of the natural lottery. How exercised should we be, after all, by the effects of the natural lottery on those born into the upper or middle classes? At that level it doesn't seem very unjust, and it certainly doesn't seem remotely comparable in injustice to racial or religious discrimination against persons at the same level.

Perhaps discrimination is worse because it is deliberately imposed out of ugly motives. But if we consider instead the priority of positive equality of opportunity, that factor is out of the picture. Making positive equality of opportunity lexically prior to the difference principle is equivalent to regarding the unequal effects of class as more unjust than the unequal effects of talent. It is difficult to see how such a rule would be chosen in the original position by persons who did not know which of the two effects they were more likely to suffer from.

This priority means something only if there is a potential conflict between the two parts of the second principle. The idea is that preservation of equal opportunity can warrant the *sacrifice* of the interests of the worst-off class and the sacrifice of more general socioeconomic equality. Such a conflict could arise if the costs in public expenditure of providing fair equality of opportunity across the board (notably to the middle class) were really substantial—in widely available and excellent public higher education, for example—and if they had to be traded off against the level of the publicly guaranteed minimum standard of living. If in these circumstances one gave priority to equal chances for those who are capable of advanced education over a rise in the social minimum for those who are not, it would mean that one regarded the arbitrary influence of class on people's life prospects as more unfair than the arbitrary influence of the natural lottery—that one thought it was more important to protect social mobility than to diminish inequalities of reward.

All this suggests that two different ideas are at work in Rawls's conception of justice as fairness. One is the general idea, expressed by the original position, that all causes of social inequality for which the individual is not responsible are morally arbitrary. The other is an idea of differential illegitimacy of different types of causes of inequality, ranging from deliberate oppression to the unplanned effects of natural differences. The second idea, unlike the first, lends itself to different ways of drawing the line between what is illegitimate and what is not. Within that framework, I would assign to the natural causation of social inequalities a lesser importance than it has in Rawls's theory.

III

Let me return to a brief consideration of the original position. At the outset of *A Theory of Justice*, Rawls explains why he calls the theory "justice as fairness" by reference to the hypothetical social contract which is its ostensible foundation: "The original position is, one might say, the appropriate initial status quo, and thus the fundamental agreements reached in it are fair. This explains the propriety of the name 'justice as fairness': it conveys the idea that the principles of justice are agreed to in an initial situation that is fair."[7] We have here two or perhaps three applications of the concept of fairness: (1) The initial situation, an imaginary condition of radical equality, is described as fair; (2) therefore the agreements reached in it are fair, that is, (2a) the principles agreed to (the objects of those agreements) are fair. The fairness of the principles (and also presumably the fairness of the actual institutions of a society that conforms to those principles) derives from the fairness of the situation in which those principles would be chosen.

Rawls argues that his principles would be chosen in the original position, which, if true, would show that they are fair in the derivative sense.

---

7. *A Theory of Justice*, rev. ed., p. 11

But I have always thought that the more direct arguments discussed above have independent force and that they show the idea of fairness at work in a more transparent way.

In drawing back to the Archimedean standpoint of the original position, Rawls has attempted to apply the idea of fairness at the highest possible level, with the thought that any results obtainable at that level will transmit their fairness to more specific and concrete consequences of those results. But the complete absence of distinguishing information under the veil of ignorance and the identity of assumed motivation of the parties amounts to the assumption that fairness requires that all causes of inequality be instrumentally justified by reference to their contribution to everyone's interest.

If there is genuine controversy about whether differences in natural endowment can be permitted a noninstrumentally justified role in a fair system of distributive justice, or whether the influence of choice in combination with other factors has independent legitimating force, the question cannot be settled in an illuminating way by referring it to a procedure of choice of principles in an original position defined as Rawls defines it. If the fairness of the original position is interpreted in such a way as to make all differences between people irrelevant, because morally arbitrary, then the result will be clear in advance. No procedures will be fair except those that are instrumentally effective to everyone's advantage, and perhaps to the advantage of the worst off. Fairness that inheres in the procedures themselves will disappear.

An instrumentally justified principle for identifying fair procedures is very different, as a moral conception, from the deontological idea that some features of a process can legitimize or delegitimize the outcome in themselves, whereas others cannot. The case is analogous and closely related to that of the substitution of a purely instrumental criterion of responsibility and desert for a retributive one in the domain of punishment. There, too, one starts from the idea that people are responsible for causing harm to others, and deserve punishment for it, in the absence of any of a specific set of excusing conditions. But then, psychological and social and even metaphysical reflection may lead to a gradual expansion of the range of excusing conditions, until at the limit some people reach the position that no one is ever responsible for what he does or deserving of punishment for harm done, in the original, deontological sense. (We do not create ourselves.) Such a conclusion is likely to be followed by the adoption of an alternative instrumental justification of the practice of holding people responsible and punishing them (not necessarily a utilitarian one—it might well be egalitarian or involve other ends). But that is clearly a different moral idea—a replacement.

The two examples are connected by the concept of desert. Both theories of social justice and theories of punishment and responsibility try to tell us when what someone gets is deserved and when it isn't. But that means something very different in a theory that accords intrinsic legitimizing or delegitimizing force to the conditions that lead to the result from what it means in a theory that says someone deserves what he gets if it is what he is entitled or liable to by the procedures of an economic or legal system that is justified by its general consequences. The difference in meaning remains even if the consequences in question are evaluated by a strongly egalitarian and nonaggregative standard of the kind favored by choice in the original position, as Rawls interprets it. That standard embodies the judgment that all social inequalities are sufficiently tainted by arbitrary influences so that none of them can be regarded as intrinsically fair: Hence only instrumentally justified departures from equality are legitimate.

In a view of that kind, the requirements of justice quickly expand to fill all of social space. What I want to do is to describe a credible alternative deontological position that restricts injustice to certain specifically social causes of inequality, whose avoidance takes precedence over the general welfare and other goals, but which still leave a good deal of space free.

As I have indicated, this doesn't mean that we need not be concerned about other inequalities. It means only that the concern will not take the deontological form of a judgment of intrinsic procedural unfairness. It will instead reflect humanitarian concern for those in need or a general concern for human welfare or a pure priority ranking of more basic interests over less urgent ones.

IV

We can distinguish deontological conceptions of justice according to the way in which they assign systematic influences on how people fare under a social system to three categories: the good, the bad, and the neutral—depending on whether the influence legitimates, delegitimates, or does not affect the legitimacy of the process in question. Minimalist conceptions put much more into the neutral category. The idea is that a great deal about human life has to be regarded as part of the given, the luck of the draw, the arbitrary but morally neutral background that forms the starting point from which moral evaluation can then proceed. Free choice legitimates, and coercion or discrimination delegitimates, but a great deal else is fate or luck—the given, from a moral point of view—so that the space for justice or injustice in the operation of society is relatively small, including only certain kinds of direct human causation.

Expansive conceptions, by contrast, are reluctant to assign elements of the human condition to fate or luck if they are susceptible to change by social action. Injustice on these views consists not only in certain kinds of interference but also in tolerance—the refusal to interfere with a system that permits certain background conditions to have their unequal effect. Every social system depends on conventions and rules and laws that the members uphold, and if these have foreseeable consequences of a systematic kind, then the society is responsible for those consequences and they cannot be placed out of the reach of judgments of justice and injustice. That is the thought that brings class, natural endowment, and handicap within the range of objectionable causes of inequality in life prospects. The other important feature of more expansive conceptions is that when inequality results from a mixture of unchosen background conditions and choice, the arbitrariness of the background conditions tends to dominate in determining the injustice of the result.

What should we take as given—as background—in thinking about justice? Though it is clear to me that what is accepted as given by a libertarian outlook is too broad and exempts too much socially produced inequality from criticism on grounds of justice, I am not sure what to think about natural differences. Although a just society will not impose differential status or advantage on the basis of natural differences, is the charge of injustice defused if responsibility for an inequality can be assigned, at least substantially, not to society but to nature?

To pose the question, we have to be able to give sense to the idea that a difference in social outcomes is due primarily to a natural difference. Let us suppose that the outcome is not identical with the natural difference and, furthermore, that it could not even have appeared without the social institutions that create the dimensions of variation in which it arises. Here is one possible account of what needs to be the case for the claim to be nevertheless plausible that the outcome is due primarily to a natural difference. This is true if

1. There is a variable natural property of individuals that plays a significant causal role in the generation through social institutions of outcomes that differ substantially in value for those individuals.
2. The institutions do not aim to produce the differential results but have an independent and legitimate purpose.
3. To achieve that purpose without generating such differences would be significantly more difficult or costly.

I am not here offering conditions under which the resulting differences are legitimate but only defining an explanatory relation that would have to be invoked by someone who wanted to ascribe primary responsibility for those differences to nature. Thus, the reference to a "legitimate purpose" in clause (2) does not settle the question of whether the *institution* is legitimate. Someone disinclined to pass the buck to nature might reject the moral conclusion that such an explanation tended to show that the differences were not unjust, arguing instead that society retains responsibility for avoiding such differences even if it can do so only through institutions that would achieve the same purpose with much more difficulty or not at all. I assume that people can agree about the proposition that a social difference is primarily due to nature while disagreeing about its moral significance. The core of the idea that nature is an illegitimate cause of inequality is that other social goods must be sacrificed, if necessary, to inhibit the operation of that cause—hence the above definition.

What is the moral conception according to which nature limits the writ of justice? As the thin end of the wedge, consider an imaginary case of purely natural inequality: Suppose that 10 percent of the population—distributed randomly over other significant groups—were the bearers of a gene that expresses itself in an incurable degenerative condition that appears between the ages of thirty and forty and kills the victim within five years. Even if the gene were detectable early on, would justice demand some compensatory social policy to make up to these people for their tragically shortened lifespans? And if the effects of the gene could be slowed down, but only at very great cost, would it be *unjust* of the society not to provide such treatment at public expense?

Clearly, a decent society would invest in research to seek an affordable method of genetic correction. Clearly, sufferers from this condition would be very unfortunate. But it seems to me morally intelligible to hold that because it is nature that has dealt them this blow, a social system that does not engage in significant rectification of the inequality is not guilty of injustice. That would be an example of the view that justice does not always require that we share one another's fate.

That is a fanciful and extreme example, but it has real analogues. Some people suffer from congenital disabilities, mental and physical, which are not only burdens in themselves but also affect the capacity to gain benefits through social interaction. Others suffer from diseases, like kidney failure, that require expensive treatment. I do not think society has the same kind of responsibility, under justice, with respect to those inequalities that it has with respect to others that are socially caused. Straightforward humanitarian concern for the welfare of those afflicted will not be undermined by the fact that nature is responsible for their disadvantage, but the kinds of deontological judgments of justice that *take precedence* over the general welfare may be.[8]

---

8. It seems to me a mindless abuse of the ideal of equality, for example, that advocates for the disabled have blocked the installation of freestanding pay toilets on Manhattan streets (of the kind that are common in Europe) unless they could all be large enough for wheelchair access (*New York Times*, January 27 and 28, 1993).

I want to concentrate, however, on two sorts of differences whose societal impact is very deep and pervasive. The first is the natural lottery of talent, already discussed. The second is sex.

I have already said something about the relation between the natural lottery and income, but let me make clear what I am not saying. I am not saying that those whose talents have higher market value deserve a higher reward for their efforts, so that it would be wrong to try to implement the difference principle. To come as close as possible to an equal society would be *pro tanto* a good thing. My doubts have to do with whether this goal should have the kind of moral priority associated with justice. On the other side of the balance, I have in mind not the freedom of marketable individuals to make money but rather the value of other goods that have nothing to do with equality; they belong to the pursuit of excellence, and are therefore naturally associated with inequality—education, for example.

In a modern society education is to a considerable extent a public function, and the ideal of providing equal educational opportunities for all persons of equal ability, regardless of their financial resources, is an important part of social justice. That is consistent, however, with unequal opportunities for persons of different abilities, so we are faced with the question of what a just allocation of opportunities or resources is, corresponding to the variation in abilities. A hierarchical educational system that allows people to go as far as their abilities and efforts will take them in the pursuit of objective intellectual excellence will apportion both opportunities and resources very unequally. Does that create a problem of prima facie injustice—to be laid to rest only if the policy can be shown to be maximally beneficial, in its long-term effects, for the less talented?

I don't think so. A reasonable answer to the charge that unequal benefits from the educational system are unfair is that once the society provides fair equality of opportunity, it is nature, not society, that is responsible for the unequal capacity of individuals to benefit from it. Educating individuals to the limit of their capacity is a legitimate aim, and social inequality generated in the pursuit of a legitimate aim is not unjust if natural differences among the persons involved are its primary cause. (Effects on third parties are another matter, so this argument works better in defense of educational inequalities per se than for resulting economic inequalities.) An alternative would be to construe this case as a form of *equal* treatment of individuals by society, with equal treatment defined in a way that is proportional to the person's natural educational potential. But that seems to stretch the idea of equality too far out of shape. It is pretty clear that the good of education is unequally distributed by such a system. I believe a similar antiegalitarian position is appropriate for support for the arts, scientific research, exploration, pure scholarship, architecture, and so forth.

V

To get into deeper and hotter water, let me turn to the responsibility of nature for the difference between the sexes. Sex is not a dimension along which people vary, like intelligence or athletic ability. People simply come in two sexes, whatever other categories they are divided into. The purely natural differences do not give a clear advantage to one sex or the other. Their learning abilities are similar. Women can bear children and men can't, but women can become pregnant against their will, and childbirth can be painful and dangerous. Women are on average smaller and less strong than men, but they are also physically tougher and longer-lived.

But when we think of the differences between the lives of men and of women we are thinking of differences that result from the ways in which social, political, and economic institutions accommodate the biological facts of reproduction. The natural division of reproductive labor has enormous consequences in all actual societies, and it is the responsibility of every society to reflect on what those consequences should be. The question is whether the responsibility of nature for the fundamental difference that is at the root of it all should affect our judgment about what kinds of social differences or inequalities between men and women are unjust.

We are familiar by now with the pervasive effects of the difference between the sexes on the status of women even in liberal modern societies: political weakness, lower earnings, economic dependence, lesser educational and employment opportunities and expectations, sharp drop in standard of living when a marriage breaks up, not to mention less tangible psychological burdens—all these disadvantages are common when the traditional domestic division of labor is the norm.

Does it mean anything to divide or factor the responsibility for these inequalities between nature and society? Obviously the social contribution is large and affords a substantial foothold for judgments of injustice on most conceptions. In any case, many of the results are bad considered merely from the point of view of the general welfare, without regard to procedural justice. But that is not the end of the story. The question remains, how far justice requires a society to go in eliminating the social expression of sexual differences—specifically, whether this goal requires, if necessary, the sacrifice of substantial aggregate social benefits or other benefits considered by comparison optional. How much resistance to the effects of the reproductive difference between the sexes does justice require, and what form should the ideal of equality take? (I take it for granted that evaluatively equal treatment and equal opportunity for men and women would in any case have to be defined in a way that takes into account biological differences, but I set that aside.)

The problem I am talking about presents itself only under the following conditions:

1. There is a social arrangement—not necessarily a very rigid one—that assigns different probabilistic occupational expectations to men and women as a result of the statistically normal division of labor within the family.
2. The results are on average better for men than for women at all social levels.
3. Elimination or reduction of the difference would require sacrifices in aggregate welfare or in general socioeconomic equality.

Perhaps the third condition is never satisfied; perhaps the elimination of differential gender expectations will always advance welfare and general equality. In that case the problem does not arise. But I am interested in the question of whether sexual inequality has the deontological weight to trump those other values.

It certainly looks as though the path of least resistance for most contemporary societies is to accept a defeasible presumption that women, except upper-class women who can afford servants, will be the primary caregivers for the children they bear and perhaps nurse, and will therefore have more limited occupational opportunities outside the home than men. Is this natural? It seems to be an inertial consequence of the facts of pregnancy, childbirth, and nursing. For a society to depart substantially from this path of least resistance requires effort and resources, so it is not inaccurate to say that nature is a major cause of the usual situation.

As usual, two diametrically opposed responses offer themselves. One could say that the responsibility of nature defuses the charge of injustice by diminishing the responsibility of society. Or one could say that the fact that people are not responsible for their sex makes it almost as unfair for a society to permit sex to differentially affect expectations as it would be to impose such an inequality.

In economically undeveloped societies, a severe limitation of occupational choice will often be unavoidable. Perhaps most people have to be peasants—with no opportunity even for secondary education and no chance of social mobility—simply so that there will be enough to eat. The economic surplus above subsistence may be sufficient to support only a military and administrative structure and a tiny educated class. In such circumstances it is likely that some sexual division of labor will also be part of the inescapable fate of almost everyone, and it couldn't be called unjust.

But what about the modern world? Is it really conceivable that we should accept a situation in which being a woman and having children is on average a disadvantageous position, socially and economically, unless that situation can be altered without net social costs? That seems particularly hard to swallow. Perhaps not all natural differences are equal. Perhaps sex is unique.

This is essentially a question of fair equality of opportunity. Justice plausibly requires that hereditary socioeconomic class not be allowed to impose big differences in life chances on persons of similar natural ability. Should it not also rule out the imposition of big differences in the life chances of men and women of similar natural ability—regarding this as unjust at whatever socioeconomic level it occurs?

In this case I believe the answer is yes. But I also believe that this answer is consistent with the exclusion of naturally caused inequalities from the domain of injustice. The reason is that the role of social institutions in generating inequality between the sexes is too deep. In the case of a handicap or a natural ability, different social outcomes are (or could be) produced by interaction between those features and a labor market that depends not at all on differences in the prior social status of the potential employees. By contrast, most differences in employment and economic opportunities for women are parasitic on a more fundamental social fact, the sexual division of labor, and not on the direct interaction between biological sexuality and the nonsexual labor market. Social institutions do not in this case merely create a dimension of variation in occupational roles that then interacts with natural differences between men and women to produce different results, on average. Rather, the labor market interacts with the *status* difference between men and women. The causes of inequality are social all the way down.[9]

This shows itself also in the fact that the differential consequences for the two sexes are substantially independent of whether, in the particular case, the individual occupies the traditional role in procreation and child-rearing. Every woman, whether or not she will have children, grows up deeply affected by the general expectations and opportunities that prevail in a social order in which almost all women who have children are primarily responsible for their care and for the maintenance of a home, and thus require the economic support of a man. Consequently, although the purely biological facts often have a direct effect on an individual woman's life, it is the pervasive social institutions that arise partly in response to the biological facts that have a systematic effect on all women's life prospects and opportunities. Regarding those inequalities as due to nature is really the wrong way to look at the matter.

This case may be more like class or even caste than it is like other natural differences that interact with the social system to generate inequalities. The influence of nature here is at one remove: It has an effect on the social structure itself and not merely on how different individuals fare under it. If we think of the difference in social and economic expecta-

---

9. I am indebted to Janos Kis for clarification on this point.

tions for men and for women as a denial of fair equality of opportunity—due not to the socioeconomic status of one's parents but to the position to which one is assigned at birth in society's great enterprise of reproducing and continuing itself—then it looks like a strong case of deontological injustice, with all the concomitant priorities. And unlike the effects of the natural lottery, it seems equally wrong at every socioeconomic level. If every woman is seen by society as a presumptive bearer and primary caretaker of children, and if this presumption carries with it substantially diminished educational, economic, and professional expectations of other kinds, then we are closer to a caste system than to the vagaries of the natural lottery.

It is very unclear, however, what a just alternative would be. The "disappearance of gender"[10] doesn't seem a reasonable or realistic hope. There will inevitably be some general social expectations, of a rough kind, about the division of domestic labor between the sexes. Even the expectation that there will be no "normal" division of labor whatever would be an expectation that society, through laws and conventions, would have to impose on its members, and it might burden some individuals just as unfairly as an alternative norm. This is a platitude, but the aim of justice in this area should be not to eliminate differences but to devise a system that treats men and women comparably by some measure that takes into account their differences. Equivalence of opportunities and life prospects, in evaluative terms, can be only roughly defined, given the importance of the differences, but it is the only reasonable goal if the deontological standard of justice is to be applied to this case.

That means two things: First, women who do not have children should have exactly the same opportunities as men, so that the range of results depends entirely on the variation in ability and inclination. Second, women who do have children, even if this inevitably affects the shape of the rest of their lives, should not thereby end up worse off than men. But to even define this condition, let alone to say how it is to be realized and at what cost, is the real task. Some combination of enhanced opportunities, flexible working conditions, shared or assisted child care, and economic compensation or security is clearly necessary to approximate fair equality of opportunity.

But the consequences of nature are always, I suspect, going to be significant. To put it abstractly, the type of criterion of equal treatment that I am suggesting would imply that if there are natural differences of inclination or aptitude between men and women that produce social consequences whereby men and women fare differently, then those

<hr>

10. See Susan Moller Okin, *Gender, Justice, and the Family* (New York: Basic Books, 1989), p. 171. "Gender" here means not sex but the conventional and institutional differences in status, role, and expectations accorded to the sexes by collective social understanding.

consequences are unjust only if they arise through the interaction of the natural differences with institutions that provide evaluatively unequal opportunities to women and men (or what is the same thing, to those who are potential bearers of children and those who are not). Of course, the application of such a criterion involves difficult judgments not only about evaluative comparability but also about which differences are natural and which are themselves socially produced. But it would be amazing if none were natural.

VI

Whatever may be said about the sexes, there remains a general moral issue over what it is for different persons with widely different natural characteristics to nevertheless be treated by a society on equal terms. How strongly does the equality of the terms have to resist the effects of the differences? According to minimalist views, we come to the societal table with our differences, and equality or inequality of terms is judged by what society adds above that baseline. According to more expansive views, everything is fair game, and the responsibility of society is not limited. I have tried to describe a credible view that limits the strict deontological force of requirements of justice to the avoidance of inequalities for which social institutions are primarily responsible.

When it comes to evaluating inequalities that are not caused by one of the deontologically forbidden factors, there are many options. One might consider only efficiency; one might consider whether the inequalities are consistent with the welfare of society as a whole, measured by some kind of utilitarian standard; or one might consider whether they leave some people in conditions of absolute deprivation or need that no decent society should tolerate, whatever the cause. One might even adopt a standard extensionally equivalent to the difference principle, accepting social inequalities only if they are as advantageous as possible to the worst-off group in the society—but in that case the principle would be a consequentialist standard rather than a deontological one, based not on the wrongness of certain *causes* of inequality but rather on a pure priority for the interests of the worse off over those of the better off, whatever the causes.

But with the exception of the condition of decency, which mandates a social minimum, I would favor none of the above. If justice is a strict but not all-encompassing requirement, then it does not tell us what to do with the leeway that is left once its conditions are met. The elimination of injustice may leave us with many possible goals and reasons for social policy or private action, none of them mandatory and many of them in conflict with one another. This gives us important social, political, and individual choices, but they may be less constrained by the need to avoid arbitrary inequalities or to resist the social consequences of natural differences than I was once inclined to think. Justice and individual rights set an indispensable standard of what every society owes its members, but that in itself is a reason to be wary of their indefinite expansion or of the elevation of any other comprehensive value into a strict requirement.

11

Raz on Liberty and Law

Liberalism of one kind or another is the dominant political tradition of Western culture; that is why it is under such constant attack. But while the conflicts between liberalism and various authoritarian, repressive, radical, romantic, or theocratic alternatives produce a good deal of excitement on a world scale, a quieter and intellectually more demanding argument has gone on within the tradition about the best way to interpret liberalism, both theoretically and in application to concrete social and political problems. One of the most important issues in this debate is how liberalism justifies its distinctive toleration for multiple different and inconsistent forms of life and systems of value—its remarkable impartiality, in political terms, among diverse conceptions of the human good and its commitment to allow individuals to seek their own salvation or self-realization provided they do not interfere with the same freedom of others. Unlike those French secularists who forbid Muslim girls from wearing head scarves to school, true liberals are reluctant to interfere even with antiliberal cultures in their midst. This is sometimes foolishly thought to depend on moral skepticism, but it doesn't: The commitment to toleration, if it is not a mere compromise imposed by the balance of power, can be justified only by a strong moral conviction that it is right—otherwise why not suppress what we don't like?

On this question the Oxford moral and legal philosopher Joseph Raz is a distinguished defender of a view that, in its logical structure and basic values, adheres to the tradition of John Stuart Mill. Raz believes that liberal institutions are justified because, for those civilizations capable of sustaining them, they provide the best way of promoting human well-being: their value, in other words, is instrumental. The argument depends both on a definite view of the nature of human well-being, human good, or human happiness—in which autonomy has a central place—and on a belief that liberal toleration increases the likelihood that people will attain that good. This was precisely the structure of justification, in its original utilitarian version, that John Rawls set out to oppose with his contractarian alternative and his motto that "the right is prior to the good." Raz believes, on the contrary, that the system of individual rights is a means of achieving the good and cannot be explained as an independent part of ethics or political theory. The issue between them is whether recognition of liberal rights is in itself a way of treating people as equals—an end in itself—or whether it is a consequence of equal concern for their welfare—a mere means.

Ethics in the Public Domain[1] offers an excellent exposure to Raz's thoughts not only about such general questions of moral and political philosophy, but also about concrete issues such as multiculturalism, free speech, and national self-determination (in an essay written jointly with Avishai Margalit) and about the nature of law and its relation to morality (a subject on which he is in the positivist tradition of H. L. A. Hart). The essays use and develop ideas set out in his earlier books, particularly *The Authority of Law* (1979) and *The Morality of Freedom* (1986).

Though Raz believes that rights are valuable because they promote the good, he is not a utilitarian because he does not believe that all human good can be reduced to a single, experiential common denominator, such as pleasure or happiness or satisfaction of desire. Nor does he think that the good life requires the kind of individualistic freedom of choice in professional, personal, and aesthetic matters that typifies modern, economically and politically liberal cultures. His position, which he calls "value pluralism," is that many different and incompatible ways of life are good in their own (incompatible) terms. Since he thinks that secure membership in a community is very important, he finds value in all kinds of relatively closed cultures. Autonomy is a general condition of well-being only because the value of a way of life, even one that does not include constant opportunities for choice, is greatly enhanced if it is as a whole freely chosen or freely accepted by someone to whom other options were available.

Our moral duty to foster the well-being of others therefore requires us, in Raz's view, not to promote a particular form of life, but to make available the conditions of free pursuit of any of those forms of life that are capable of being good for their participants. Liberalism is the political fulfillment of that duty. Governments cannot make people's lives good; they can only make available, to as many people as possible, a range of valuable options that will permit them to make something of their lives. It won't be the same range of options for everyone in the

---

1. Joseph Raz, *Ethics in the Public Domain: Essays in the Morality of Law and Politics* (Oxford: Clarendon, 1994).

society, nor will it include the same range of options in every liberal society, but this is no cause for regret. The very plurality of valuable forms of life and the incompatibility of their conditions make it inevitable that they cannot all coexist, because every social arrangement will rule out many of them. Raz says, for example, that the legal recognition of homosexual marriage, even if it is a good idea, would entail the passing away of the current type of marriage, whose exclusive heterosexuality is part of its essence. But his value pluralism is very generous: He thinks that many cultural forms typically repellent to liberals, including religious orthodoxies that assign strictly differentiated sex roles, can give people good lives, provided they socialize their members appropriately. That is why he supports toleration.

This is an attractive position, so why have Rawls and others found it unsatisfactory? One reason is that many liberals don't share Raz's value pluralism, and even those who do want to find a justification for liberal institutions that could be accepted by those who do not—by persons whose views about what constitutes a good life are much less latitudinarian than that, whether their conception is religious, hedonistic, ascetic, or communitarian, or even, for that matter, individualistic. The idea that there are principles of right independent of specific, comprehensive conceptions of the good for human beings envisions a common ground for the evaluation of the basic structure of political institutions that does not depend on settling all basic value disagreements. If liberalism had to depend on the acceptance of value pluralism, or perhaps of some narrower doctrine about the nature of human well-being, then it could not command the ethical allegiance of those with conflicting convictions—those who assign much less value to alternatives incompatible with their own form of life than Raz does and who would choose very different means for promoting the well-being of other members of their society.

That prompts the search for a different kind of political theory, driven not by the desire to advance everyone's well-being as we see it but rather by an independent duty to respect them as autonomous equals, at least in the design of our common political institutions. Such a theory would explain why people have a right to live as they choose even if it will not promote their well-being, provided it doesn't interfere with the equivalent right of others. In particular, none of us may impose our own, contested conception of well-being as the basis for the political order—and that applies even to a conception like Raz's value pluralism.

The difference between Rawls's view, based on the requirement to treat people as equals, and Raz's view, based on the duty to promote their well-being pluralistically conceived, is that the former aims for broader moral appeal. It can be equally accepted by people who disagree about the ends of life, as they inevitably will in a pluralistic society. Of course, people also disagree about the existence and definition of the right to be treated as an equal, and no justification of liberalism can avoid imposing a regime of toleration on some people who reject its fundamental values. But an equality-based conception of rights aims to rely on a more restricted, and therefore more widely acceptable, foundation than any specific conception of the good or the ends of life.

Admittedly this strategy has something paradoxical about it, because it requires us to subordinate the pursuit of the good for everyone as we see it to another value that is more obscure, in spite of its intuitive appeal. It has always been a puzzle why people's rights should be more ethically important than their welfare. Raz's position removes the problem by explaining rights as a means to the good as he understands it. Rawls, by contrast, finds in liberal rights an ethical and political common ground acceptable to parties who can't agree about the good or about the best means of achieving it. Liberal institutions enable them to show respect for one another nonetheless.

To take a current example: What should be the attitude of political liberals toward religious fundamentalist communities in their own societies—Islamic fundamentalists in Britain and Christian fundamentalists in the United States? Raz was strongly affected by the Rushdie affair, and in a superb essay on multiculturalism he addresses with great sensitivity the question of how liberalism should deal with the kind of cultural diversity that puts religious fundamentalists cheek by jowl with secular individualists. He argues that with the sort of cultural pluralism that has resulted from the labor migrations of this century, mere toleration for minorities is no longer enough. It is necessary to adopt a positive liberal multiculturalism—the ideal of a political society that embraces diverse communities "and belongs to none of them." Raz believes we should support the equal standing of rival groups on the basis of a value pluralism those groups themselves do not share—because, while fundamentalists are mistaken in thinking that theirs is the privileged gateway to human fulfillment, nevertheless their communities provide one among many forms of well-being. Liberals "should not take cultures at their own estimation" but should recognize value even in those whose claims to absolute superiority they reject.

Although Raz's pluralism opposes the forcible detachment of children from the culture of their parents and recognizes the deep desire of most parents to understand their children and share their world, it also implies that such communities should not be permitted to prevent their members from leaving or from acquiring the capacities (through education) that would make it possible to move to another form of life. Finally (to come to the Rushdie case) it does not require that others should be prevented from condemning or denigrating those cultures, since hostility between rival forms of life is inseparable from commitment, and the state does not endorse such hostility merely by tolerating its expression.

Raz cannot expect the fundamentalists to endorse tolerant political institutions (except as a form of self-protection where they are weak), since that would require them to accept a value pluralism incompatible with their deepest beliefs. Yet he hopes that liberal multiculturalism would produce changes in its component subcultures that could lead them to support it. He says it requires a common political culture of mutual toleration and respect, which permits participation in a shared political arena. But how is this possible, in Raz's theory? If such a society "belongs to none" of its subcultures, that must mean its common political framework is something they all have reason to accept, rather than an imposition of the values of one of them. Raz is faced with a dilemma: Either the liberal framework depends on value pluralism, in which case it is imposed by a subgroup, or else it depends, as in Rawls's theory, on an independent conception of right, in which case it isn't just an instrument for the promotion of well-being.

Raz has excellent things to say about freedom of speech, commonly derided by authoritarian governments as a right that is of interest only to writers and intellectuals. He makes the important point that the protection of freedom of expression contributes to the common good, vastly beyond the interests of those who take advantage of it to express themselves on controversial subjects, because it is a vital tool in the detection and prevention of the worst forms of abuse of power through cruelty, massacre, neglect, or sheer incompetence and stupidity. The interests of speakers or writers are only a small part of it, as we can see by looking around at the sorts of things, from mass famine to genocide, that seem to happen with such ease in closed societies. Raz says, strikingly:

> If I were to choose between living in a society which enjoys freedom of expression, but not having the right myself, or enjoying the right in a society which does not have it, I would have no hesitation in judging that my own personal interest is better served by the first option. I think that the same is true for most people. (p. 39)

This instrumental justification of the right explains why its importance is much greater than its direct contribution to the well-being of the rightholder would suggest. Many familiar rights, including property rights and freedom of contract or occupation, are justified partly by this kind of contribution to the common good.

Yet I doubt that it is the whole story. The idea of equal respect for persons, for their autonomy and sovereignty over their thoughts, utterances, and personal choices, is a value distinct from concern for their general well-being, and it justifies the protection of individual rights of liberty not just instrumentally but also as something we owe to each person for its own sake. That is part of what it means to treat others as moral equals. But this is part of a continuing argument—an argument that has certainly not been won by either side.

Half the book is taken up with the philosophy of law, and as Raz's political theory stands in opposition to Rawls's, in legal theory his position contrasts with Ronald Dworkin's. Raz is a positivist about law in the following sense: He believes that the content of the law can be identified by reference to social facts only, without resort to moral argument. Law is the directive of a suitably constituted authority, telling its subjects how they ought to behave. This doesn't mean that moral argument has no role in the law. First, it will often be part of the reason for legislation: Conduct may be made illegal because it is wrong. But one can tell that it is illegal even without agreeing that it is wrong. Second, application of the law by the judiciary may require moral reasoning, particularly if the law includes general concepts like reasonable care or equal protection of the laws, which have evaluative meaning. But here again, says Raz, the identification of the law on the basis of a judicial decision does not require that one agree with the moral reasoning that led to it. Third, there are, according to Raz, gaps in the law—cases in which the social facts, including the language of the relevant statutes and the precedents, do not by themselves determine a verdict. In such cases it is appropriate for the judge to make new law, filling the gap, and he should be guided by the moral aim of producing the best outcome, all things considered. Fourth, there may be cases in which the law is so bad that not only should private individuals disobey it but even judges should refuse to enforce it.

The main contrast with Dworkin's position has to do with adjudication. Where Raz sees gaps in the law, Dworkin sees demands for interpretive discovery, in which moral reasoning plays a role. Dworkin denies that a judge should regard himself as making law when he produces a new decision in a difficult case: Rather he must regard his reasons for the decision as showing that that is what the law is—and this in turn constrains the reasons on which he can rely. On Raz's theory, a judge who relies on moral reasoning is creating law, and it is only after the decision has been rendered that others can base on it the judgment that that is what the law is. The process of judicial deliberation may include moral reasoning; the process of discovering what the law is does not.

This is not just a disagreement about how to describe what judges do; it is a disagreement about what they ought to do. Raz believes that Dworkin's interpretive method, of deciding hard cases in light of the morally best construction that fits with the existing legal system, is objectionable because "it advocates acting on principles which may never have been considered or approved either explicitly or implicitly by any legal authority and which are inferior to some alternatives in justice and fairness" (p. 309). In other words, he finds Dworkin's method too conservative: Raz believes that when a decision is not dictated by the prior acts of legal authority, a judge should not be required to decide the case on principles extrapolated from the existing legal system, if there is a morally superior alternative. This is precisely a rejection of the value that Dworkin calls "integrity": The moral fit between the system of law as a whole and a particular decision that is not positivistically determined by that system is a constraint on adjudication that Raz does not accept.

He believes that courts should be regarded as frankly political, except that they are charged primarily with advancing the common good— what's good for everyone—rather than the overall balance of conflicting interests. But how that is to be done, what rights it requires us to protect, is an issue on which people will disagree for the same types of reasons that divide them politically elsewhere. So there is no deep difference between criticizing a court for a bad interpretation and criticizing the legislature for a bad law. Here, again, I find Raz too suspicious of fundamental divisions between different forms of legal, moral, and political reasoning. In spite of his value pluralism, he retains the reductionist impulse to analyze morality in all its aspects as a way of making things better on the whole.

But this is an important viewpoint, and Raz offers his sharp opinions in clear and unpretentious prose that is accessible to anyone who cares about the moral dimension of politics and the law.

12

Waldron on Law and Politics

Jeremy Waldron's assertive and engaging book *The Dignity of Legislation*[1] has a chip on its shoulder—hence the title. In the academic culture of legal theory that Waldron partly inhabits, legislatures come in for a lot of distrust, or even contempt, in comparison with courts. Courts are widely thought to arrive at their results by reasoning, whereas legislatures are thought to operate by the crude clash of partisan interests. In the United States there is substantial support for the role of courts in guarding individual rights from the depredations of legislative majorities that would otherwise trample them underfoot: This is the famous institution of judicial review, whereby laws passed by Congress or the state legislatures can be struck down as unconstitutional if they violate certain individual rights—to personal freedom, as in the case of abortion, or to equal treatment, as in the case of racial segregation. Britain, too, may soon acquire some version of this system, in the form of a Bill of Rights.

No one who followed the impeachment of President Clinton can find it easy to associate the U.S. Congress with the concept of dignity. But Waldron has an important argument to make, which applies even more sharply to the ideological pandemonium of the United States than to the relatively civilized conflicts of British politics. He believes that the defining "circumstances of politics" are such as to make the legislature, and not the courts, the appropriate arena for deciding the most fundamental questions that face a society. The reason is that there is no consensus about basic principles of justice in modern societies, and it is better that these conflicts be argued out in a larger, representative body than in a smaller, highly selective one like the U.S. Supreme Court. Since that

1. (Cambridge: Cambridge University Press, 1999).

Court also operates by voting and often decides cases by a five-to-four majority, the issue is not whether majorities should be permitted to decide fundamental disputes of justice and rights but who it should be a majority of, how the members of the group should be selected, and what kind of debate should lead to the vote. Courts and legislatures are very different in these respects, and many liberty-loving Americans would be profoundly uneasy if the protection of freedom of speech, for example, were entrusted entirely to elected representatives of the popular will like Henry Hyde and Trent Lott. But that uneasiness doesn't prove they're right.

The question concerns the relation between theories of justice and conceptions of institutional design. Waldron faults John Rawls for treating the institutional question only for the case of a "well-ordered society," one whose members are agreed on the fundamental principles of justice and committed to supporting institutions that conform to them. Waldron says that since there are no well-ordered societies, the real problem is how to design institutions that will command the allegiance of people who *disagree* over fundamental questions of justice—not just over means or interests or purely personal values—but who nevertheless have to live together and arrive at collective decisions that will be "resilient to disagreement," decisions that even the losers can accept with good grace.

What is the best way to insure this resilience to disagreement: a system of legislative supremacy or a constitution with substantive protections immune to legislative revision and enforced by judicial review? Of course, neither of these may work, as we can see from the failure of democratic governments in various countries with beautifully drafted democratic constitutions. On the other hand, given the right traditions of political culture, either method may produce stability. The question, however, is not just a practical but also a normative one: What procedural or substantive guarantees would effectively justify us in accepting and supporting the results of a collective decision when it goes against us—when we think the result is not just practically but also morally wrong?

That is something that will inevitably happen in politics. A state can certainly survive and function without meeting this condition of legitimacy; historically, most states have not even tried to meet it. But Waldron argues, against the contemporary current, that a system of legislative supremacy can do so, and is better suited for the purpose than a system that includes substantive antimajoritarian provisions enforced by the courts.

The case for substantive guarantees, exempt from legislative revision, is that there are certain outcomes a minority cannot be expected to accept just because they have lost a vote. Experience gives us good reason to fear our fellow human beings. If I were a secular Turkish citizen, I would be grateful that the secular character of the Turkish state is constitutionally guaranteed—and enforced by the army! No doubt those who want to make the *sharia* the law of the land find this procedure completely unacceptable. But there is no way to design a system that will command the actual acceptance of all the conflicting parties. At some level, the institutions by which decisions are taken in controversial cases must reflect a particular conception of justice or fairness or equity that will itself be controversial. There is no way to step back or up to a level so purely procedural that everyone can be expected to accept and support its contingent results, whatever they may be.

Waldron recognizes that we cannot separate issues of institutional design entirely from issues of justice, but he does want to keep substantive justice as much as possible within the political arena, for resolution by legislative conflict, rather than embodying it in constitutional provisions that are resistant to change and interpreted by judicial reflection and argument. The problem is to identify the conditions under which this can be done fairly. So there is a hard kernel of justice in the defense of majority rule as a way to handle the bulk of those other, more substantive disagreements about justice that will inevitably divide a modern society. Waldron's defense appeals to a particular conception of fairness, but though he presents it almost as a formal solution to the problem, it is really no less controversial than the substantive positions that it is supposed to enable us to decide among.

His defense draws on some classic writers in political theory, not all of whom were convinced democrats—Aristotle, Hobbes, Locke, and Kant—and the book is a contribution to the history of political thought, as well as to contemporary debate. (He is very good, for example, on the Hobbesian structure of Kant's political theory.) The argument has two parts: a defense of the superior wisdom of larger decision-making bodies over smaller groups or single individuals and a defense of majority rule as fair and respectful of the equality of the participants.

There is the purely probabilistic point, due to Condorcet, that if each of a group of individuals has a better than even chance of being right about something, a majority vote of that group has a better chance of being right than the average individual has. More specific to politics is the advantage, noted by Aristotle, of starting from the range of existing and conflicting opinions in search of the truth and trying to arrive at a conclusion that accounts for those disagreements and preserves what is valuable in them, rather than relying on the a priori reasoning of a single mind.

Related to this is the importance of being exposed directly to the points of view of others who will be affected by a policy or law, to overcome the natural limitations of imagination and make realities vivid. (Waldron has an interesting aside here about affirmative action: The use of diversity rather than purely individual merit as a factor in appointment to a law faculty, for instance, can still be defended as a form of decision based on merit—"only now, our starting point is the merit of the department or faculty as a whole;" that is, we are deciding among individual candidates on the basis of which one will enable the faculty as a whole to perform its function better.)

Waldron wants to go beyond the defense of majority rule as a mere mechanism for aggregating preferences or interests—a kind of electoral algorithm for cost-benefit calculation. His image of the dignity of legislation gives to each deliberator the role of trying to arrive at the objectively right answer, and not just to advance the interests of his particular constituents. They must contribute a forceful representation of those interests to the debate, but they should seek a solution that gives appropriate weight to all interests, and it is not to be assumed that utilitarian maximizing of some aggregate total is the answer that accords with justice.

There is no guarantee that this procedure will produce the right answer, and even when it does, not everyone will be convinced. But that, rather than a tradeoff among competing interests, should be the aim of the process and the aim of its participants. It is interesting that Waldron finds in Locke the suggestion that this openness holds true of the interpretation of the law of nature and that the legislature is the right place to develop a collective understanding of what it requires—not just to choose means to the implementation of a law universally available to introspection. He argues that the legislative is for Locke the supreme power because a representative body is needed to decide fundamental issues of justice and right.

The fact that any question can in principle be reopened and that there is unanimity about nothing does not help us, however, to decide what normative assumptions we may rely on in fixing the framework within which collective decisions on disputed questions will be made—perhaps even to the extent of excluding the possibility of certain changes through the framework that we have established. Waldron is presumably prepared to fix in stone some kind of representative democracy based on universal suffrage, even though there are still people who think women shouldn't be allowed to vote. If he is prepared to enforce a condition of equal citizenship for women in defining the group whose majority opinion should be decisive, that obviously cannot be explained by the fact that it would be chosen by the majority of that group—why that group rather than another, for example, men? This is an institutional rock bottom, based on an assumption about justice that is nonetheless controversial—more in some societies than in others. But then why not also hardwire into the system other strict conditions, like freedom of religion or freedom of speech or the prohibition of racial caste, putting them out of the reach of legislative majorities?

Clearly majority rule does make sense for many matters that have to be decided collectively, but Waldron's explanation of its completely general fairness is unconvincing. In a chapter called "The Physics of Consent," he argues that majority rule is the decision method by which persons who regard one another as equals can best express their mutual respect. He develops from passages in Hobbes and Locke the idea that if there is a majority that favors one side of a dispute, the opposing voices on the two sides will cancel each other out up to the number of the minority, leaving the surplus voices in the majority unopposed—and clearly the group should act when some members favor a course of action and their wishes are unopposed.

But these "extra" majority votes are not unopposed. They are opposed by the minority, whose opposition has not vanished just because it can be paired with an equal number of votes on the other side. It is sleight of hand to assimilate the preferences of the unpaired members of the majority to those of a member or subgroup with a preference on a matter on which everyone else is neutral.

The defense of majority rule has to be more complex than this—starting from the need for collective decision and the impossibility of unanimity and then assessing the probability of error for different methods of decision and the dangers of unfairness or prejudice in the particular issue to be decided. If we have to decide whom to throw out of an overcrowded lifeboat, it would be better to draw lots. But more important for our purposes, sometimes it may be better—fairer—to exclude from simple majority rule certain matters that, though controversial, have to be settled for a society in a uniform fashion and should be settled in one way rather than another. This depends on a substantive normative judgment, but so does the principle of universal adult suffrage, which underlies majority rule. If we think it unreasonable to expect people to support the decision of a majority that deprives them of their freedom of religion or their freedom of speech, we have grounds for making this institutionally impossible, as we have grounds for making it institutionally impossible for a majority to deprive a minority of its vote.

The buck has to stop somewhere, though whether judicial review or a constitutional council or something else is the best way of implementing this kind of countermajoritarian protection is another question. There is no a priori answer to any of these questions of institutional design, and conceivably Waldron is right that more of the contested issues of justice and rights should be in legislative hands than are now put there under the U.S. system. I only think he is too confident of having demonstrated this. In reply to Charles Beitz's criticism of the purely procedural interpretation of equal respect as implausibly narrow, he says:

> It is because we disagree about what counts as a substantively respectful outcome that we need a decision-procedure; in this context, folding substance back into procedure will necessarily privilege one controversial view about what respect entails and accord-

ingly fail to respect the others. Thus in the circumstances of politics, all one *can* work with is this "implausibly narrow understanding" of equal respect; and I hope I have convinced the reader that majority-decision is the only decision-procedure consistent with equal respect in this *necessarily* impoverished sense. (p. 162)

There is a whiff of the a priori in those italicized words *can* and *necessarily*. Every institutional design, however purely procedural, privileges one controversial view about justice, fairness, or respect over others. That by itself does not tell us how much should be so privileged in the design of the political and legal system and how much should be left to explicitly political decisions within that constitutional framework.

I admit that my doubts about Waldron's desire to expand the political to embrace as many of our collective disagreements as possible are largely due to pessimism, which is a matter of temperament and contingencies of experience. Waldron is originally from New Zealand, and I can't help thinking this has something to do with his relative optimism. Perhaps for some societies he is right.

13

Scanlon's Moral Theory

On occasion we are faced with acute moral choices—whether to join the Resistance or stay at home and care for our widowed mother; whether to run off with Vronsky or remain with Karenin. But largely, morality shapes our lives in ways we don't even think about; in fact, it does so partly by excluding certain options from our thoughts. Most of us, for instance, wouldn't even consider (1) threatening to expose a colleague's adulterous affair to his wife unless he votes our way on a contested appointment or policy issue; (2) extracting some cash from the pocketbook of an interior decorator as she inspects our house because we think she is overcharging us; (3) stealing a kidney for a friend who needs a transplant; (4) selling all we have and giving it to the poor. It isn't that we weigh the pros and cons and determine that the cons outweigh the pros. These things are not on the menu of options among which we feel we must choose. Such exclusions, as well as restrictions on what may legitimately be taken into account in some decisions but not in others (prohibitions against nepotism, for instance), typify the complexity of moral standards and suggest that an accurate account of morality and its role in life will not be simple.

T. M. Scanlon's understanding of this complexity and of its sources in the variety of human relations and values is one of the virtues of his original and illuminating book, *What We Owe to Each Other*.[1] Scanlon has been one of the most influential contributors to moral and political philosophy for years but, with overdeveloped diffidence, has never published even a collection of his most important essays. The appearance of his first book, a complex and powerful argument for the moral theory

---

1. (Cambridge, Mass.: Harvard University Press, 1998).

first sketched in his essay "Contractualism and Utilitarianism,"[2] is a philosophical event. Scanlon sets out an understanding of the nature and content of morality that is both original and credible, and he makes a strong case for its advantages over rival theories. The careful attention he gives to alternatives provides an accurate picture of the current state of the field as well.

The book is about morality rather than politics, though its general method can be applied to the political domain, where some of the most heated moral arguments and controversies take place. Recent work in political theory is more widely known, but moral philosophy has been an intensely active field over the past three decades, and Scanlon's theory addresses a number of its central questions: first, the question of the objectivity or truth of moral claims, their relation to reason, and whether or not they should be regarded as in some sense relative or subjective; second, the question of the kind of concern or respect for persons that is at the foundation of morality—what kinds of motives it calls on when it requires us to forgo certain means that would advance our personal aims and how much it can ask that we sacrifice for the sake of others; third, the question of how and to what extent individual rights, liberties, and prerogatives are morally shielded from encroachment in the name of the general good; fourth, the question of whether modest advantages to each of a large number of people can be aggregated to outweigh a large cost to each of a much smaller number for purposes of moral justification—a besetting problem for the intuitive acceptability of utilitarianism.

Scanlon's answers to these and other questions are presented in a theory of right and wrong that gets some support from particular moral intuitions but that is also deeply unifying, foundational, and systematic. It is not a general theory of value and the ends of life: Scanlon believes that morality—the standard of right and wrong in our dealings with other persons—forms a distinctive and uniquely important subpart of ethics more broadly conceived. That is the significance of his title.

The central claim is that the motivational source of morality is something quite different from the impartial universal benevolence most naturally expressed by a utilitarian system—a system whose ultimate standard is the maximization of overall, aggregate well-being. In fact he sets himself against the natural but simplistic idea that well-being is the dominant value or that any other measure of the good, conceived as an end to be promoted by everyone, is the basic form of value. Value takes many forms other than that of something to be promoted or maximized. One would not, he observes, show an appreciation for the value of friendship by betraying one friend in order to make several new ones.

2. T. M. Scanlon, "Contractualism and Utilitarianism," in Amartya Sen and Bernard Williams, eds., *Utilitarianism and Beyond*, (Cambridge: Cambridge University Press, 1982).

Morality, too, is not identified with promoting the good—human happiness, for example. Its motivating aim, according to Scanlon, is a certain kind of relation with our fellow human beings, the relation of being able to justify our conduct to each other, as individuals, in what he describes as a form of "codeliberation." That is how we show our appreciation of the distinctive value of persons—not by promoting a collective human good in which the interests of a minority may be outweighed by the greater aggregate interests of a majority.

The big question about such a proposal is where we are to find the standards that will enable us to justify our conduct to one another. Doesn't this just postpone by one step the search for the right standards? The originality of Scanlon's answer, and what will arouse the most critical resistance, is that he thinks the search for conditions of mutual justification will itself lead us to the right standards by combining diverse reasons in an appropriate framework for the identification of acceptable principles. But for such a method to succeed, it must uncover forms of justification that avoid circularity—that is, avoid appealing surreptitiously to precisely those moral principles that the process of mutual justification is supposed to warrant. It must appeal to something more fundamental.

Here is how Scanlon formulates his contractualism: "It holds that an act is wrong if its performance under the circumstances would be disallowed by any set of principles for the general regulation of behavior that no one could reasonably reject as a basis for informed, unforced general agreement." (p. 153). The idea is that if our aim is to be able to justify our conduct to others, we will want it to conform to principles that none of them could reasonably reject, because then everyone who shares our interest in justification would in effect be prepared to license what we do insofar as it accords with those principles. If we deliberately do something that is in this sense wrong, we are in effect saying that we don't care about its admissibility to reasonable others.

The term "contractualism" should not mislead: No *actual* contract is supposed to give rise to moral principles—only an imaginary agreement by persons imagined to be both reasonable and motivated by the desire for such an agreement. This is in the tradition of Kant's categorical imperative, which also tests principles of conduct by their hypothetical acceptability from all points of view, suitably harmonized. And as with Kant's method, the application of Scanlon's contractualism requires further value judgments since the question of what constitute *reasonable* grounds for rejection of a principle is an irreducibly normative one.

The nerve of Scanlon's position is that reasonable grounds for rejecting a principle come from the points of view of distinct individuals rather than from any collective or impersonal point of view. Utilitarianism would require us to accept principles that maximize the expected sum of human well-being, and reject those that do not, because the point of view from which acceptance or rejection is determined is that of impartial benevolence toward all. Scanlon, by contrast, believes one could reasonably reject certain principles that would maximize total well-being in favor of other principles that would produce a lower expected total but that have other virtues—they are less unfair, they do not impose such severe burdens on anyone, or they do not require the abandonment of important values not reducible to well-being. The reasonableness of an individual's rejection of a principle depends on his taking the points of view of other individuals into account, but it does not depend on conformity to the verdict of an external point of view that is not that of any individual.

Here is one of his examples:

Suppose that Jones has suffered an accident in the transmitter room of a television station. Electrical equipment has fallen on his arm, and we cannot rescue him without turning off the transmitter for fifteen minutes. A World Cup match is in progress, watched by many people, and it will not be over for an hour. Jones's injury will not get any worse if we wait, but his hand has been mashed and he is receiving extremely painful electrical shocks. Should we rescue him now or wait until the match is over? Does the right thing to do depend on how many people are watching—whether it is one million or five million or a hundred million? (p. 235)

Scanlon thinks that we shouldn't wait and that his contractualist approach explains why. The agony of Jones is vastly greater than the frustration any one of the viewers would feel at the interruption, so none of them could reasonably pose an objection to being deprived of fifteen minutes of the game merely to relieve Jones. And in Scanlon's model, it is only individuals whose objections can knock out a principle. There is no collective point of view that combines the frustration of all those viewers (a billion watched the final match between France and Brazil in 1998) and by reference to which Jones's pleas for rescue can be reasonably rejected—or even be counted unreasonable. If, on the other hand, Jones could be rescued immediately only by a maneuver that would kill Smith, also pinned down by the equipment, then it wouldn't be reasonable for him to object to Smith's being freed first. The comparisons that determine what is reasonable must, according to Scanlon, be individual rather than collective.

The same applies when we are evaluating moral principles in advance: We have to imagine their prospective impact on the lives of individuals, and if a proposed principle would generate reasonable individual complaints more severe than the alternatives, it is to be rejected. For example, suppose that in the course of construction of a new movie theatre in New York, an accident injures a pedestrian as severely as Jones has been injured. Here we have to compare the burden on each individual of a general slight risk of injury from construction accidents with the burden on each of those same individuals of ruling out all construction in cities, even with high but not foolproof levels of care to minimize the risk. As Scanlon points out, it is clear that no one could reasonably reject a rule that allows construction projects with due care—not even someone injured as a result. This is not because the aggregate pleasure of the moviegoers outweighs the agony of the accident victim but because a ban on construction would be pervasively and certainly constraining for almost everyone, including those who know it would save them from a small chance of being the victim of a construction accident.

To move to a more difficult example, let us ask how Scanlon's contractualism would handle the question of whether, in the present global situation of inequality, misery, and indifference, a well-off person who wished to do the right thing would have to devote most of his energy and resources to combating the acute misery that exists in the world (with the implication that most of us in the rich countries are living morally unacceptable lives). Utilitarianism makes it difficult to avoid this conclusion, and it is accepted by some utilitarians, like Peter Singer. There are so many people you could save, each at a modest cost.

Scanlon mentions this problem without offering an unqualified answer, but here is a suggestion: While no one could reasonably reject some requirement of aid from the affluent to the destitute, the cumulative effect on an individual life of an essentially unlimited requirement to give to those who are very much worse off than yourself, whatever other affluent people are doing, would simply rule out the pursuit of a wide range of individualistic values—aesthetic, hedonistic, intellectual, cultural, romantic, athletic, and so forth. Would the certain abandonment of all these things provide reasonable grounds for rejection of a principle that required it—even in the face of the starving millions? The question for Scanlon's model would be whether it could be offered as a justification to *each one* of those millions, and my sense is that perhaps it could, that one could say, "I cannot be condemned as unreasonable if I reject a principle that would require me to abandon most of the substance of my life to save yours."

This sounds hard, and I am not sure whether Scanlon would accept it. But if he would, it illustrates two important things about the method. First, as already indicated, it resists aggregation of the value of all the lives I could save by radically transforming mine and makes the reasonableness of my rejection depend on a one-to-one comparison. Second, it gives a result with regard to the demand for self-sacrifice different from the result it gives with regard to principles that govern the conduct of impartial third parties. For in the latter type of case, Scanlon holds that it is right to save the larger number when the threatened losses are comparable (as they are not in the case of poor Jones versus the soccer fans).

If, for example, a disinterested third party somehow had to choose between preventing the loss to me of all the resources and opportunities that permit me to lead an agreeable life and saving numerous other people from starvation, it is clear that no one could reasonably reject a principle that required him to save the greater number.

Differences of this kind, depending on the relations of the actors and victims in a situation, are common in the morality most of us intuitively take for granted. That morality treats very differently (1) the choice of a disinterested third party about which of two groups of people to rescue and (2) the choice of one party to rescue himself or a loved one, as opposed to some strangers, or (3) the choice of a third party whether to harm someone not otherwise in danger as a means of saving someone else from a greater harm or several other people from comparable harm. Potentially, the contractualist focus on individual points of view may be able to shed light on these complex standards.

As an example of (3), it seems clear that it would be wrong to cut up a healthy person to provide organ transplants that would save the lives of five other people and that a society that condoned such a practice would be monstrous; but why? Scanlon might say that any principle that permitted this would be reasonably rejected by everyone, in advance of their knowing the likelihood of their needing an organ transplant, simply because it is essential for each person's secure sense of self that the possible usefulness of his body parts to others should be ruled out of consideration absolutely. This is not actually circular, because it rests the general principle of bodily integrity on the vital importance of the sense of bodily inviolability for each individual. But it may seem a bit wobbly as a justification, since the ground, in a normative judgment about what it is reasonable to reject when bodily integrity conflicts with probable increases in ex ante life expectancy, seems just about as uncertain as the answer to the original question and not so different from it in character. In the face of the uncertainty that opens up when we try to apply the contractualist method to difficult cases with conflicting individual points of view, those who want answers may conclude that only a move back to a more impersonal level can determine what it is and is not reasonable for individuals to reject and that the contractualist framework is an unnecessary detour.

Others will find such crosscurrents and uncertainties true to the complexity of the moral life. Or perhaps the right thing to say, with Aristotle, is that one should not demand from the philosophical treatment of a subject more certainty than the subject admits. Scanlon's method is highly controversial, and so is its application to specific questions. It requires not just the plugging in of factual premises but also moral thinking all the way down. Its value lies not in providing a decision procedure but in identifying a very specific type of moral reasoning, as well as a special set of questions that must be posed in the course of it. Through its structure, Scanlon's method tries to explain what moral questions are questions about. If such an account succeeds, one of the things it will explain is why some of those questions are so difficult.

The most basic level of normative thought concerns the reasons people have—reasons for acting or refraining, for rejecting or accepting a principle, for taking into account or excluding from consideration other reasons in this or that context, and so forth. These are not just reasons "for" and "against" doing something. Scanlon makes an illuminating comparison between reasons for action and reasons for belief:

> We all recognize that reasons for belief do not . . . simply count *for* a certain belief with a certain weight, and deciding what to believe is not in general simply a matter of balancing such weights. There certainly are cases in which deciding what to believe is a matter of "weighing" evidence for and against the proposition in question, but this is so only because our other beliefs about the nature of the case identify those considerations as relevant for a belief of the kind in question. In general, a given consideration counts in favor of a certain belief only given a background of other beliefs and principles which determine its relevance. . . . Because of these connections, accepting a reason for or against one belief affects not only that belief, but also other beliefs and the status of other reasons. . . . My claim is that reasons for action, intention, and other attitudes exhibit a similarly complex structure. I do not mean to deny that deciding what to do is sometimes a matter of deciding which of several competing considerations one wants more or cares more about. My point is rather that when this is so in a particular case it is because a more general framework of reasons and principles determines that these considerations are the relevant ones on which to base a decision. Much of our practical thinking is concerned with figuring out which considerations are relevant to a given decision, that is to say, with interpreting, adjusting and modifying this more general framework of principles of reasoning. (pp. 52–53)

Reasons at a multiplicity of levels are what shape our conduct and our morality. Scanlon takes the existence of reasons as basic and indefinable in terms of anything else. They are not, in particular, reducible to desires or motives, and the reasons we have do not derive from desires.

We find out about what reasons we have by thinking about it. Since reasons are general, we can test the plausibility of a hypothesis about what we have reason to do or want by considering the credibility of its implications for other cases. Deciding what we have reason to do, like deciding what we have reason to think, is what makes us rational beings, and for a rational being, recognizing a sufficient reason to do something can by itself motivate that action.

So Scanlon is what would be called a realist about moral truth, but his realism has no metaphysical implications: It falls entirely within the realm of reasons and morality, and it rightly avoids the strategy of reducing these to anything else more ontologically or scientifically "respectable." As he puts it:

> The question at issue is not a metaphysical one. In order to show that questions of right and wrong have correct answers, it is enough to show that we have good grounds for taking certain conclusions that actions are right or are wrong to be correct, understood as conclusions about morality, and that we therefore have good grounds for giving these conclusions the particular importance that we normally attach to moral judgments. (pp. 2–3)

His defense of objective truth in morality is therefore to be found in his substantive moral theory and in the arguments he offers for particular results—much of which I haven't touched, in particular the detailed discussions of promises and of the conditions of responsibility.

There is room in Scanlon's theory for a degree of relativism, in two senses. The first is what he calls "parametric universalism," according to which the appropriate ways to show respect for certain general values such as privacy or loyalty will vary with different social conventions or traditions. The second is that people in different social circumstances or from different traditions may have reasons to accept or reject different principles. Some things, like killing people because of their membership in an ethnic or religious group you don't like, are wrong everywhere, whatever people may think. But other things may be wrong in one culture but not in another, because of different conceptions of personal honor, for example. Neither form of relativism is inconsistent with the objective correctness of moral judgments. These are just ways in which morality includes some relativity in its content.

Of course, realism about morality does not mean that the truth is what we now believe. As in any field where we are trying to get things right, or less wrong, we can never say that we have reached a point where openness to further revision is no longer necessary. As Scanlon observes, "Working out the terms of moral justification is an unending task" (p. 361). Moral philosophy should be interested in answers but even more in fully understanding the questions, so that the search for answers can be less blind. To this aim Scanlon has made what I believe will be an enduring contribution. Philosophy, like everything else, proceeds by the comparison of alternatives. Scanlon has presented a distinctive conception of the nature of morality that is compelling in itself, but which will deepen the understanding even of those who are not persuaded by it.

PART III

Reality

14

Rorty's Pragmatism

Truth and Progress,[1] the third volume of Richard Rorty's philosophical essays, can be recommended not only to Rorty's admirers and to those who regard him as a leading enemy of reason but also to anyone who wants to get a sense of a significant intellectual phenomenon. Rorty must be the contemporary anglophone philosopher most read by non-philosophers. His position resembles that of A. J. Ayer at the start of his career—a representative of philosophy to the larger world who offers a revolutionary view of the subject that suddenly makes it easy. For Ayer, the view was logical positivism; for Rorty, it is pragmatism; in both cases, they are just the messengers since the basic idea comes from others. And in both cases, the view has an almost irresistibly liberating appeal, especially to those who find philosophy a bore anyway, because it reveals that most of the philosophy of the past 2,500 years was a waste of time and that we don't have to worry any more about the problems that occupied the great figures of the past, even if those figures themselves retain a certain historical interest. At one point in the book Rorty says, "Perhaps it may clarify matters if I say that I hope that people will never stop reading, e.g., Plato, Aristotle, Kant, and Hegel, but also hope that they will, sooner or later, stop trying to sucker freshmen into taking an interest in the Problem of the External World and the Problem of Other Minds" (p. 47).

I would have been inclined to describe Rorty as suffering from what Wittgenstein called "loss of problems," but this remark suggests that his intuitive susceptibility to the basic questions of philosophy may always have been weak—that he was introduced to them by his teachers and

1. (Cambridge: Cambridge University Press, 1998).

feels put upon. Most philosophers, and many people who never become philosophers, think up the problem of the external world and the problem of other minds on their own, in early adolescence, without having read any philosophy or taken a course; they arise naturally. But Rorty apparently finds it easy to just drop these and other problems—the mind-body problem, the problem of the foundations of ethics, the problem of the nature of mathematical truth, and so on—like tiresome acquaintances who are cluttering up his social life.

Truth and Progress contains seventeen essays, some reacting to a dozen contemporary figures (Donald Davidson, Crispin Wright, Hilary Putnam, John Searle, Charles Taylor, Daniel Dennett, Robert Brandom, John McDowell, Michael Williams, Jürgen Habermas, and Jacques Derrida), others on the history of philosophy, and several on the relation of philosophy to ethics and politics. Rorty's distinctive tone and point of view come across strongly, and he works hard to dispel misunderstandings and identify agreements and disagreements with others. His comments on particular thinkers are never polemical, even if his more sweeping judgments are.

Rorty, unlike Ayer, did not start out as a prophet of philosophers' lib. He was once a sober scholar with a particular interest in the philosophy of mind, if anything somewhat overprofessional in trying to construct positions that responded to all the current arguments in the field at once. He was different from most young analytic philosophers mainly in the breadth of his interest and knowledge in both the history of philosophy and contemporary philosophy outside the analytic tradition. This reflected his training at Chicago and Yale before he began to teach at Princeton, that analytic hothouse where he gradually became disaffected with the enterprise.

The disaffection is not complete, because some of Rorty's heroes are analytic philosophers—Wittgenstein, Quine, Sellars, and Davidson in particular. They are cited as sources for Rorty's version of pragmatism along with Nietzsche, James, Dewey, Heidegger, Habermas, Derrida, and Kuhn. There's room for disagreement with his interpretation of some of these authors, but that is relatively unimportant, because Rorty's magic formula isn't hard to describe. It is a Darwinist outlook on language and thought:

> By "Darwinism" I mean a story about humans as animals with special organs and abilities (e.g., certain features of the human throat, hand, and brain that let humans coordinate their actions by batting marks and noises back and forth). According to this story, these organs and abilities have a lot to do with who we are and what we want, but have no more of a *representational* relation to the intrinsic nature of things than does the anteater's snout or the bowerbird's skill at weaving. (pp. 47–48)

This means that statements and beliefs are just items in the toolkit we use to survive and get what we want. They are justified if they serve our contingent purposes and not if they don't. Though truth is not their aim, we call them true if we and others are inclined to adopt them. We also acknowledge that they might turn out to be false, but this means only that something might persuade us to change our minds—not that they might not correspond to the way things really are. The latter idea presupposes the dread correspondence theory of truth, which is responsible for so much criminal waste of philosophical energy—on the problem of the external world and the problem of other minds, for example. There is no such thing as the way things really are, and the idea of comparing our concepts and beliefs with the world makes no sense. All there is is a bunch of us batting marks and noises back and forth, and once in a while some creative artist or scientist or social critic—Albert Einstein, Catharine MacKinnon, Elvis Presley—will come up with some new marks or noises, which other people will repeat or imitate and which will be interwoven with practices that some of us find we prefer to some of the old ones.

Such a view invites two charges that Rorty is concerned to rebut: the charge of relativism and the charge of inconsistency. The first seems to follow from his position that justification is always relative to a purpose or aim, so that it would appear that we must say a policy of genocide was right for the Nazis. To this Rorty replies that his position is not relativism but ethnocentrism; the pragmatic justification of all his statements depends on his own desires and values, and these imply that the Nazis' values and actions were wrong, period. There is no room in his language for a judgment that does not express his point of view, and hence no room for the thought of what was "true for the Nazis." For the same reason he holds, at least in one essay, that it was true that women should not be subjugated, even in the distant past when almost no one thought this, and that it was true before Newton said so that gravitational attraction accounted for the movements of the planets. The causal independence of the facts from our beliefs is one of our firmest beliefs, even though it makes no sense to say that our beliefs are true because they correspond to the facts.

The second charge, of inconsistency, arises because he seems to support his denial that there is a way things really are by appealing to a claim about the way things really are—namely, his Darwinian story. But he replies that this is not offered as an objective claim but only as a change in our self-image that may improve our lives:

> I stoutly deny thinking that Darwin describes reality, or even just us human beings, better than anybody else. But his way of describing human beings, when supplemented . . . by a story about cultural evolution, does give us a useful gimmick to prevent people

from overdramatizing dichotomies and thereby generating philosophical problems. By pressing an analogy between growing a new organ and developing a new vocabulary, between stories about how the elephant got its trunk and stories about how the West got particle physics, we neo-Darwinians hope to fill out the self-image sketched by the Romantic poets and partially filled in by Nietzsche and Dewey. (p. 152)

Rorty is also emphatic that pragmatism is not the view of common sense and that it is not supported by ordinary intuitions. It is offered as a revolution in progress, whose slogans he hopes may one day become common sense: that all experience is shaped by language, that language is contingently formed by history, and that therefore everything we think should be accompanied by a large dose of historicist self-consciousness or irony. The idea that our beliefs, about mathematics or chemistry or psychology or morality or anything else, could be in any strong sense objectively true or false should simply be abandoned.

I always feel when reading Rorty that his philosophical position must reflect his own mental experience, which is very different from the norm. He seems genuinely to find it possible to change his beliefs at will, not in response to the irresistible force of evidence or argument, but because it might make life more amusing, less tedious, and less cluttered with annoying problems. It's like moving the living-room furniture around. The policy of tailoring your beliefs and truth claims to suit your interests is the source of well-known horrors. Rorty has no use for any orthodoxies of that kind—his values are impeccably liberal—but he really doesn't feel the force of reason as a barrier to accepting a belief that would make life easier. And I think that without some feeling for the way in which conclusions can be forced on us by the weight of evidence and reasons, it is impossible to make sense of many of the linguistic and reflective practices that Rorty tries to capture in his pragmatist net.

He might reply that science easily lends itself to pragmatic interpretation. For example, Einstein's general theory of relativity is handy because it enables us to predict the displacement of the images of stars near the sun during an eclipse, whereas Newton's theory of gravity doesn't. But the only reason anyone cares about the results of those observations is that they show that Einstein's theory is an improvement on Newton's as an account of what the universe is really like. No basic science could be done by anyone who really took up Rorty's ironic historicism as an attitude to his own activities. Nor, of course, could most philosophy, but that's fine with Rorty, who hopes that the mind-body problem will one day seem as quaint as disputes over the relation between the first and second persons of the Trinity do to atheists.

Rorty cares about politics, the elimination of cruelty, humiliation, and want, and the preservation of liberty. I couldn't agree more with his vision of a liberal utopia "in which everybody has a chance at the things only the richer citizens of the rich North Atlantic democracies have been able to get—the freedom, wealth, and leisure to pursue private perfection in idiosyncratic ways." But he thinks that moral and political theory, insofar as they hope to defend anything like objective and universally valid principles, are worse than useless in support of these aims. In a perfectly awful essay on human rights, he compares moral philosophers with universalistic hopes to Serbian torturers, because both take themselves to be acting in the interests of true humanity by purging the world of what is not really human. Both parties, he says, use the term "men" to mean "people like us." This is one of those spasms of vulgarity to which Rorty is occasionally prone. Another occurs later in the same essay when he says we should "see Kant's *Foundations of the Metaphysics of Morals* as a placeholder for *Uncle Tom's Cabin*."

Rorty may be right that in politics, sentiment is often a more effective tool than reason. But too much of his broad appeal comes from the folksy scorn with which he encourages people to believe that they can stop worrying about difficult questions, liberate themselves from what he calls the "authoritarian" control of the image of a reality independent of themselves that they may or may not get right, and go with the flow, be it communal or idiosyncratic. This serves some of the worst elements in contemporary culture. Abandoning the aim of justification that is more than local in ethics and politics would not be beneficial in the long term. Not only ethical theory but also our resources for moral reflection would be much poorer if Kant had never written the *Grundlegung*.

Apart from philosophy, Rorty has all the right views. He even acknowledges that "the bad guys," those, for example, "who have no qualms about converting academic departments and disciplines into political power bases," tend to favor his side of the argument about the purely social nature of objectivity. But he thinks that the connection is not necessary and that one can remain attached to the virtues of disinterested research while holding a pragmatic conception of truth. Well, Rorty is living proof that it can be done, but that is of interest only if we want to evaluate pragmatism by pragmatist standards. Whether it succeeds or fails by its own standards, there remains the question of whether it is correct. That question, which Rorty regards as unintelligible, can't be avoided by those in his audience who are not already converted. They can't just take up his view as they might take up a new dance step.

Rorty does offer what he calls a "hackneyed" argument against the realistic alternative that he thinks should be abandoned. The argument is that we cannot directly compare our beliefs about electrons, for example, with electrons themselves. All we can do is justify them by reference to other beliefs or observations that are also usable as evidence only insofar as they can be captured in language. There is no "mind-independent" or "language-independent" world for our beliefs and statements to corre-spond to: The idea is completely empty, except in the sense that elec-trons are not *caused* to exist by our beliefs—but that is just another of our beliefs.

Rorty acknowledges that this argument on behalf of pragmatism is the same as the argument formerly used to support idealism, the view that everything is mental. It's just that Rorty holds that the mind isn't something with a nature of its own independent of its representation by language, so he gets the conclusion that everything is linguistic. The trouble with the argument for either conclusion is that it relies on a plat-itude that is consistent with both sides of the dispute to support one side against the other. A realist will agree with a pragmatist that when he talks about the relation between language and the world he continues to use language. That was never in doubt. The question is how some of these statements should be understood.

The statement that the hydrogen atom contains one electron is an as-sertion about how the physical world is, independent of our representa-tion of it. To be sure, the statement itself is a representation. But it is a representation not of another representation but of a physical element. Rorty seems prepared to say that hydrogen atoms would have had one electron even if human beings and language had never existed, but his explanation of the significance of this is just mirrors and smoke. To insist that it is one of our beliefs, and part of the language game we play with the word "electron," is to substitute a philosophical mantra for the un-qualified commonsense idea that the statement is true because it cor-rectly describes a nonlinguistic physical fact.

Pragmatism is offered as a revolutionary new way of thinking about ourselves and our thoughts, but it is apparently disabled by its own character from offering arguments that might show its superiority to the common sense it seeks to displace. Rorty says to us, "Try it, you'll like it!" But we can't try it unless we are persuaded to believe it, and for that kind of belief—belief that has truth rather than comfort as its object—pragmatism leaves no room.

15

The Sleep of Reason

I

You will remember that in 1996 a physicist at New York University named Alan Sokal brought off a delicious hoax that displayed the fraudulence of certain leading figures in cultural studies. He submitted to the journal *Social Text* an article entitled "Transgressing the Boundaries: Toward a Transformative Hermeneutics of Quantum Gravity," espousing the fashionable doctrine that scientific objectivity is a myth and combining heavy technical references to contemporary physics and mathematics with patently ridiculous claims about their broader philosophical, cultural, and political significance, supported by quotations in a similar vein from prominent figures such as Lacan and Lyotard and references to many more. The nonsense made of the science was so extreme that only a scientific ignoramus could have missed the joke. The article expressed deep admiration for the views of two editors of *Social Text*, Stanley Aronowitz and Andrew Ross, quoting at length from Aronowitz's crackbrained social interpretations of quantum theory. The article was published in a special issue of *Social Text* devoted to science studies, Sokal revealed the hoax, and nothing has been quite the same since. We may hope that incompetents who pontificate about science as a social phenomenon without understanding the first thing about its content are on the way out and that they may some day be as rare as deaf music critics.

Fashionable Nonsense: Postmodern Intellectuals' Abuse of Science,[1] published originally in French under the title *Impostures Intellectuelles*,[2] is a

---

1. Alan Sokal and Jean Bricmont, *Fashionable Nonsense: Postmodern Intellectuals' Abuse of Science* (New York: Picador, 1998).
2. Sokal and Bricmont, *Impostures Intellectuelles* (Paris: Editions Odile Jacob, 1997).

follow-up to the article. Sokal and his coauthor, Jean Bricmont, a physicist at the University of Louvain, decided to produce a fuller discussion of witless invocations of science and math by intellectuals in other fields. Because the most prominent culprits were French, they first published their book in France, but since the influence of these figures on American literary theory, feminism, and cultural studies is substantial, it is good that it has been translated into English.

Nearly half the book consists of extensive quotations of scientific gibberish from name-brand French intellectuals, together with eerily patient explanations of why it is gibberish. This is amusing at first but becomes gradually sickening. There is also a long and sensible chapter on skepticism, relativism, and the history and philosophy of science. An introduction and an epilogue discuss the political and cultural significance of the affair. Sokal's hilarious parody, with its 109 footnotes and 219 references, is reprinted as an appendix, together with comments explaining many of the travesties of science that appear in it.

There are a few differences from the French version. Apart from minor changes, the authors have left out a chapter on Henri Bergson and his misunderstanding of the theory of relativity, thought not to be of sufficient interest to English-speaking readers, and have added an article Sokal published in *Dissent* about his reasons for producing the parody. (This second article was submitted to *Social Text* but rejected "on the grounds that it did not meet their intellectual standards"—an unintended compliment.) The book is somewhat repetitive: The basic idea is contained in the parody and Sokal's comments on it. But the parody alone is worth the price of the volume:

> Postmodern science provides a powerful refutation of the authoritarianism and elitism inherent in traditional science, as well as an empirical basis for a democratic approach to scientific work. For, as Bohr noted, "a complete elucidation of one and the same object may require diverse points of view which defy a unique description"—this is quite simply a fact about the world, much as the self-proclaimed empiricists of modernist science might prefer to deny it. In such a situation, how can a self-perpetuating secular priesthood of credentialed "scientists" purport to maintain a monopoly on the production of scientific knowledge? (pp. 246–47)

> A liberatory science cannot be complete without a profound revision of the canon of mathematics. As yet no such emancipatory mathematics exists, and we can only speculate upon its eventual content. We can see hints of it in the mutidimensional and nonlinear logic of fuzzy systems theory; but this approach is still heavily marked by its origins in the crisis of late-capitalist production relations. Catastrophe theory, with its dialectical emphases on

smoothness/discontinuity and metamorphosis/unfolding, will indubitably play a major role in the future mathematics; but much theoretical work remains to be done before this approach can become a concrete tool of progressive political praxis. (pp. 252–53)

The chapters dealing in more detail with individual thinkers reveal that they are beyond parody. Sokal could not create anything as ridiculous as this, from Luce Irigaray:

Is $E = Mc^2$ a sexed equation? Perhaps it is. Let us make the hypothesis that it is insofar as it privileges the speed of light over other speeds that are vitally necessary to us. What seems to me to indicate the possibly sexed nature of the equation is not directly its uses by nuclear weapons, rather it is having privileged what goes the fastest. . . . (p. 110)

We are offered reams of this stuff, from Jacques Lacan, Julia Kristeva, Bruno Latour, Jean-Francois Lyotard, Jean Baudrillard, Gilles Deleuze, Régis Debray, and others, together with comments so patient as to be involuntarily comic. For example in response to Irigaray, they say, "Whatever one may think about the 'other speeds that are vitally necessary to us', the fact remains that the relationship $E = Mc^2$ between energy (E) and mass (M) is experimentally verified to a high degree of precision, and it would obviously not be valid if the speed of light (c) were replaced by another speed" (p. 110).

The writers arraigned by Sokal and Bricmont use technical terms without knowing what they mean, refer to theories and formulae that they do not understand in the slightest, and invoke modern physics and mathematics in support of psychological, sociological, political, and philosophical claims to which they have no relevance. It isn't always easy to tell how much is due to invincible stupidity and how much to the desire to cow the audience with fraudulent displays of theoretical sophistication. Lacan and Baudrillard come across as complete charlatans, Irigaray as an idiot, Kristeva and Deleuze as a mixture of the two. But these are delicate judgments.

Of course anyone can be guilty of this kind of thing, but there does seem to be something about the Parisian scene that is particularly hospitable to reckless verbosity. Humanists in France don't have to learn anything about science, yet those who become public intellectuals typically appear on stage in some kind of theoretical armor. Listen to Baudrillard:

In the Euclidean space of history, the shortest path between two points is the straight line, the line of Progress and Democracy. But this is only true of the linear space of the Enlightenment. In our non-Euclidean *fin de siècle* space, a baleful curvature unfailingly deflects all trajectories. This is doubtless linked to the sphericity of time (visible on the horizon of the end of the century, just as the earth's sphericity is visible on the horizon at the end of the day) or the subtle distortion of the gravitational field. (p. 150)

Sokal and Bricmont emphasize that their criticism is limited to the abuse of science and mathematics and that they are not qualified to evaluate the contributions of these writers to psychology, philosophy, sociology, political theory, and literary criticism. They only suggest, cautiously, that the dishonesty and incompetence shown in the passages they examine might lead one to approach the writers' other work with a critical eye. Clearly all this name-dropping is intended to bolster these writers' reputations as deep thinkers, and its exposure should arouse skepticism.

Sokal and Bricmont are playing it close to the vest here. They could no doubt find in these same works passages having nothing to do with science that are nonsensical, irresponsible, and indifferent to the meanings of words. But since there is no direct way to refute a fogbank, they have adopted the safer strategy of focusing on the occasions when these writers rashly try to invoke the authority of science and mathematics by using a vocabulary that does have a clear meaning and that could not serve their purposes, literal or metaphorical, unless it were being used more or less correctly. That also allows Sokal and Bricmont to explain why the scientific material introduced, even if it were not completely garbled, would be irrelevant to the literary, psychological, or social topics being discussed.

I am not sure how many admirers of these writers, or of postmodernist thought generally, will read this book. It is important to follow up on the positive effects of the original hoax, but will teachers of cultural studies and feminist theory go through these long-suffering explanations of total confusion about topology, set theory, complex numbers, relativity, chaos theory, and Gödel's theorem? The scientifically literate will find them amusing up to a point, but for those whose minds have been formed by this material, it may be too late. Or they may claim that these particular writers are not as important as the sales of their books suggest and that other postmodern theorists don't misappropriate science. Derrida, for example, is conspicuously absent from the book except for one quote in the original parody, because that was an isolated instance, produced in response to a question at a conference.

Yet the effect of a hatchet job like this, if it succeeds, is not just to undermine the reputations of some minor celebrities but also to produce a shift in the climate of opinion, so that insiders with doubts about the intelligibility of all this "theory" are no longer reluctant to voice them, and outsiders who have grumbled privately to one another for years have something concrete to which they can point. Anyone who teaches in an American university has heard similar inanities from students and colleagues in comparative literature or cultural studies. This episode should at least have an impact on the next generation of students.

II

Although Sokal and Bricmont focus on the abuse and misrepresentation of science by a dozen French intellectuals and on the cognitive relativism of postmodern theory, their book broaches a much larger topic—the uneasy place of science and the understanding of scientific rationality in contemporary culture.

The technological consequences of mathematics, physics, chemistry, and biology permeate our lives, and everyone who has been around for a few decades has witnessed the most spectacular developments. That alone would give science enormous prestige, but it also reinforces the purely intellectual aura of science as a domain of understanding that takes us far beyond common sense, by methods that are often far more reliable than common sense. Yet it is not easy for those without scientific training to acquire a decent grasp of this kind of understanding, as opposed to awareness of its consequences and the ability to parrot some of its terminology. One can be infatuated with the idea of theory without understanding what a theory is.

To have a theory it is not enough to throw around a set of abstract terms or to classify things under different labels. Whether it is true or false, a theory has to include some general principles by which fresh consequences can be inferred from particular facts—consequences not already implied by the initial description of those facts. The most familiar theories embody causal principles that enable us to infer from present observation what will happen or what has already happened, but there are other kinds of theories—mathematical, linguistic, or ethical, for example—that describe noncausal systematic relations. A successful theory increases one's cognitive power over its domain, power to understand why the particular facts are as they are and to discover new facts by inference from others that one can observe directly. Most important of all, it provides an understanding of the unifying reality that underlies observed diversity.

You don't have to understand quantum mechanics to appreciate the nature of science. Anyone who has taken introductory chemistry and is familiar with the periodic table of the elements has some idea of how powerful a theory can be—what an extraordinary wealth of specific consequences can be derived from a limited number of precise but general principles. And understanding classical chemistry requires only a basic spatial imagination and simple mathematics, nothing counterintuitive. Yet it should be clear that not everything in the world is governed by general principles sufficiently precise and substantive to be embodied in a theory. Theories in the social sciences may depend on principles that apply to large numbers of people, even if the principles are only probabilistic; but to employ theoretical-sounding jargon in talking about literature or art has about as much effect as putting on a lab coat, and in most cases the same is true for history.

Unfortunately, the lack of familiarity with real scientific theories sometimes results in imitation of their outward forms together with denigration of their claim to provide a specially powerful source of objective knowledge about the world. This defensive iconoclasm has received crucial support from a radical position in the history and philosophy of science whose authority is regularly invoked by writers outside those fields: the epistemological relativism or even anarchism found in the writings of Thomas Kuhn and Paul Feyerabend.

As Sokal and Bricmont explain, Kuhn and Feyerabend were writing in the context of an ongoing dispute over the relation of scientific theories to empirical evidence. The logical positivists tried to interpret scientific propositions so that they would be entailed by the evidence of experience. Karl Popper denied that this was possible but held that if scientific propositions were to have empirical content, they had to be such that at least their falsehood could be entailed by the evidence of experience. Yet neither of these direct logical relations appears to hold, because the evidentiary relation pro or con between any experience and any theoretical claim always involves auxiliary hypotheses—things apart from the proposition and the evidence themselves that are assumed to be true or false. There is nothing wrong with relying on many assumptions in the ordinary case, but it is always logically possible that some of them may be false, and sometimes that conclusion is forced on us with regard to an assumption that had seemed obvious. When that happens with a truly fundamental aspect of our worldview, we speak of a scientific revolution.

So far none of this implies that scientific reasoning is not objective or that it cannot yield knowledge of reality. All it means is that a scientific inference from evidence to the truth or falsity of any proposition involves in some degree our whole system of beliefs and experience and that the method is not logical deduction alone, but also a weighing of which elements of the system it is most reasonable to retain and which to abandon when an inconsistency among them appears. In normal inquiry this is usually easy to determine; but at the cutting edge it is often difficult, and a clear answer may have to await the experimental production of further evidence or the construction of new theoretical hypotheses.

This means that most of our beliefs at any time must in some degree be regarded as provisional since they may be replaced when a different balance of reasons is generated by new experience or theoretical ingenuity. It also means that an eternal set of rules of scientific method cannot be laid down in advance. But it does *not* mean that it cannot be true that a certain theory is the most reasonable to accept, given the evidence available at a particular time, and it does not mean that the theory cannot be objectively true, however provisionally we may hold it. Truth is not the same as certainty or universal acceptance.

Another point sometimes made against the claim of scientific objectivity is that experience is always "theory-laden," as if that meant that any experience that seemed to contradict a theory could be reinterpreted in terms of it, so that nothing could ever rationally require us to accept or reject a theory. As Sokal and Bricmont point out, however, nothing of the kind follows.

Suppose I have the theory that a diet of hot fudge sundaes will enable me to lose a pound a day. If I eat only hot fudge sundaes and weigh myself every morning, my interpretation of the numbers on the scale is certainly dependent on a theory of mechanics that explains how the scale will respond when objects of different weights are placed on it. But it is not dependent on my dietary theories. If I concluded from the fact that the numbers keep getting higher that my intake of ice cream must be altering the laws of mechanics in my bathroom, it would be philosophical idiocy to defend the inference by appealing to Quine's dictum that all our statements about the external world face the tribunal of experience as a corporate body rather than one by one. Certain revisions in response to the evidence are reasonable; others are pathological.

Much of what Kuhn says about great theoretical shifts, and the inertial role of long-established scientific paradigms and their cultural entrenchment in resisting recalcitrant evidence until it becomes overwhelming, is entirely reasonable, but it is also entirely compatible with the conception of science as seeking, and sometimes finding, objective truth about the world. What has made him a relativist hero is the addition of provocative remarks to the effect that Newton and Einstein, or Ptolemy and Galileo, live in "different worlds," that the paradigms of different scientific periods are "incommensurable," and that it is a mistake to think of the progress of science over time as bringing us closer to the truth about how the world really is.

Feyerabend is more consistently outrageous than Kuhn, deriding the privileged position of modern science as a way of understanding the world. "All methodologies have their limitations," he says in *Against Method*, "and the only 'rule' that survives is 'anything goes.'"[3] As Sokal and Bricmont point out, the first clause of this sentence may be true, but it does not in any way support the second. I was a colleague of Feyerabend's at Berkeley in the 1960s, and once it fell to the two of us to grade

---

3. Paul Feyerabend, *Against Method* (London: New Left Books, 1975), p. 296.

the German exam for the philosophy graduate students. About twenty of them took it, and their papers were numbered to preserve anonymity. We discovered that the department secretary who assigned the numbers had considerately left out the number thirteen, and Feyerabend was appalled and outraged by this display of rank superstition. But his views developed, and both he and Kuhn have a lot to answer for.

Both of them are repeatedly cited in support of the claim that everything, including the physical world, is a social construct, existing only from the perspective of this or that cognitive practice; that there is no truth but only conformity or nonconformity to the discourse of this or that community; and that the adoption of scientific theories is to be explained sociologically rather than by the probative weight of reasoning from the experimental evidence. Scientists don't believe this, but many nonscientists now do. For example, Sokal and Bricmont tell us that the sociologist of science Bruno Latour recently challenged as anachronistic the report, from French scientists who examined the mummy, that Pharaoh Ramses II had died of tuberculosis—because the tuberculosis bacillus came into existence only when Robert Koch discovered it in 1882.

I don't think this is just a case of malign influence from bad philosophy: The radical relativism found in Kuhn and Feyerabend fell on fertile ground. The postmodernist doctrine that there is nothing outside the text, no world to which it is tied down, seems plausible to the consumers of postmodernist writings because it is so often true of those writings, where language is simply allowed to take off on its own. Those who have no objective standards themselves find it easy to deny them to others.

III

As Sokal and Bricmont point out, the denial of objective truth on the ground that all systems of belief are determined by social forces is self-refuting if we take it seriously, since it appeals to a sociological or historical claim that would not establish the conclusion unless it were objectively correct. Moreover, it privileges one discipline, sociology or history, over the others whose objectivity it purports to debunk, such as physics and mathematics. Given that many propositions in the latter fields are much better established than the theories of social determination by which their objectivity is being challenged, this is like using a ouija board to decide whether your car needs new brake linings.

Relativism is kept alive by a simple fallacy, repeated again and again—the idea that if something is a form of discourse, the only standard to which it can answer is conformity to the practices of a linguistic community and that any evaluation of its content or justification must somehow be reduced to that. This is to ignore the differences between types of discourse, which can be understood only by studying them from inside. There are certainly domains, such as etiquette or spelling, where what is correct is completely determined by the practices of a particular community. But empirical knowledge, including science, is not like this. Where agreement exists, it is produced by evidence and reasoning, and not vice versa. The constantly evolving practices of those engaged in scientific research aim beyond themselves at a correct account of the world and are not logically guaranteed to achieve it. Their recognition of their own fallibility shows that the resulting claims have objective content.

Sokal and Bricmont argue that the methods of reasoning in the natural sciences are essentially the same as those used in ordinary inquiries like a criminal investigation. In that case we are presented with various pieces of evidence; we use lots of assumptions about physical causation, spatial and temporal order, basic human psychology, and the functioning of social institutions; and we try to see how well these fit together with alternative hypotheses about who committed the murder. The data and the background assumptions do not entail an answer, but they often make one answer more reasonable than others. Indeed they may establish it, as we say, "beyond a reasonable doubt."

That is precisely what scientists strive for. Although reasonable indubitability is not the position of theories at the cutting edge of knowledge, many scientific results achieve it over time through massive and repeated confirmation, together with the disconfirmation of alternatives. Even when the principles of classical chemistry are explained at a deeper level by quantum theory, they remain indispensably in place as part of our understanding of the world.

And yet there is something else about the science produced over the past century that makes it more than a vast extension of the employment of commonsense rationality. The fact is that contemporary scientific theories describing the invisible physical reality that underlies the appearances no longer represent a world that can be intuitively grasped, even in rough outline, by the normal human imagination. Newtonian mechanics, the atomic theory of matter, and even the basic principles of electricity and magnetism can be roughly visualized by ordinary people. Quantum theory and the theory of relativity cannot be so visualized, because they introduce concepts of space, time, and the relation between observed and unobserved states of affairs that diverge radically from the intuitive concepts that we all use in thinking about our surroundings.

Scientific progress has accustomed us to the idea that the world has properties very different from those presented to our unaided senses, but classical theories can still be understood through models that are based on what we can see and touch. Everyone understands what it is for something to be composed of parts, and there is no difficulty in extending this idea to parts too minute to be seen but inferable from other evidence, such as that of the chemical reactions between different types of substances. We can perceive the action of gravity and magnetic attraction, and electric currents can be roughly imagined by analogy with the flow of liquids. But the world of Einstein's special theory of relativity, in which the interval between two widely separated events cannot be uniquely specified in terms of a spatial distance and a temporal distance, is not one that can be intuitively grasped, even roughly, by a layman.

Our natural idea, an idea entirely suitable for the scale of ordinary experience, that things happen in a unique, three-dimensional space and along a unique, one-dimensional time order is so deep a feature of our intuitive conception of the world that it is very hard to make the transition, required by relativity theory, to seeing this as just the way things appear from the point of view of a particular frame of reference. To account for the different spatiotemporal relations that the same events appear to have from different frames of reference in uniform motion relative to one another, it is necessary to postulate a reality of a different kind, relativistic space-time, which can be precisely mathematically described but not really imagined.

Special relativity is not a theory whose interpretation is contested. It reveals an objective reality very different from the way the world appears, but one with clear and definite properties. Quantum theory, by contrast, though it is extremely successful in predicting the observable facts—deriving from physics the phenomena described by classical chemistry, for example—seems to present conceptual problems even to the physicists who work with it, problems about how to conceive the underlying reality that the theory describes, which is so different from the observed reality that it explains. If one tries to use ordinary physical imagination to grasp the reality that underlies the observations, the result always contradicts the observations. It is impossible to convey the problem without discussing the theory, but one gets a flavor of the difficulty from the usual gloss that in quantum mechanics, we seem forced to think of the basic facts as indeterminate among mutually incompatible observable states—as if a 50 percent chance of rain, for example, could be the most accurate description of yesterday's weather.

Physics continues to develop, of course, but these two theories have taken us to a conception of the real character of the world that can be grasped only through mathematical formulations and not even roughly by imagination. As a result, scientific journalism often reads like mumbo jumbo. Not only does this prevent the assimilation of modern physics into the general educated understanding of the world, but it also leads to grotesque misuse of references to these theories by those who think of them as a kind of magic.

Thus quantum theory, via the Heisenberg indeterminacy principle, and, to a lesser extent, relativity, are often invoked to show that today even science has had to abandon the idea of an objective, mind-independent reality. Yet neither theory has this significance, however strange may be the reality that they describe and its interaction with observers. And this alienation will only increase if, as seems likely, science penetrates to less and less intuitively imaginable accounts of the reality that lies behind the familiar manifest world, accounts that rely more and more on mathematics that only specialists can learn.

IV

Sokal and Bricmont are as much concerned with the general rise of irrationalism and relativism as with the abuse of science, and one of their motives is political. Sokal says that what motivated him to produce his parody was a belief that the infestation of the academic Left in America with postmodernist relativism badly weakened their position as critics of the established order. To challenge widely accepted practices, it is not enough to say there is no objective truth and then present an alternative point of view.

Sokal in particular emphasizes that he is an old leftist and that he taught math in Nicaragua during the Sandinista government. Clearly he doesn't want to be confused with Allan Bloom. As Sokal and Bricmont observe, there is no logical connection between any abstract theory of metaphysics or epistemology and any particular political position. Objectivity with regard to the facts ought to be seen as essential for any view, Left, Right, or center, that presents itself as an account of how societies should be organized. Objectivity is implied by every claim that the justification for one system is better than that for another because justification always involves, in addition to values that may be contested, appeals to the facts that reveal how well a particular system will serve those values. Objectivity should be valued by anyone whose policies are not supported by lies.

The embrace of relativism by many leftist intellectuals in the United States, although it may not be politically very important, is a terrible admission of failure and an excuse for not answering the claims of their political opponents. The subordination of the intellect to partisan loyalty is found across the political spectrum, but usually it takes the form of blind insistence on the objective truth of certain supporting facts and refusal to consider evidence to the contrary. So what explains the shift, at least by a certain slice of the intellectual Left, to this new form of obfuscation?

Sokal and Bricmont attribute it partly to despair brought on by the course of history:

The communist regimes have collapsed; the social-democratic parties, where they remain in power, apply watered-down neo-liberal policies; and the Third World movements that led their countries to independence have, in most cases, abandoned any attempt at autonomous development. In short, the harshest form of "free market" capitalism seems to have become the implacable reality for the foreseeable future. Never before have the ideals of justice and equality seemed so utopian. (p. 206)

This is a disturbing bit of rhetoric. Anyone whose hopes were dashed by the collapse of communism had either a very feeble grip on reality or a very distasteful set of values, and it is simply playing to the galleries to say that we are now all doomed to the harshest form of free-market capitalism. A return to old-fashioned standards of objectivity of the kind this book favors would require the abandonment of a lot of left-wing cant, which is not the same as abandoning the ideals of justice and equality.

Perhaps Sokal and Bricmont are right, and the appeal of relativism comes when one gives up the will to win and settles for the license to keep saying what one has always said, this time without fear of contradiction. But I think there is a more direct link between postmodernism and the traditional ideas of the Left. The explanation of all ostensibly rational forms of thought in terms of social influences is a generalization of the old Marxist idea of ideology, by which moral principles were all debunked as rationalizations of class interest. The new relativists, with Nietzschean extravagance, have merely extended their exposure of the hollowness of pretensions to objectivity to science and everything else. Like its narrower predecessor, this form of analysis sees "objectivity" as a mask for the exercise of power, and so provides a natural vehicle for the expression of class hatred.

Postmodernism's specifically academic appeal comes from its being another in the sequence of all-purpose "unmasking" strategies that offer a way to criticize the intellectual efforts of others, not by engaging with them on the ground, but by diagnosing them from a superior vantage point and charging them with inadequate self-awareness. Logical positivism and Marxism have in the past been used by academics in this way, and postmodernist relativism is a natural for the role. It may now be on the way out, but I suspect there will continue to be a market in the huge American academy for a quick fix of some kind. If it is not social constructionism, it will be something else—Darwinian explanations of virtually everything, perhaps.

16

Davidson's New *Cogito*

Skepticism depends on the claim that one could be in a subjectively indistinguishable state while the objective world outside one's mind was completely different from the way it appears, and not just temporarily but permanently—past, present, and future. Call this the skeptical possibility.

There are two traditional methods of refuting skepticism. One is subjective reductionism—the reduction of the objective to the subjective, in one form or another—so that facts about the objective world are analyzed, in some more or less complicated way, in terms of how things appear to us. This includes various forms of phenomenalism, verificationism, pragmatism, transcendental idealism, and "internal" realism. Reductionism denies that the skeptical possibility is a real possibility.

The other response is to leave unchallenged the logical possibility of a gap between appearance and reality but to argue that we are justified in believing that the world is in fact largely as we take it to be. This response includes arguments as various as Descartes's route to objective knowledge through God's benevolence and Quine's naturalized epistemology.

Donald Davidson has produced a third response to skepticism. Like reductionism, it denies the skeptical possibility. But it does not reduce the objective to the subjective; and although in a sense it goes in the opposite direction, it does not proceed by reducing the subjective to something else that is objective, in the fashion of behaviorist philosophies of mind. It is not reductionist at all. Rather, Davidson insists on certain consequences of the fact that thought and subjective experience, the entire domain of appearances, must be regarded as elements of objective reality and cannot be conceived apart from it. The subjective is in itself objective, and its connections with the objective world as a whole are such that the radical disjunction between appearance and reality that skepticism requires is not a genuine logical possibility.

The argument is that our thoughts depend for their content on their relations to things outside us, including other thinkers and speakers. And since we can't doubt that we are thinking, we can't doubt that the world contains our thoughts and that it is of such a character as to be capable of containing those thoughts. Specifically, to have the content that they have, and that we cannot doubt that they have, our thoughts must be largely true of what they are about. Therefore our beliefs must be largely true, and the skeptical possibility is an illusion.

Though the argument from thought to the objective world is a little longer and the conclusion much more comprehensive, the spirit is Cartesian: Not *je pense, donc je suis* but *je pense, donc je sais*. It is Cartesian in the sense of the *cogito* itself because it depends on the impossibility of doubting that one is thinking the thoughts one thinks one is thinking.

This is my interpretation of Davidson's refutation of skepticism, which is most fully set out in his essay "A Coherence Theory of Truth and Knowledge"[1] but whose elements appear in many of his writings.[2] He might not want to put it quite this way. In particular, he would certainly resist the dramatic structure that makes it an argument *from* thought *to* objective reality—on which the parallel with Descartes depends. Davidson's aim is anti-Cartesian: Instead of getting us out of the egocentric predicament, he is trying to show that we can't get into it:

> There are of course some beliefs that carry a very high degree of certitude, and in some cases their content creates a presumption in favor of their truth. These are beliefs about our own present propositional attitudes. But the relative certitude of these beliefs does not suit them to be the foundation of empirical knowledge. It springs, rather, from the nature of interpretation. As interpreters we have to treat self-ascriptions of belief, doubt, desire and the like as privileged; this is an essential step in interpreting the rest of what the person says and thinks. The foundations of interpretation are not the foundations of knowledge, though an appreciation of the nature of interpretation can lead to an appreciation of the essentially veridical nature of belief.[3]

On the other hand, he also says, taking up the point of view of the subject, "The agent has only to reflect on what a belief is to appreciate that most of his basic beliefs are true."[4]

1. In E. LePore, ed., *Truth and Interpretation* (Oxford: Blackwell, 1986).
2. See especially Davidson, "On the Very Idea of a Conceptual Scheme," *Inquiries Into Truth and Interpretation* (New York: Oxford University Press, 1984).
3. Donald Davidson, "Empirical Content," in E. LePore, ed., *Truth and Interpretation* (Oxford: Blackwell, 1986), p. 332.
4. "A Coherence Theory of Truth and Knowledge," p. 319.

I find that when the argument for the "essentially veridical nature of belief," based on the nature of interpretation, is pressed against a seriously resisting skeptical doubt, it inevitably takes the form I have given it. At any rate, this is how I would express the deeply interesting refutation of skepticism contained in Davidson's views, and it is the argument I want to discuss. Sometimes Davidson talks as if the claim were almost mundane. In resisting this tendency, emphasizing its heroic character, and drawing a parallel with the *cogito*, I mean to express my sense of how remarkable it would be if it succeeded.

One does not beg the question against skepticism by claiming that it must admit objective ideas from the start. Skepticism always depends on the possibility of forming an objective conception of the world in which one is placed, a conception that partitions the world between one's mind and the rest of it in such a way as to admit the logical possibility of radically different alternatives on the other side of the divide, while the contents of one's mind remain the same. The possibilities that one is dreaming or hallucinating stand in for these skeptical alternatives, but a mere temporary dream or hallucination is not the real skeptical possibility and is not ruled out by Davidson's argument. Skepticism requires the possibility of systematic and general failure in the correspondence between appearance and reality, so that the world is not and never has been more or less as it appears to be. This would be satisfied by Descartes's evil demon story, or certain versions of the brain in the vat (those in which I have always been a brain in a vat, rather than having recently been envatted after an otherwise normal life).

The skeptic maintains that he can form the objective conception of a world that contains someone who is subjectively just like himself but whose perceptions and thoughts do not and never have corresponded to the way the world is. He concludes that he can have no grounds for ruling out the possibility that he himself is that person. Clearly, then, the skeptic is committed to at least one assumption about objective reality: namely, a strong form of logical independence of the contents of minds from the general character of the world in which they are situated.

Davidson's challenge to this independence is posed initially in terms of the conditions of interpretation that govern the ascription of mental states to others. Someone who actually knew what was going on in the world—the evil demon himself, for example—could not, according to Davidson, ascribe beliefs to anyone else in it except as part of a systematic interpretation in which those beliefs were largely true, making it possible to understand errors against a background of truth. That is because interpretation must try to make sense of the other person's point of view, and the only way to do that is to ascribe to him representations of and beliefs about the world that you observe him reacting to. Even false beliefs must be formulated in terms of concepts whose content is established by their connections to the world in the context of other, true beliefs. So the evil demon couldn't systematically deceive me even if he were omnipotent: It is logically impossible.

This way of putting the argument may seem to leave open the possibility of doubt on the ground that these are merely conditions of *interpretation* and there is a gap between interpretation and reality, just as there is a gap between appearance and reality. Interpretations can be mistaken, even if they are supported by the evidence. And if it is logically possible that the appearances in a mind might diverge radically from reality, then it is equally possible that an interpretation of what is in that mind, supported by Davidson's charitable principles of interpretation, should nevertheless diverge radically from the mind's actual contents. Davidson's principles might yield no coherent interpretation whatever, for example, even though the person was actually thinking about some completely nonexistent world. Therefore, it may seem that this argument can't refute the skeptic without assuming in advance that his crucial premise, the skeptical possibility, is mistaken.

I believe, however, that this reply mistakes the character of Davidson's principles of interpretation.[5] They are intended to belong not just to epistemology but also to metaphysics, and to govern not only the ascription of mental states to others on the basis of observational evidence but also, in a sense, the ascription of mental states to oneself. The objection to the skeptic is that he cannot really conceive of the strange objective world whose possibility he must suppose, because he cannot conceive of *himself* having the thoughts he now has, in that situation. And since he is entitled to the equivalent of Cartesian certainty about roughly what is going on in his own mind, he cannot intelligibly doubt that most of his beliefs are true. The argument against the skeptical possibility is that it violates the conditions for ascription of beliefs to anyone, including oneself. The would-be skeptic can conceive of a situation in which he would be incapable of having the thoughts he now has, just as he can conceive of his own nonexistence; but he can no more conceive that he is *now* incapable of having those thoughts than he can conceive that he may now not exist.

In discussing this argument, I shall not take up the difficult question of precisely how the "external" conditions for the possession of beliefs, perceptions, and so forth are best specified—how large a subset of beliefs, and of what kind, needs to be true to provide the leverage needed to interpret the false ones; what kinds of causal and other relations to the world and other people need to be present; or how large a space for error this leaves. The general idea of such a theory is sufficient for our purposes without a detailed interpretation, which in any case presumably

---

5. Cf. "A Coherence Theory of Truth and Knowledge," p. 315: "What a fully informed interpreter could learn about what a speaker means is all there is to learn; the same goes for what a speaker believes."

cannot be given in the abstract but would be revealed differently in relation to different areas of thought. I also won't consider independent reasons for and against the correctness of this theory of interpretation. My concern is with an argument based on it, so I will consider only the consequences for skepticism and not the theory of interpretation itself. My aim is to understand better the face-off between Davidson's argument and the subjective certainty of the skeptic (or a provisional skeptic, like Descartes) that he is able to conceive of skeptical possibilities that Davidson claims are illusory. This investigation will inevitably have some implications for the theory of mental content, but that is not its main purpose.

Let's suppose the skeptic says that it is consistent with what he knows is going on in his mind that there are not and never have been any material objects, including his own body. Davidson will reply that in saying this, he is making use of the concept of a material object and that he could have that concept and use those words to express it only if he and his language were in a systematic objective relation, causal and referential, to actual material objects: For his thoughts to be thoughts about material objects, real or imaginary, it is not enough that some episode occur within the confines of his mind. For any such episode to be a thought about material objects, it must reach beyond itself, representing the world outside. And it cannot do that unless it has a role in a complex system of real interactions between the individual who has the thought, the kinds of things the thought is about, and other thinking individuals. This is a priori.

Now the skeptic will find it difficult to avoid the feeling that this argument must have something wrong with it, simply because the conclusion is too strong. Even if the conditions Davidson claims for possession of the concept of material object are correct, it would seem that there ought to be a way of formulating an alternative, weaker, disjunctive conclusion. But if the skeptic tries to express that conclusion, he will immediately get into trouble. Suppose he says, "Either there are material objects and I can talk and think about them; or else there aren't, in which case I don't have the concept and am thinking something else." This doesn't make sense. I don't have *what* concept? Or else there aren't *what*? The second disjunct seems inexpressible—and yet it also seems to be there, tantalizingly awaiting expression as part of a suitable weakening of the conclusion.

Suppose the skeptic tries this instead: "I am thinking about the possibility that there might not be any material objects only if there are material objects (and other people), and my thoughts are suitably related to them." But then what is the alternative? It will have to be, "Otherwise I am talking gibberish to myself, and these images I am having and symbols I am juggling fail to represent anything." But is that a thought I can have? The things going through my mind *seem* to me to be thoughts about material objects. Could I possibly be mistaken about this? And if I were mistaken, what mistake would I be making? That is, what would I be *thinking* my thoughts were about?

The skeptic might try another tack: to concede the conclusion of Davidson's argument but dismiss it as trivial, on the ground that the principle of charity in interpretation requires that the concept of material object be taken to refer to *whatever* it needs to refer to to make his beliefs largely true.[6] To know on this ground that his beliefs about material objects are largely true would be to know nothing about what the world is actually like: It would be analogous to the knowledge that I am *here*—wherever that is—which tells me nothing about my location.

This objection fails because in order to think, "There are material objects—whatever *they* are," the skeptic would have to employ the concept of a range of possible referents for his concept of material object, none of which he can identify or form any true beliefs about, and that is something Davidson's view rules out. Indeed, even to have the thought that I am here—wherever that is—I must have the concept of a range of possible locations to which "here" may refer, and that is possible only if I can make other correct judgments about spatial location.

The skeptic always relies on the idea that however far he is pushed into his subjective corner by the elimination of objective knowledge, there will always be something for him to fall back on as a way of describing the contents of his own mind. But Davidson's argument seeks to prevent him from retreating into that corner, by showing that his conception of himself and his thoughts is necessarily objective, and with much broader objective implications than Descartes' *cogito* establishes. So there is no place in the mind for him to retreat *to* from the objective external world.

Now this seems like too strong a result to be possible. If ordinary claims about the contents of one's mind have strong objective implications, it must, one would think, be possible to doubt the implications, and therefore by inference the subjective claims, and still find something even more subjective that remains and that is logically detachable from the large, objective world picture that burdens ordinary psychological concepts. Can we really not describe the *inner surface* of our minds (the cognitive analogue of sense data) without all that? Surely we can fall back on the certainty that we at least *think* we are thinking about material objects—which might be enough to support a form of skepticism. Otherwise we seem to be faced with the dilemma of either maintaining

6. See Donald Davidson, "Knowing One's Own Mind," *Proceedings of the American Philosophical Association*, 60, (1987), p. 456: "The agent . . . is in no position to wonder whether she is generally using her own words to apply to the right objects and events, since whatever she regularly does apply them to gives her words the meaning they have and her thoughts the contents they have."

very strong claims of certainty for which we lack adequate warrant or being totally skeptical even about the contents of our own minds.

The acute problem of there being nowhere to retreat to is vividly expressed by Wittgenstein, in the course of his argument that without objective conditions, it would be impossible for a term to name a sensation.

> "Well, I *believe* that this is the sensation S again."—Perhaps you *believe* that you believe it![7]

> What reason have we for calling "S" the sign for a *sensation*? For "sensation" is a word of our common language, not of one intelligible to me alone. So the use of this word stands in need of a justification which everybody understands.—And it would not help either to say that it need not be a *sensation*; that when he writes "S", he has *something*—and that is all that can be said. "Has" and "something" also belong to our common language.—So in the end when one is doing philosophy one gets to the point where one would like just to emit an inarticulate sound.—But such a sound is an expression only as it occurs in a particular language-game, which should now be described.[8]

Wittgenstein is talking about the impossibility of retreat from the public language, rather than from causal relations to the external world, but it is the same point. Faced with Davidson's argument, the skeptic who is trying to say or to think what it is that he can be certain he *has*, in conceiving of material objects—which does not imply their existence or the existence of anything at all outside his mind—will likewise be reduced to emitting an inarticulate sound, because he cannot describe what he has as an idea of a material object, or even as an impression of an idea of a material object. What justifies him in calling it an impression of *that* idea? He will be reduced to trying to describe the conception without its content, which on the face of it looks impossible.

If this avenue of retreat is closed off, and he cannot find a core of subjective certainty that does not carry excessively strong objective implications, can the skeptic instead achieve a radical skepticism even about his own mind? It won't help to take as a model Lichtenberg's response to Descartes, namely, a refusal even to admit *cogito* in the sense in which it implies *sum*. Something more radical than this would be needed to resist Davidson's conclusion: It would not be enough to say that all I can be sure of is that thoughts are going on, not that I am having them—for even that would require, for the thoughts to have content, that they be related to an objective world. Skepticism in the face of Davidson's argument

---

7. Ludwig Wittgenstein, *Philosophical Investigations*, (Oxford: Blackwell, 1953) sec. 260.
8. *Philosophical Investigations*, sec. 261

would have to take the form of the hypothesis that the truth is inexpressible by me and that I do not have real thoughts at all. But since this is something I cannot think, it can appear only as an unimaginable abyss, which is the alternative to continuing to maintain that I have extensive knowledge of the world that may be inadequately grounded but which I cannot abandon because I cannot think that I am not thinking.

Perhaps the closest it is possible to come to expressing this form of skepticism would be just to observe that we have no alternative to thinking that our system of beliefs is largely true. While we can (indeed must) think that some of our beliefs are probably false, we cannot on Davidson's view hold that all or most of them might be, so long as we think anything at all. And the aspiring skeptic might say that simply to recognize the unavoidability of this ought to undermine our confidence. Even if the alternative is literally unthinkable, the objective conception of the world that we are stuck with is tainted by its inescapability. Let me explain why this is so. An explanation is needed because not all inescapable beliefs are equally disturbing.

The nub of the problem is that Davidson has produced an a priori argument for a conclusion that is not a necessary truth and is not claimed by the argument to be a necessary truth. It may be a necessary truth that *if* a being has beliefs, the bulk of them must be true. But that is just a premise of the argument against the skeptic. The conclusion is that a particular body of beliefs, the ones I actually hold, consisting mostly of contingent propositions, is largely true. And that is not a necessary truth but an enormous and remarkable natural fact, a fact about the world as a whole and not just about my own mind. The argument for it is a priori, however, because in addition to the necessary general principle that is one of the premises, the only other premise is that I have certain thoughts—which, while it is not a necessary truth, is still something that, for Cartesian reasons, I cannot doubt.

Such an a priori argument seems miraculous. More miraculous than the *cogito* itself, whose immediate conclusion, though contingent, seems relatively modest—and also more miraculous than a priori arguments, based on inconceivability of the alternatives, for the necessary truths of logic and mathematics. After all, the arguments for most necessary truths have to be a priori; but it is absolutely amazing that there should be an a priori argument that proves that *this* set of propositions, which I believe, covering vast tracts of history, natural science, and ordinary lore about the world, is largely true.

There are, of course, more particular grounds, of a familiar, empirical kind, for the particular contingent claims that make up the set of my beliefs about the world. But these establish only their likelihood relative to one another, since the grounds for my beliefs are always other beliefs. The claim that they are largely true, rather than just being a coherent set

of propositions, is a further contingent claim. It is just this which Davidson's argument is designed to establish, by ruling out the possibility
that, though coherent, they might be largely false. Because they are our
actual beliefs, we cannot regard them simply as a coherent set of propositions, nor can we regard their truth as simply consisting in that coherence, which in itself is not sufficient for truth (since I can formulate coherent sets of propositions that I do not believe and that are not true).

Of course, if Davidson is right, then the ordinary empirical grounds
are the only grounds needed for true beliefs, and coherence among our
beliefs yields truth. But if the skeptic questions this, proposing to sus-
pend belief and consider the possibility that this is merely a coherent
system of thoughts, Davidson's ground for refuting him is an a priori argument for the contingent truth that most of the things I in fact believe
are true. Not just that *if* I have a body of beliefs, most of them must be
true (this necessary truth is a premise of the argument) but that *these* beliefs, which I in fact have, are largely true.

The picture is that we have a rich objective conception of the world,
which includes ourselves, complete with all the thoughts that go into
that conception. The whole thing, including our own existence and the
fact that we think all these things, is largely contingent. But it is not contingent that the parts have to hang together in a certain way, in particular that the existence of our thoughts requires that various things be true
of our relation to the rest of the world, including the other people in it.[9]
So if there is any part of the picture that we cannot doubt, and it is attached with sufficient firmness and leverage to the rest, we get an a priori argument for the rough accuracy of the whole thing. This role is sup-
plied by the contents of our own thoughts.

The a priori argument is needed because the empirical reasons for
particular beliefs are not by themselves sufficient. It makes sense to
think about each of a great many of my beliefs, taken one at a time, that it
might be false, in spite of the evidence. Some reason must be given to
show that these individual possibilities can't be combined into the possibility that most of them are false. That reason can't be just the sum of
the particular reasons for each of them, since these are just further beliefs
in the set, and the whole question is whether most of them might be
false.[10] If they were, their apparent support of one another would be systematically misleading. So we cannot demonstrate empirically that this
is not the case, as is proposed by naturalized epistemology; it must be
proved to be impossible, if skepticism is to be ruled out. We need an a pri-

---

9. How these things hang together is described in Donald Davidson, "Three Varieties
of Knowledge," in A. Phillips Griffiths, ed., *A. J. Ayer: Memorial Essays* (Cambridge: Cambridge University Press, 1991).

10. Cf. "A Coherence Theory of Truth and Knowledge," p. 309.

ori argument, and Davidson has given us one. It is an argument that does *not* rely on the reduction of truth to coherence.[11]

My feeling about it somewhat resembles the feeling one has about a major paradox, in which you are faced with an argument that leads to an unacceptable conclusion, but you can't figure out what has gone wrong. In this case the problem is not that the conclusion seems obviously false but that it is too strong to have been established with the kind of certainty that this argument appears to provide. Skepticism seems to have been repressed and rendered mute, rather than really refuted; it is still there, trying to find an outlet.

One way of resisting the argument would be to deny that the ascription of thoughts to ourselves carries objective implications about our relation to the rest of the world, but I am not inclined to take this way out. Even if these objective relations to our surroundings do not constitute the whole nature of thought (and how could they, given the normative character and infinite reach of intentionality?), still they seem to be among its necessary conditions. Even in thinking about my own sensations I use concepts that I believe to be part of a public language that I learned from others who could tell what I was feeling. And when it comes to thinking about tables and chairs, the objective story is even plainer. Such thoughts need some foothold in a relation to what is outside us. Yet once I have acquired these concepts, I cannot doubt that I am employing them if I seem to myself to be doing so, even though the attribution carries strong objective commitments.

At the same time, I can employ those concepts, given that the objective necessary conditions of my having them are met, to imagine a world in which those conditions do not obtain—either a world without any material objects or at least one in which the external reality is totally different from the actual world. And if I then go on to imagine this world containing someone who, apart from external relations, is exactly like me, what is one to say about such a creature? It doesn't seem right to describe him as believing that George Bush lost the 1992 election; but is there any mental condition at all that we can ascribe to him?

For him to have any beliefs at all, something going on in his mind must be such as to be rendered true or false by the way the world is. For example, for him to believe that there are material objects, or chairs, even though there aren't any, his thought would have to be of such a character as to be true if it occurred in the counterfactual situation in which there were some. His mental expression for material objects, or chairs, would have to apply correctly only to them, and his images would have to be images of them. But what could make this true if there were none and neither the expression nor the images had ever had any

11. A coherent set of propositions could be largely false, on Davidson's principles, provided it were not believed.

occurrent relation to such a thing? What would make his mental word a word for chairs?

It is possible for someone to think about frescoes, for example, even though he has never seen a fresco, believes falsely that the murals by Chagall in the Metropolitan Opera House are frescoes, and also believes that Michelangelo's paintings on the Sistine ceiling are not frescoes. But this requires that he know something about the defining features of a fresco, so that with enough further information he would be able to recognize his error. To refer to frescoes, his thought has to be connected with other things, like wet plaster, which could in turn connect him with frescoes. What could it mean to say of someone who had no true beliefs about what was wet or dry, what had any colors or shapes, or what was made of plaster, wool, or whipped cream, that he has the concept of a fresco? Even though it is possible to acquire some concepts by learning their definitions, this must lead eventually to ideas that are grasped in themselves and can be applied directly to their objects. It doesn't really mean anything to say of a disembodied mind in a world without matter that he could identify wet plaster if he encountered it or that he believes that frescoes are applied onto wet plaster.

If this is right, then Descartes was mistaken in thinking that his ideas of space and his idea of a piece of wax were independent of the existence of space and material objects and of his real relations to them. Even the evil demon, in an immaterial and nonspatial world, would not have those concepts, whatever else might be going on in its mind.

It seems to me that there are only two alternatives to accepting Davidson's argument. One is Platonism, the view that we can grasp directly a system of necessarily existent universals by the pure operation of our minds, independently of any contingent facts about the world and our contingent relations to it. This means that we can have a priori knowledge about the necessary structures of the world but not a priori knowledge that our empirical beliefs are largely true, as Davidson contends—because my concept of a piece of wax does not require my ever having come in contact with wax, matter, space, or any actual samples of anything that might come into the definition of wax. It is enough to apprehend the pure ideas of those things. This does still require that we have a critical core of true beliefs about the world to have any thoughts at all—beliefs about the universals and their relations—but the core has been shrunk and pulled inward, even though the beliefs are in a sense still about the external world. Given how mysterious thought is, It seems to me that Platonism must always be a candidate for the truth; but in a sense, it's not a real theory but just an expression of hope for a theory.

The alternative to Platonism as a way of escaping from Davidson's argument would be to admit a form of skepticism about whether one was really capable of significant thought, while at the same time admitting that it is inexpressible and strictly unthinkable since it is equivalent to saying, "Perhaps the sentence I am uttering right now means nothing at all." This seems a distinctly unattractive alternative, but perhaps there is a way of redescribing it. It would be a genuinely new form of skepticism—based on the belief that it is impossible to conceive of the contents of any mind, including one's own, except as part of a conception of the whole world in which it is situated and to which it is related. Although the skeptic would not be able to describe a skeptical possibility in the traditional sense, he would be able to observe that the proposition that his actual empirical beliefs are largely true—a proposition he now realizes he cannot conceive to be false—involves a huge set of nonnecessary truths, which he can't possibly know a priori. By revealing the a priori character of our attachment to the set, Davidson's argument actually points us toward this inexpressible form of skepticism.

17

Stroud and the Quest for Reality

Barry Stroud's strange and absorbing book *The Quest for Reality*[1] sets out to undermine the central metaphysical ambition that has dominated philosophy since the seventeenth century—that of reaching what Bernard Williams calls an "absolute conception of reality." The aim is to achieve a comprehensive understanding of the world, consistent with modern science, which distinguishes between what exists objectively, independent of our minds, and what is merely subjective—due to the effects of the world on our minds and our responses to it.

In resisting the metaphysical conclusions that result from this quest, Stroud writes against the temper of the times and very much in the spirit of the later Wittgenstein, who was also self-consciously out of step with the times and who remains for the most part unassimilated by contemporary philosophy, in spite of being conventionally venerated as one of the few great philosophers of the twentieth century. Stroud's philosophical style, however, except for its lack of ornament and strict avoidance of technical language, is completely unlike Wittgenstein's, which was gnomic and indirect. Stroud is clear, explicit, methodical, and relentless. He tries to block every exit and to say exactly what has been shown and what has not. The result is deliberately frustrating, for his aim is to baffle a desire for understanding of our true relation to the universe, which is at the root of philosophy and which Stroud himself recognizes we cannot get rid of.

Like all of his writings—on skepticism, on Hume, on Kant, on Wittgenstein—this book displays a profound grasp of the history and

---

1. Barry Stroud, *The Quest for Reality: Subjectivism and the Metaphysics of Color* (New York: Oxford University Press, 2000).

logical structure of philosophical problems and theories and a feeling for the derangement of thought that underlies them. He insists that the understanding sought by metaphysics is distinct from scientific understanding, for we could attain it only by answering a question that remains after all scientific results are in. Yet the metaphysical outlook he wants to resist arose and continues to be widely accepted because it seemed to so many people obvious from the beginning that the results of modern physical science reveal a distinction between subjective appearance and objective reality, one that demands formulation as a comprehensive philosophical worldview. Before explaining why Stroud believes that this is not the case, let me describe the view more fully.

The new science of the seventeenth century was brought into existence when Galileo and Newton developed a quantitative geometrical understanding of the physical world and the laws governing it, a description that left out the familiar qualitative aspects of things as they appear to the separate human senses: their smell, taste, sound, feel, and color. Colors and smells did not enter into physics, and in spite of the look and aroma of a typical chemistry lab, they didn't enter into chemistry either, when it subsequently developed into a theory of the true composition of everything around us from a limited number of elements. Stroud quotes Galileo: "If the ears, the tongue, and the nostrils were taken away, the figure, the numbers and motions of bodies would indeed remain, but not the odours or the tastes or the sounds, which, without the living animal, I do not believe are anything else than names." This view was taken up by Descartes and then enshrined by Locke as the now familiar distinction between primary and secondary qualities—the primary qualities of size, shape, and motion being those that belong to things as they are in themselves, and the secondary qualities of color, sound, taste, feel, and smell being mere appearances, produced by the action of these things on our senses.

This conception of the world, as Stroud says, "came to seem like nothing more than scientifically enlightened common sense." And it has survived changes in physical science that have long since rendered obsolete the original catalogue of primary qualities. A modern Locke has to accommodate charge, spin, superstrings, and space-time of many more than three dimensions, but the idea is the same: The physical world as it is in itself is describable in quantitative, spatiotemporal terms; everything else we say about it depends on how it affects us or how we react to it. Objective, mind-independent reality is the now totally unfamiliar world described by a rapidly developing physics; the familiar world that we live in, from colors to values, is subjective and mind-dependent.

Stroud attacks this "unmasking" form of explanation, as he aptly names it, through what has always been its most seductive example, that of color. It is very easy to agree to the philosophical commonplace that ripe lemons are not really yellow in themselves: They just look yellow to human beings, and the explanation for this is that their surface reflects light in such a way that when it strikes a human eye, it produces the characteristic visual experience that we call seeing yellow. The reflective properties of lemons are due to their primary qualities, describable entirely in the language of physics—chemical surface structure, photons, quantum theory— without any reference to color.

Physics does not purport to explain the operations of the human mind, but those who accept the standard view that colors are subjective base it on a rough idea that is not actually an explanation, but rather a belief that the true explanation has a certain form. This rough idea is that physics accounts for everything that happens when light is reflected from a lemon to a human eye, thus triggering physical effects on the retina which in turn produce physical effects in the brain; and the brain, in some way we don't yet understand, produces a visual experience. Nothing about color enters into the first part of the story, which is pure physics.

By contrast, when we see a lemon, its actual physical shape is part of the explanation of the pattern of reflected light it throws on the retina, and therefore of our visual perception of it as ovoid. So lemons really have the shape they appear to have but not the color. Or perhaps, alternatively, we could say that color can be ascribed to lemons but only in a dispositional sense: Their yellowness consists in the fact that they are disposed to affect human vision in a certain way. In any event, the conclusion that lemons are not really in themselves yellow seems very like a direct consequence of modern science.

Stroud has a great deal to say about this picture. He points out, first, that nothing about the colors of things follows from physics because physics simply does not mention colors. It describes the specifically physical properties of things and the relations among them, but it does not say that these are all the properties there are. To reach the conclusion that physical objects are not really colored requires a further, philosophical step. We have to separate out from the world described by physics our perceptions of and beliefs about the colors of things, and determine that the most plausible account of these phenomena does not involve the attribution of color to physical objects.

It seems to me that Stroud is right to reject dispositional analyses of color. Nothing could have the disposition to affect human observers in the typical way if there were no such thing as vision. Dispositional analyses imply that if creatures with vision had never been on the evolutionary menu, nothing would ever have had any color at all. This seems inconsistent with the meaning of the word: There may be an independent metaphysical argument to show that gold is not yellow, but if it is yellow now, it was yellow before there were any human beings and would have been yellow even if creatures with vision or living organisms were not among the possibilities of nature. The dispositional analysis of color fails, because it is really equivalent to the elimination of color from the external world.

But Stroud's main claim against the unmasking project is much more fundamental and philosophically radical. He believes that the theory is an answer to a question that we cannot ask. The reason is this: To find out whether it is possible to carve out from the totality of the things we ordinarily believe a subset—the description in terms of primary qualities—that tells what the external world is really and objectively like, we have to begin by acknowledging the appearances to the contrary. The whole point of the unmasking explanation is to show that those appearances are merely subjective. So at the start of the investigation, we have to recognize that people have visual perceptions of color and beliefs about the colors of things, while suspending judgment about the truth of those perceptions and beliefs, in order to see whether we can develop an account of the situation that dispenses with their objective truth. But this, according to Stroud, is something we cannot do. His arguments depend on a view of psychological concepts that he shares with Wittgenstein and Donald Davidson:

> We identify what different people think, believe, and perceive in ways that are as rich and complex as our conception of the nonpsychological world onto which those thoughts, beliefs, and perceptions are directed . . . we who inhabit the world can understand someone in that world as believing something or as perceiving something only if we can somehow connect the possession of the psychological states we attribute to the person with facts and events in the surrounding world that we take the beliefs and perceptions to be about. (pp. 150–51)

These arguments, he says,

> strongly suggest that no one could abandon all beliefs about the colors of things and still understand the color terms essentially involved in ascribing perceptions and beliefs about the colors of things. If that is so, no one competent to understand and acknowledge the perceptions and beliefs he hopes to unmask could free himself completely from all commitment to a world of colored things. So no one could succeed in unmasking all those perceptions and beliefs as giving us only "appearance," not "reality." (p. 168)

Although individual color beliefs and impressions can be false, Stroud holds that we cannot ascribe them at all unless we believe that many of them are true, because we couldn't give any content to the belief or impression—we couldn't identify it—without some conception of its object. The unmasker can't separate out these psychological states as pure subjective events, detached from the world. He can't understand them apart from the world that they are about.

However—and this is the strangest part of his view—Stroud does not think that the existence of color beliefs implies that any of them are actually true; his thesis is only that we cannot *believe* that there are color beliefs unless we *believe* that many of them are true.

He likens the situation formally to what is known as Moore's paradox (after G. E. Moore, who identified it): You can't consistently assert, "I believe it is raining but it isn't," even though there is no inconsistency in your believing that it is raining when it isn't. According to Stroud, the unmasker likewise cannot consistently assert, "People believe objects are colored but they aren't." But this doesn't mean it would be contradictory or inconsistent for that to be so. It means only that he cannot pose the question that the unmasking explanation tries to answer, by admitting color appearances and then asking whether there are colors: In specifying that people have color beliefs and perceptions, he is already committed to a world with color in it.

Furthermore, because the question can't be asked, we can't reach a positive answer either—namely that color is objectively real. Color can neither be unmasked as merely subjective nor metaphysically endorsed as objectively real: Beliefs about color must remain at their nonmetaphysical, ordinary level. We know that lemons are yellow because we can see that they are, and that's the end of it.

But are they *really* yellow? Eat your broccoli and don't ask so many questions. This is, as I say, a frustrating argument. It tells us we cannot ask a question we strongly wish to ask in order to understand our relation to the world in a fundamental way—and we are deluding ourselves when we think we have posed it, let alone answered it.

Demonstrations of the limits of thought are an important element in philosophy, and Wittgenstein tried to turn philosophy into a method of showing that most of philosophy consists of doomed attempts to transgress those limits. Stroud is much more cautious. He insists that each case must be considered on its own, and he does not claim that the detailed argument he offers for the case of color can be transferred even to other secondary qualities, like sound, let alone to more distant examples, like value. But he clearly suspects that unmasking will not work in the important cases.

He briefly discusses the case of value—another prime candidate—and suggests that it may be impossible to attribute any value judgments to people without committing oneself to the truth of some of them. The problem again is what is needed to understand their content as judgments of value rather than, say, mere desires or aversions. And if we cannot even admit the existence of value judgments while suspending judgment as to whether any of them are true, we cannot get into the position to ask whether values have objective reality or are merely subjective appearances.

If Stroud is right, we are left with a world that consists of all the different kinds of things we take to be true—a world full of yellow lemons, stock market rallies, beautiful landscapes, and wicked dictators, as well as quarks, neurotransmitters, and black holes. These things are very different from one another, and we come to know about them in different ways, but there is no ground for singling out some of them for the title of objective reality.

This is an absolutely fundamental issue: Can large segments of our everyday view of the world and what is true of it be separated out and given a purely psychological interpretation? It arises everywhere in philosophy: Unmasking interpretations have been offered even for the primary qualities and matter (by Berkeley, who thought that the shape we see is as subjective as the color), for mathematics, aesthetics, causality, and of course ethics. Stroud is pressing a question that threatens to stop metaphysics before it starts, leaving us with most of our scientific and prephilosophical beliefs, as well as familiar methods of justifying and correcting them, but no overarching theory of reality.

I cannot believe that he is right, though much of what he says is convincing. One thing he seems to me to be clearly right about is that when you look at a lemon and it looks yellow to you, there is no way of correctly describing your mental state without talking about color as a property which, if it exists, is a property of physical objects. The lemon looks to you *to be yellow*. This cannot be redescribed as the lemon's producing in you a yellow visual sensation. As Stroud says, it is not like perceiving that a thumbscrew is a painful instrument by feeling pain when it is applied to your thumb. Thumbscrews would not be painful if no one could feel pain: Their painfulness really is nothing but a disposition to cause pain under certain conditions. But the yellow in your visual experience is just the color that the lemon appears to have. It looks *to be yellow* fully as much as it looks to be ovoid.

The question is whether we can acknowledge this while leaving open the possibility that all visual appearances of yellow or any other color are a kind of illusion—the illusion of perceiving a property that nothing has, a property that does not exist. It would have to be a natural illusion shared by all humans with normal sight, like other optical illusions, and it would have obvious utility, enabling us to identify and classify objects by sight, because the illusion of different colors is naturally produced in us in a systematic way by reflected light.

We can certainly see colors where nothing colored exists; Stroud gives the example of the rainbow. And in familiar optical illusions, people see differences of length or size where there are none. But as ordinarily understood, the intentional objects of these perceptions (i.e., what they appear to be perceptions *of*) are properties that, though not present in the particular case, have plenty of other true instances. No colored object is seen when I see a rainbow, but the question is whether this could be true of all color vision. Could the object—the intentional object—of a perception or belief be that something has a property that does not and never did exist, that could not be possessed by any object, and that is also distinct from a whole range of other properties of the same type, none of which exists?

It seems to me that the best reason for thinking this is still the story that physics tells about vision, surfaces, and light. One of the things that must be true if lemons are yellow is that their yellowness explains why they look yellow. This means that their being the color they look to us to be must explain the psychological effect. But this seems to be incompatible with what we know about the physical facts. We are pretty sure that what lemons contribute to the explanation of vision are just those physical properties that cause them to reflect light in certain ways; the rest of the explanation, which we don't have, is about the relation between the brain and the mind, and it doesn't include anything about lemons. So unless color is really a physical property of surfaces, describable in terms of their primary qualities, it isn't part of the explanation of what we see.

But yellowness—the property lemons *appear* to have—is, if it is anything, a property *in addition* to all their primary qualities. Since no such property of lemons plays a role in the explanation of their looking yellow to us, it is an illusion—one with which we're all familiar and which we can identify in ourselves and others through the systematic similarity of the circumstances under which it occurs. Stroud believes that admitting the possibility of a colorless world would require us also to give up the assumption that people see things as colored; I remain unpersuaded.

As Stroud says, no argument in this difficult territory can hope to be final. And as he also says, the question has to be investigated separately for each case: Note, for example, that there is no "rival explanation" argument from physics that could support an unmasking strategy about ethics; unmasking there is more likely to take the form of the reinterpretation of ostensibly objective value judgments as personal feelings. I don't think this will succeed, but again I am skeptical that the question can be stopped before it starts.

Whatever one thinks of the conclusion, it is illuminating to think through the argument. This is philosophy of an exemplary purity, tenacity, and depth.

18

The Psychophysical Nexus

I. The Mind-Body Problem after Kripke

This essay will explore an approach to the mind-body problem that is distinct both from dualism and from the sort of conceptual reduction of the mental to the physical that proceeds via causal behaviorist or functionalist analysis of mental concepts. The essential element of the approach is that it takes the subjective phenomenological features of conscious experience to be perfectly real and not reducible to anything else—but nevertheless holds that their systematic relations to neurophysiology are not contingent but necessary.

A great deal of effort and ingenuity has been put into the reductionist program, and there have been serious attempts in recent years to accommodate within a functionalist framework consciousness and phenomenological qualia in particular.[1] The effort has produced results that reveal a good deal that is true about the relations between consciousness and behavior, but not an account of what consciousness is. The reason for this failure is unsurprising and always the same. However complete an account may be of the functional role of the perception of the color red in the explanation of behavior, for example, such an account taken by itself will have nothing to say about the specific subjective quality of

---

1. See, for example, Sydney Shoemaker, "Self-Knowledge and 'Inner Sense,' Lecture III: The Phenomenal Character of Experience," in *The First-Person Perspective and Other Essays* (Cambridge: Cambridge University Press, 1996). I will use the term "functionalism" throughout this essay in an unsophisticated way, to refer to theories that identify mental states by their typical causal roles in the production of behavior—also called their "functional" roles. I shall leave aside the version of functionalism that identifies mental states with computational states.

the visual experience, without which it would not be a conscious experience at all.

If the intrinsic character of conscious experience remains stubbornly beyond the reach of contextual, relational, functional accounts, an alternative strategy seems called for. The exploration of such an alternative should be of interest even to those who remain convinced that functionalism is the right path to follow, since philosophical positions can be evaluated only by comparison with the competition. The alternative I wish to explore can be thought of as a response to the challenge issued by Saul Kripke at the end of *Naming and Necessity*:

> That the usual moves and analogies are not available to solve the problems of the identity theorist is, of course, no proof that no moves are available. . . . I suspect, however, that the present considerations tell heavily against the usual forms of materialism. Materialism, I think, must hold that a physical description of the world is a *complete* description of it, that any mental facts are "ontologically dependent" on physical facts in the straightforward sense of following from them by necessity. No identity theorist seems to me to have made a convincing argument against the intuitive view that this is not the case.[2]

Kripke's view of functionalism and causal behaviorism is the same as mine: that the inadequacy of these analyses of the mental is self-evident. He does not absolutely rule out a form of materialism that is not based on such reductionist analyses, but he says that it has to defend the very strong claim that mental phenomena are strictly necessary consequences of the operation of the brain; moreover, the defense of this claim lies under the heavy burden of overcoming the prima facie modal argument that consciousness and brain states are only contingently related, since it *seems* perfectly conceivable about any brain state that it should exist exactly as it is, physically, without any accompanying consciousness. The intuitive credibility of this argument, which descends from Descartes's argument for dualism, is considerable. It appears at first blush that we have a clear and distinct enough grasp on both phenomenological consciousness and physical brain processes to see that there can be no necessary connection between them.

That is the position that I hope to challenge. It seems to me that post-Kripke, the most promising line of attack on the mind-body problem is to see whether any sense can be made of the idea that mental processes might be physical processes necessarily but not analytically. I would not, however, try to defend the claim that "a physical description of the

---

2. Saul Kripke, *Naming and Necessity* (Cambridge, Mass.: Harvard University Press, 1980), p. 155.

world is a *complete* description of it," so my position is not a form of materialism in Kripke's sense. It is certainly not a form of physicalism. But there may be other forms of noncontingent psychophysical identity. So I shall argue.

Because I am going to be talking about different kinds of necessity and contingency throughout the argument, I should say something at the outset about my assumptions, which will not be universally shared. The set of ideas about necessity and contingency with which I shall be working derives largely from Kripke. This means that the semantic category of analytic or conceptual truths, the epistemological category of a priori truths, and the metaphysical category of necessary truths do not coincide—nor do their complements: synthetic, a posteriori, and contingent truths.

I believe that there are conceptual truths and that they are discoverable a priori, through reflection by a possessor of the relevant concepts—usually with the help of thought experiments—on the conditions of their application. Often the process of discovery will be difficult and the results controversial. Conceptual truths may or may not be necessary truths. In particular, conceptual truths about how the reference of a term is fixed may identify contingent properties of the referent, though these are knowable a priori to a possessor of the concept.

Not everything discoverable a priori is a conceptual truth; for example, the calculation of the logical or mathematical consequences that follow from a set of theoretical premises is a priori but not, I would say, conceptual. And although some conceptual truths are necessary, not all necessary truths are conceptual. This applies not only to mathematical or theoretical propositions discoverable by a priori reasoning but also, as Kripke showed, to certain identity statements that cannot be known a priori, such as the identity of heat with molecular motion or that of water with H_2O.

The relations among these different types of truths are intricate. In the case of the identity of water with H_2O, for example, as I shall explain more fully later, the following appears to hold. First, there are some conceptual truths about water—its usual manifest physical properties under the conditions that prevail in our world. These are the properties by which we fix the reference of the term "water," and they are knowable a priori. Most of them are contingent properties of water, because they depend on other things as well, but some of them may be necessary if they follow from the intrinsic nature of water alone. Second, there are theoretical truths, derivable from principles of chemistry and physics, about the macroscopic properties, under those same conditions, of the compound H_2O. These are necessary consequences of premises that are partly necessary (the nature of hydrogen and oxygen) and partly contingent. Third, there is the a posteriori conclusion, from evidence that the manifest properties of the water with which we are acquainted are best explained in this way, that water is in fact nothing but H_2O. This is a necessary truth, though discovered a posteriori, because *if* it is true, then any other substance with the same manifest properties that did not consist of H_2O would not be water. And this last conditional clause, following "because," is a conceptual truth, discoverable by reflection on what we would say if we encountered such a substance.

In the context with which we are concerned here, the mind-body problem, functionalism is the claim that it is a conceptual truth that any creature is conscious and is the subject of various mental states, if and only if it satisfies certain purely structural conditions of the causal organization of its behavior and interaction with the environment—whatever may be the material in which that organization is physically (or nonphysically) realized. I do not believe that this is a conceptual truth, because I do not believe that the conceptual implication from functional organization to consciousness holds.

I don't doubt that all the appropriately behaved and functionally organized creatures around us are conscious, but that is something we know on the basis of evidence, not on the basis of conceptual analysis. It may even be impossible in fact for a creature to function in these ways without consciousness; but if so, it is not a conceptual impossibility but some other kind. The functional organization of purely physical behavior, without more, is not enough to entail that the organism or system has subjective conscious experience, with experiential qualities. I make this claim particularly about sensations and the other qualities of sentience, rather than about higher-order intentional states like belief or desire—though I am inclined to think that they too require at least the capacity for sentience. My rejection of functionalism is based on the conviction that the subjective qualitative character of experience—what it is like for its subject—is not included or entailed by any amount of behavioral organization and that it is a conceptually necessary condition of conscious states that they have some such character.

On the other hand, I will argue later that there *is* a conceptual connection between consciousness and behavioral or functional organization, but in the opposite direction. I deny the functionalist biconditional because of the falsity of one of its conjuncts, but I think a weak version of the opposite conjunct is true. I believe it is a conceptual truth about the visual experience of colors, for example, that it enables a physically intact human being to discriminate colored objects by sight, and that this will usually show up in his behavior in the appropriate circumstances, provided that he meets other psychological and physical conditions. This is a conceptual truth about color vision analogous to the conceptual truths about the manifest properties of water in our world: In both cases the manifestations are contingent properties of the thing itself, dependent on surrounding circumstances. Functional organization is not a conceptually sufficient condition for mental states, but it is part of our concept of mental states that they in fact occupy something like the roles in relation to behavior that functionalists have insisted upon. Such roles permit us to fix the reference of mental terms. But they are, at least in general, contingent rather than necessary properties of the conscious mental states that occupy them.

Finally, and this is the main point, while it is obviously not conceptually necessary that conscious mental states are tied to specific neurophysiological states, I contend that there are such connections and that they hold necessarily. They are not conceptual, and they are not discoverable a priori, but they are not contingent. They belong, in other words, to the category of a posteriori necessary truths. To explain how, and to characterize the type of necessity that could hold in such a case, is the problem.

Kripke argued that if the psychophysical identity theory is to be a hypothesis analogous to other empirical reductions or theoretical identifications in science, like the identification of heat with molecular motion or fire with oxidation, it cannot be a contingent proposition. It must be necessarily true if true at all, since a theoretical identity statement tells us what something *is*, not just what happens to be true of it. In the vocabulary introduced by Kripke, the terms of such an identity are both rigid designators, and they apply or fail to apply to the same things in all possible worlds.

Kripke observes that there is an appearance of contingency even in the standard cases of theoretical identity. The identification of heat with molecular motion is not analytic, and it cannot be known a priori. It may seem that we can easily conceive of a situation in which there is heat without molecular motion or molecular motion without heat. But Kripke points out that this is a subtle mistake. When one thinks one is imagining heat without molecular motion, one is really imagining the feeling of heat being produced by something other than molecular motion. But that would not be heat; it would merely be a situation epistemically indistinguishable from the perception of heat. "Heat," being a rigid designator, refers to the actual physical phenomenon that is in fact responsible for all the manifestations on the basis of which we apply the concept in the world as it is. The term refers to that physical phenomenon and to no other, even in imagined situations in which something else is responsible for similar appearances and sensations. This is so because the appearances and sensations of heat are not themselves heat, and can be imagined to exist without it.

Kripke then points out that a similar strategy will not work to dissipate the appearance of contingency in the case of the relation between sensations and brain processes. If I seem to be able to imagine the taste of chocolate in the absence of its associated brain process or the brain process unaccompanied by any such experience, we cannot say that this is merely to imagine the *appearance* of the experience without the experience, or vice versa. There is, in this case, no way of separating the thing itself from the way in which it appears to us, as there is in the case of heat. We identify experiences not by their contingent effects on us but by their intrinsic phenomenological qualities. So if they are really identical with physical processes in the brain, the vivid appearance that we can clearly conceive of the qualities without the brain processes, and vice versa, must be shown to be erroneous in some other way.

My hope is to show that this can be done, without abandoning a commitment to the reality of the phenomenological content of conscious experience. If the appearance of contingency in the mind-body relation can be shown to be illusory, or if it can be shown how it might be illusory, then the modal argument against some sort of identification will no longer present an immovable obstacle to the empirical hypothesis that mental processes are brain processes.

The hypothesis would resemble familiar theoretical identities, like that between heat and molecular motion, in some respects but not in others. It would be nonanalytic, discoverable only a posteriori, and necessarily true if true. But, of course, it could not be established by discovering the underlying physical cause of the *appearance* of conscious experience, on analogy with the underlying physical cause of the appearance of heat—since in the case of experience, the appearance is the thing itself and not merely its effect on us.

Clearly this would require something radical. We cannot at present see how the relation between consciousness and brain processes might be necessary. The logical gap between subjective consciousness and neurophysiology seems unbridgeable, however close may be the contingent correlations between them. To see the importance of this gap, consider how the necessary connection is established in other cases.

To show that water is H_2O or that heat is molecular motion, it is necessary to show that the chemical or physical equivalence can account fully and exhaustively for everything that is included in the ordinary prescientific concepts of water and heat—the manifest properties on the basis of which we apply those concepts. Not only must the scientific account explain causally all the external effects of water or heat, such as their effects on our senses. It must also account in a more intimate manner for their familiar intrinsic properties, revealing the true basis of those properties by showing that they are *entailed* by the scientific description. Thus, the density of water, its passage from solid to liquid to gas at certain temperatures, its capacity to enter into chemical reactions or to appear as a chemical product, its transparency, its viscosity, its electrical conductivity, and so forth must all be accounted for in a particularly strong way by its chemical analysis as H_2O, together with whatever laws govern the behavior of such a compound. In brief, the essential intrinsic properties of water on the macro level must be properties that simply *follow* from the behavior of H_2O under normal conditions.

Otherwise it will not be possible to say that water is *constituted* of H_2O and nothing else.

In what sense must the familiar, manifest properties of water follow from the properties of H_2O to support the claim of constitution? To require a strict logical entailment would be far too demanding. We do not find that even in the case of reduction of one scientific theory to another, more fundamental theory. There is always a certain amount of slippage and deviation around the edges. But what we can expect is that the reducing theory will entail something close enough to the familiar properties of the thing to be reduced, allowing for the roughness of ordinary concepts and perceptual observations, to permit us to conclude that nothing more is needed to explain why H_2O, for example, has the macroscopic features of water.

To illustrate: One reason for the absence of strict entailment is that the relation between the physics of H_2O and the macroscopic properties of water is probabilistic. It is, I am assured by those who know more about these matters than I, physically possible for H_2O to be a solid at room temperature, though extremely unlikely. That means that if water is H_2O, it is possible for water to be a solid at room temperature. And similar things can apparently be said about the other manifest properties of water by means of which the reference of the term is fixed. Yet I think these esoteric facts do not remove the element of necessity in the relation between the properties of H_2O and the macroscopic properties conceptually implied by our concept of water. Those macroscopic, manifest properties are not really inconsistent with an interpretation under which they are merely probabilistic, provided the probabilities are so astronomically high that their failure is for all practical purposes impossible, and it would never be rational to believe that it had occurred. It is enough if the physics of H_2O entails that the probability of water having these properties under normal background conditions is so close to 1 as makes no experiential difference. Let me take this qualification as understood when I speak of entailment from now on.[3]

This rough variety of "upward entailment" is a necessary condition of any successful scientific reduction in regard to the physical world. It is the *a priori* element in *a posteriori* necessary theoretical identities. We begin with an ordinary concept of a natural kind or natural phenomenon. This concept—*heat* or *water*—refers to the actual examples to which we apply it and with which we are in some kind of direct or indirect con-

---

3. One further point: Even if there are laws governing the behavior of molecules in large numbers that are genuinely higher order and not merely the statistical consequences of the probabilistic or deterministic laws governing the individual particles—holistic laws, so to speak—it still does not affect the point. Facts about the macroscopic properties of a substance like water or an event like a thunderstorm would still be *constitutively* entailed by the facts about the behavior of the microscopic or submicroscopic constituents—whatever kinds of laws might be required to account for this behavior.

tact through our occupation of the world. To establish that those examples are in fact identical with something not directly manifest to perception but describable only by atomic theory, we must show that the pre-scientifically familiar intrinsic features of heat and water are nothing but the gross manifestations of the properties of these physicochemical constituents—that the liquidity of water, for example, consists simply of a certain type of movement of its molecules with respect to one another. If the properties of the substance that we refer to by the term "water" can be exhaustively accounted for by such a microanalysis, and if experiment confirms that this is in fact the situation that obtains, then that tells us what water really is.

The result is a posteriori because it requires not only the a priori demonstration that H_2O *could* account for the phenomena but also empirical confirmation that this and not something else is what *actually* underlies the manifest properties of the substance we refer to as water. That would come from experimental confirmation of previously unobserved implications of the hypothesis and disconfirmation of the implications of alternative hypotheses, for example, that water is an element. Thus it is not a conceptual reduction. Nevertheless, it is a necessary identity because our concept of water refers to the actual water around us, whatever it is, and not to just any substance superficially resembling water. If there could be something with the familiar manifest properties of water that was not H_2O, it would not be water. But to reach this conclusion, we must see that the behavior of H_2O provides a true and complete account, with nothing left out—an approximate entailment—of the features that are conceptually essential to water, and that this account is in fact true of the water around us.

It is this "upward entailment" that is so difficult to imagine in the case of the corresponding psychophysical hypothesis, and that is the nub of the mind-body problem. We understand the entailment of the liquidity of water by the behavior of molecules through geometry, or more simply the micro-macro or part-whole relation. Something analogous is true of every physical reduction, even though the spatiotemporal framework can be very complicated and hard to grasp intuitively. But nothing like this will help us with the mind-body case, because we are not dealing here merely with larger and smaller grids. We are dealing with a gap of a totally different kind, between the objective spatiotemporal order of the physical world and the subjective phenomenological order of experience. And here it seems clear *in advance* that no amount of physical information about the spatiotemporal order will entail anything of a subjective, phenomenological character. However much our purely physical concepts may change in the course of further theoretical development, they will all have been introduced to explain features of the objective spatiotemporal order, and they will not have implications of this radically different logical type.

But without an upward entailment of some kind, we will not have a proper reduction, because in any proposed reduction of the mental to the physical, something will have been left out—something essential to the phenomenon being reduced. Unless this obstacle can be overcome, it will be impossible to claim that the relation between sensations and brain processes is analogous to the relation between heat and molecular motion—a necessary but a posteriori identity.

Yet I believe that is the region in which the truth probably lies. The evident massive and detailed dependence of what happens in the mind on what happens in the brain provides, in my view, strong evidence that the relation is not contingent but necessary. It cannot take the form of a reduction of the mental to the physical, but it may be necessary all the same. The task is to try to understand how that might be the case.[4]

II. Subjectivity and the Conceptual Irreducibility of Consciousness

The source of the problem—what seems to put such a solution out of reach—is the lack of any intelligible internal relation between consciousness and its physiological basis. The apparent conceivability of what in current philosophical jargon is known as a "zombie"—that is, an exact physiological and behavioral replica of a living human being that nevertheless has no consciousness—may not show that such a thing is possible, but it does show something about our concepts of mind and body. It shows that those concepts in their present form are not logically connected in such a way that the content of the idea of consciousness is exhausted by a physical or behavioral-functional specification.

But the rejection of conceptual reduction is only the beginning of the story. The problem is to look for an alternative account of the evidently very close relation between consciousness and the brain that does not in any way accord a diminished reality to the immediate phenomenological qualities of conscious experience. Because of the causal role of mental events in the physical world and their association with specific organic structures and processes, Cartesian dualism is implausible. Physicalism, in the sense of a complete conceptual reduction of the mental to the physical, is not a possibility, since it in effect eliminates what is distinctive and undeniable about the mental. Ostensibly weaker forms of physicalism seem always to collapse into behavioristic reductionism.

---

4. My position is very like that of Colin McGinn, but without his pessimism. See McGinn, *The Problem of Consciousness* (Oxford: Blackwell, 1991). What I have to say here is also a development of a suggestion in Nagel, *The View from Nowhere* (New York: Oxford University Press, 1986), pp. 51–53.

For that reason I have occasionally been drawn to some kind of property dualism; but like substance dualism, it seems just to give a name to a mystery and not to explain anything: Simply to say that mental events are physical events with additional, nonphysical properties is to force disparate concepts together without thereby making the link even potentially intelligible. It suggests pure emergence, which explains nothing. But I believe these dead ends are not exhaustive and that starting from our present concepts of mind and body, another approach is possible.

When we try to reason about the possible relations between things, we have to rely on our conceptual grasp of them. The more adequate the grasp, the more reliable our reasoning will be. Sometimes a familiar concept clearly allows for the possibility that what it designates should also have features not implied by the concept itself—often features very different in kind from those directly implied by the concept. Thus ordinary prescientific concepts of kinds of substances, such as water or gold or blood, are in themselves silent with regard to the microscopic composition of those substances but nevertheless open to the scientific discovery, often by very indirect means, of such facts about their true nature. If a concept refers to something that takes up room in the spatiotemporal world, it provides a handle for all kinds of empirical discoveries about the inner constitution of that thing.

On the other hand, sometimes a familiar concept clearly excludes the possibility that what it designates has certain features: For example, we do not need a scientific investigation to be certain that the number 379 does not have parents. There are various other things that we can come to know about the number 379 only by mathematical or empirical investigation, such as what its factors are or whether it is greater than the population of Chugwater, Wyoming, but we know that it does not have parents just by knowing that it is a number. If someone rebuked us for being closed-minded, because we can't predict in advance what future scientific research might turn up about the biological origins of numbers, he would not be offering a serious ground for doubt.

The case of mental processes and the brain is intermediate between these two. Descartes thought it was closer to the second category, and we could tell just by thinking about it that the human mind was not an extended material thing and that no extended material thing could be a thinking subject. But this is, to put it mildly, not nearly so self-evident as that a number cannot have parents. What does seem true is that the concept of a mind or of a mental event or process fails to plainly leave space for the possibility that what it designates should turn out also to be a physical thing or event or process as the result of closer scientific investigation—in the way that the concept of blood leaves space for discoveries about its composition. The trouble is that mental concepts don't obviously pick out things or processes that take up room in the spatiotemporal world to begin with. If they did, we could just get hold of some of those things and take them apart or look at them under a microscope. But there is a prior problem about how those concepts might refer to anything that could be subjected to such investigation: They don't give us the comfortable initial handle on the occupants of the familiar spatiotemporal world that prescientific physical substance concepts do.[5]

Nevertheless, it is overconfident to conclude, from one's inability to imagine how mental phenomena might turn out to have physical properties, that the possibility can be ruled out in advance. We have to ask ourselves whether there is more behind the Cartesian intuition than mere lack of knowledge, resulting in lack of imagination.[6] Yet it is not enough merely to say, "You may be mistaking your own inability to imagine something for its inconceivability." One should be open to the possibility of withdrawing a judgment of inconceivability if offered a reason to doubt it, but there does have to *be* a reason, or at least some kind of story about how the illusion of inconceivability may have arisen.

If mental events really have physical properties, we need an explanation of why they seem to offer so little purchase for the attribution of those properties. Still, the kind of incomprehensibility here is completely different from that of numbers having parents. Mental events, unlike numbers, can be roughly located in space and time and are causally related to physical events, in both directions. The causal facts are strong evidence that mental events have physical properties, if only we could make sense of the idea.[7]

Consider another case in which the prescientific concept did not obviously allow for the possibility of physical composition or structure—the case of sound. Before the discovery that sounds are waves in air or another medium, the ordinary concept permitted sounds to be roughly located and to have properties like loudness, pitch, and duration. The concept of a sound was that of an objective phenomenon that could be heard by different people or that could exist unheard. But it would have been very obscure what could be meant by ascribing to a sound a precise spatial shape and size, or an internal, perhaps microscopic, physical structure. Someone who proposed that sounds have physical parts, without offering any theory to explain this, would not have said anything understandable. One might say that in advance of the development of a physical theory of sound, the hypothesis that sounds have a physical microstructure would not have a clear meaning.

Nevertheless, at one remove, the possibility of such a development is evidently not excluded by the concept of sound. Sounds were known to

5. See Colin McGinn, "Consciousness and Space," *Journal of Consciousness Studies*, 2 (1995), 220–30.

6. This is the objection that Arnauld made to Descartes in the fourth set of objections to the *Meditations*.

7. Compare Donald Davidson, "Mental Events," in *Essays on Actions and Events* (New York: Oxford University Press, 1980).

have certain physical causes, to be blocked by certain kinds of obstacles, and to be perceptible by hearing. This was already a substantial amount of causal information, and it opened the way to the discovery of a physically describable phenomenon that could be identified with sound because it had just those causes and effects—particularly once further features of sound, like variations of loudness and pitch, could also be accounted for in terms of its precise physical character. Yet it is important that *in advance*, the idea that a sound has a physical microstructure would have had no clear meaning. One would not have known how to go about imagining such a thing, any more than one could have imagined a sound having weight. It would have been easy to mistake this lack of clear allowance for the possibility *in* the concept for a positive exclusion of the possibility *by* the concept.

The analogy with the case of mental phenomena should be clear. They too occupy causal roles, and it has been one of the strongest arguments for some kind of physicalism that those roles may prove upon investigation to be occupied by organic processes. Yet the problem here is much more serious, for an obvious reason: Identifying sounds with waves in the air does not require that we ascribe phenomenological qualities and subjectivity to anything physical, because those are features of the perception of sound, not of sound itself. By contrast, the identification of mental events with physical events requires the unification of these two types of properties in a single thing, and that remains resistant to understanding. The causal argument for identification may make us believe that it is true, but it doesn't help us to understand it, and in my view, we really shouldn't believe it unless we can understand it.

The problem here, as with the other issue of purely conceptual reduction, lies in the distinctive first-person/third-person character of mental concepts, which is the grammatical manifestation of the subjectivity of mental phenomena. Though not all conscious beings possess language, our attribution of conscious states to languageless creatures implies that those states are of the kind that in the human case we pick out only through these distinctive concepts, concepts that the subject applies in his own case without observation of his body.

They are not pure first-person concepts: To try to detach their first-person application from the third person results in philosophical illusions. For example, from the purely first-person standpoint, it seems intelligible that the subject of my present consciousness might have been created five minutes ago and all my memories, personality, and so on transferred from a previous subject in this same body to the newly created one, without any outwardly or inwardly perceptible sign—without any other physical or psychological change. If the pure first-person idea of "I" defined an individual, that would make sense, but it seems reasonably clear that the real idea of "I" has lost its moorings in this philosophical thought experiment. The point goes back to Kant, who ar-

gued that the subjective identity of the consciousness of myself at different times does not establish the objective identity of a subject or soul.[8]

That is not to say that I understand just how the first person and the
third form two logically inseparable aspects of a single concept—only
that they do. This applies to all conscious mental states and events, and
their properties. They are subjective, not in the sense that they are the
subjects of a purely first-person vocabulary, but in the sense that they
can be accurately described only by concepts in which nonobservational
first-person and observational third-person attributions are systematically connected. Such states are modifications of the point of view of an
individual subject.

The problem, then, is how something that is an aspect or element of
an individual's subjective point of view could also be a physiologically
describable event in the brain—the kind of thing that, considered under
that description, involves no point of view and no distinctively immediate first-person attribution at all. I believe that as a matter of fact you
can't have one without the other and, furthermore, that the powerful intuition that it is conceivable that an intact and normally functioning
physical human organism could be a completely unconscious zombie is
an illusion—due to the limitations of our understanding. Nevertheless
those limitations are real. We do not at present possess the conceptual
equipment to understand how subjective and physical features could
both be essential aspects of a single entity or process. Kant expresses
roughly the same point in terms of his apparatus of phenomena and
noumena:

> If I understand by soul a thinking being in itself, the question
> whether or not it is the same in kind as matter—matter not being a
> thing in itself, but merely a species of representations in us—is by
> its very terms illegitimate. For it is obvious that a thing in itself is of
> a different nature from the determinations which constitute only
> its state.
>
> If on the other hand, we compare the thinking "I" not with mat-
> ter but with the intelligible that lies at the basis of the outer appear-
> ance which we call matter, we have no knowledge whatsoever of
> the intelligible, and therefore are in no position to say that the soul
> is in any inward respect different from it.[9]

What I want to propose, however, is that these conceptual limitations
might be overcome—that there is not a perfect fit at every stage of our

8. See Immanuel Kant, *Critique of Pure Reason*, A 363–64: The Paralogisms of Pure
Reason.

9. *Critique of Pure Reason*, A 360. McGinn, too, remarks on the similarity of Kant's view
to his own; see *The Problem of Consciousness*, pp. 81–82.

conceptual development between conceptual truths and necessary truths, and that this is the most probable interpretation of the present situation with respect to mind and brain: The dependence of mind on brain is not conceptually transparent, but it is necessary nonetheless.

III. Necessary Truth and Conceptual Creativity

The greatest scientific progress occurs through conceptual change that permits an empirically observed order that initially appears contingent to be understood at a deeper level as necessary, in the sense of being entailed by the true nature of the phenomena. Something like this must have happened at the birth of mathematics, but it is a pervasive aspect of physical science. This is the domain in which I think it is appropriate to speak of natural, as opposed to conceptual, necessity.

To take a simple and familiar example: It was observable to anyone before the advent of modern chemistry that a fire will go out quickly if enclosed in a small airtight space. Given the prescientific concepts of air and fire, this was not a conceptual truth, and there would have been no way, on purely conceptual grounds, to discover that it was anything other than a strict but contingent correlation. However, its very strictness should have suggested that it was not really contingent but could be accounted for as a logical consequence of the true nature of fire and air, neither of which is fully revealed in the prescientific concepts.

This phenomenon is itself one of the evidentiary grounds for identifying fire with rapid oxidation, and air with a mixture of gases of which oxygen is one. Those identifications in turn reveal it to be a noncontingent truth that the enclosed fire will go out. The very process of oxidation that constitutes the fire eventually binds all the free oxygen in the airtight container, thus entailing its own termination. Once we develop the concepts of atomistic chemistry and physics that enable us to see what fire and air really are, we understand that it is not really conceivable that a fire should continue to burn in a small airtight space, even though our prescientific concepts did not make this evident.

The consequence is that conceivability arguments for the contingency of a correlation or the distinctness of differently described phenomena depend for their reliability on the adequacy of the concepts being employed. If those concepts do not adequately grasp the nature of the things to which they refer, they may yield deceptive appearances of contingency and nonidentity.

The mind-brain case seems a natural candidate for such treatment because what happens in consciousness is pretty clearly supervenient on what happens physically in the brain. In the present state of our conceptions of consciousness and neurophysiology, this strict dependence is a brute fact and completely mysterious. But pure, unexplained supervenience is never a solution to a problem but a sign that there is something fundamental we don't know. If the physical necessitates the mental, there must be some answer to the question *how* it does so. An obviously systematic connection that remains unintelligible to us calls out for a theory.[10]

From the conceptual irreducibility of the mental to the physical, together with the empirical evidence of a connection between the mental and the physical so strong that it must be necessary, we can conclude that our mental concepts or our physical concepts or both fail to capture something about the nature of the phenomena to which they refer, however accurate they may be as far as they go. The conceptual development that would be needed to reveal the underlying necessary connection is of a radical and scientifically unprecedented kind, because these two types of concepts as they now stand are not already open to the possibility that what they refer to should have a true nature of the other type.

Ordinary physical concepts, like that of fire, are candidly incomplete in what they reveal about the inner constitution of the manifest process or phenomenon to which they refer: They are open to the possibility that it should have a microstructural analysis of the kind that it in fact proves to have. But nothing in the ordinary concepts of either consciousness or the brain leaves space for the possibility that they should have inner constitutions that would close the logical gap between them. Physical phenomena can be analyzed into their physical constituents, with the aid of scientific experimentation, and mental phenomena can perhaps be analyzed into their mental constituents, at least in some cases, but these two paths of analysis do not meet. The apparent conceivability of each of the correlated items without the other cannot be defused without something much more radical than the type of reduction that we are familiar with in the physical sciences.

That poses the general question of how we can attempt to develop conceptions that reflect the actual necessary connections and are therefore reliable tools for reasoning, and what determines whether there is hope of developing such concepts for a domain where we do not yet have them. After all, humans did not always have logical, geometrical, and arithmetical concepts, but had to develop them. Yet we cannot will a new conceptual framework into existence. It has to result from trying to think, in light of the evidence, about the subject we want to understand, and devising concepts that do better justice to it than the ones we have.

So how might we proceed in this case? Although I am not going to follow them, there are precedents for this revisionist project: The idea that

---

10. A similar position is endorsed by Galen Strawson in *Mental Reality* (Cambridge, Mass.: MIT Press, 1994), pp. 81–84; and by Allin Cottrell in *"Tertium datur?* Reflections on Owen Flanagan's *Consciousness Reconsidered,"* *Philosophical Psychology*, 8 (1995).

the physical description of the brain leaves out its mental essence and that we need to reform our concepts accordingly is not new. A version of it is found in Spinoza, and it is at the heart of Bertrand Russell's neutral monism, expounded in *The Analysis of Matter, An Outline of Philosophy*, and other writings. He holds that physics in general describes only a causal structure of events, leaving the intrinsic nature of its elements unspecified, and that our only knowledge of that intrinsic nature is in respect to certain physical events in our own brains, of which we are aware as percepts. He also holds that physics contains nothing incompatible with the possibility that all physical events, in brains or not, have an intrinsic nature of the same general type—though their specific qualities would presumably vary greatly. Here is what he says:

> There is no theoretical reason why a light-wave should not consist of groups of occurrences, each containing a member more or less analogous to a minute part of a visual percept. We cannot perceive a light-wave, since the interposition of an eye and brain stops it. We know, therefore, only its abstract mathematical properties. Such properties may belong to groups composed of any kind of material. To assert that the material *must* be very different from percepts is to assume that we know a great deal more than we do in fact know of the intrinsic character of physical events. If there is any advantage in supposing that the light-wave, the process in the eye, and the process in the optic nerve, contain events qualitatively continuous with the final visual percept, nothing that we know of the physical world can be used to disprove the supposition.[11]

Russell holds that both minds and bodies are logical constructions out of events. When I see the moon, my percept of the moon is one of an immense set of events, radiating out in all directions from the place where the moon is located, out of which the moon as physical object is a logical construction. The same percept also belongs to the psychologically connected set of events that constitutes my mind or mental life. And it also belongs to the set of events, centered in my skull but radiating out from there in all directions, out of which my brain as a physical object is a logical construction. (A physiologist's percept of my brain

---

11. Bertrand Russell, *The Analysis of Matter* (London: Allen & Unwin, 1927), pp. 263–64. For an excellent discussion and defense of Russell's and similar views, see Michael Lockwood, *Mind, Brain and the Quantum* (Oxford: Blackwell, 1989), chap. 10. See also Grover Maxwell, "Rigid Designators and Mind-Brain Identity," in C. Wade Savage, ed., *Minnesota Studies in the Philosophy of Science*, vol. 9 (Minneapolis: University of Minnesota Press, 1978). Maxwell argues that it is physical rather than mental concepts that are topic-neutral and that there is nothing to prevent their referring nonrigidly to what mental concepts designate rigidly.

would also belong to this set, as well as to the sets constituting his mind and his brain.)

This means that the type of identification of a sensation with a brain process that Russell advocates amounts to the possibility of locating the sensation in a certain kind of causal structure—for example, as the terminus of a sequence of events starting from the moon, and the origin of a sequence of events ending with the physiologist's observation of my brain. The import of describing it as a physical event is essentially relational. Its phenomenological quality is intrinsic in a way that its physical character is not.

This is a rich and interesting view, but it seems to me to solve the mind-body problem at excessive cost, by denying that physical properties are intrinsic. I believe that both mental and physical properties are intrinsic, and this leaves an identity theory with the problem of how to understand the internal and necessary relation between them. The theory also leaves untouched the problem of relating the subjectivity of the mental to its physical character. Russell did have something to say about this—identifying subjectivity with dependence on the specific character of the individual's brain—but I don't think it is sufficient.

Russell's view that the intrinsic nature of physical brain processes is mental would certainly explain why the apparent conceivability of a zombie was an illusion, but it seems to me not to account for the necessity of the mind-body relation in the right way. I am sympathetic to the project of reducing both the physical and the mental to a common element, but this is too much like reducing the physical to the mental.

More recent forms of reductionism are unsatisfactory in other ways. Even if we interpret the physicalist-functionalist movement in philosophy of mind as a form of conceptual revisionism rather than analysis of what our ordinary concepts already contain, I believe it has failed because it is too conservative: It has tried to reinterpret mental concepts to make them tractable parts of the framework of physical science. What is needed is a search for something more unfamiliar, something that starts from the conceptual unintelligibility, in its present form, of the subjective-objective link. The enterprise is one of imagining possibilities: Identity theorists like Smart, Armstrong, and Lewis tried to explain how the identity of mental with physical states could be a contingent truth; I am interested in how some sort of mind-brain identity might be a necessary truth.

That would require not only the imagination of concepts that might capture the connection but also some account of how our existing concepts would have to be related to these and to one another. We must imagine something that falls under both our mental concepts and the physiological concepts used to describe the brain, not accidentally but necessarily.

IV. Mental Reference

We first have to interpret the third-person and first-person conditions of reference to mental states as inextricably connected in a single concept, but in a rather special way. I have insisted that mental concepts are not exhausted by the behavioral or functional conditions that provide the grounds for their application to others. Functionalism does not provide sufficient conditions for the mental. However, in the other, "outward" direction, there does seem to be a conceptual connection between conscious mental states and the behavioral or other interactions of the organism with its environment. This is a consequence of the inseparable first-person/third-person character of mental concepts. To put it roughly, functional states aren't necessarily mental states, but it is a conceptual truth that our mental states actually occupy certain functional roles.

Imaginability and thought experiments are essential in establishing conceptual connections—or their absence. Those methods have to be used with care, but the pitfalls are not so serious here as when they are used to test for nonconceptual necessary connections, as in the case of consciousness and the brain. We can discover the presence or absence of a conceptual connection a priori because all the necessary data are contained in the concepts we are thinking with: We just have to extract those data and see what they reveal.

Sometimes, as in the case of functional characteristics of consciousness, the conceptual connection may be somewhat hidden from view. But I believe we can know a priori both (1) that specific conscious states typically occupy certain functional roles, and (2) that those functional roles do not, as a matter of conceptual necessity, entail those specific conscious states. For the latter conclusion, we only have to imagine a being whose color vision, for example, is functionally equivalent to ours but is based on a completely different neurophysiology. This may not in fact be possible, but there is no reason to believe either that it is *conceptually* excluded or that, if it were possible, such a being would have the same color phenomenology as we do.

My main interest is in the further proposition that mental states are related to certain *neurophysiological* states by an equivalence relation that is necessary but not conceptual. However, these other claims about the conceptual relation between phenomenology and behavior are an essential part of the picture. The aim is to connect phenomenology, physiology, and behavior in a single nexus.

I am denying two familiar types of functionalist view:

1. Nonrigid functionalism: Mental concepts refer contingently to whatever inner states happen as a matter of fact to occupy certain functional roles. It is analytically true that to be a mental

state of a given kind is simply to occupy a certain functional role, but it is contingently true of any particular inner state that it is a mental state of that kind. Empirical science reveals that mental concepts nonrigidly designate states that are in fact essentially physiological.[12]

2. Rigid functionalism: Mental concepts refer to functional states themselves—to the state of being in a state with a certain functional role. It is both analytically and necessarily true of a given mental state that it manifests itself in certain relations to behavior and to other mental states. Mental states are not identified with their physiological basis.[13]

The first view is unacceptable both because it analyzes mental concepts reductively and because it makes it a contingent fact that a mental state is the mental state it is. The second view is unacceptable because it analyzes mental concepts reductively and implies that they don't refer to inner states of the organism.

Consider next the following alternative:

3. Reference-fixing functionalism: The reference of our mental concepts to inner states is fixed by the contingent functional roles of those states, but the concepts apply rigidly to the occupants of those roles. It is neither necessarily true of a given mental state nor analytically equivalent to its being the mental state it is that it occupy a certain functional role, but that is how we in fact pick it out. Mental concepts rigidly designate states that are essentially physiological or phenomenological or both.[14]

This seems to me close to the truth, but it leaves out the fact that the reference of mental terms for conscious states is fixed not only by their functional role but also by their immediate phenomenological quality—an intrinsic and essential property. Something must relate these two reference fixers, one necessary and one contingent, and I believe it can be done by the following proposal:

4. Though mental concepts cannot be analyzed functionally, functional roles are needed to fix the reference of mental terms be-

12. See David Lewis, "Psychophysical and Theoretical Identifications," *Australasian Journal of Philosophy*, 50, (1972).

13. See Hilary Putnam, "The Nature of Mental States," in *Mind, Language and Reality: Philosophical Papers*, vol. 2 (Cambridge: Cambridge University Press, 1975).

14. This interesting option, which I had never heard before, was suggested to me by a New York University undergraduate, James Swoyer. A theory of similar form, but offered in the service of physicalism, is defended by Michael E. Levin, *Metaphysics and the Mind-Body Problem* (Oxford: Clarendon, 1979), pp. 113–25.

cause of the inextricable first-person/third-person character of mental concepts. It is a *conceptual* but *contingent* truth that each mental state plays its characteristic functional role in relation to behavior. It is a *conceptual* and *necessary* truth that each conscious mental state has the phenomenological properties that it has. And it is a *nonconceptual* but *necessary* truth that each conscious mental state has the physiological properties that it has.

This seems to me to do justice to the "internal" character of the relation between phenomenology and behavior. Phenomenological facts have to be in principle, though not infallibly, introspectively accessible. If two simultaneous color impressions or two sound impressions in close succession are the same or different, I ought in general to be able to tell—just because they are both mine—and this discriminatory capacity will have behavioral consequences under suitable conditions. Similarly, if a sensation is very unpleasant, I will want to avoid it, and if I am not paralyzed this will also have behavioral consequences. Although phenomenological features cannot be analyzed behaviorally or functionally, their relation to their typical functional role in the production of behavior is, in the outward direction, an a priori conceptual truth.

This is the conception of the relation between mental states and behavior—conceptual but nonreductionist—that is suggested to me by Wittgenstein's anti–private-language argument, even though it is almost certainly not Wittgenstein's conception. If each phenomenal property were in principle detectable only introspectively, there could be no concepts for such properties, for the concepts could not be governed by rules that distinguished between their correct and incorrect application. Therefore our phenomenal concepts must actually work differently, picking out properties that are detectable from both the first-person and the third-person perspective. And this seems phenomenologically accurate, so long as it is not turned into a behaviorist or essentially third-person causal-role analysis of mental concepts. Pain, color impressions, and so forth are intrinsic properties of the conscious subject, which we can identify only in virtue of their relations to other mental properties and to causal conditions and behavioral manifestations.

To state Wittgenstein's point: To name a sensation that I notice, I must have the concept of the same (type of) sensation—of its feeling the same to me—and this must be the idea of something that can hold objectively, so that if I give the name "S" to the type of sensation I am having now, that baptism sets up a rule that determines whether any particular future application of the term by me to another event will be correct or incorrect. It either will be the same—that is, will feel the same phenomenally—or it will not. That I am correctly remembering the meaning of the term must be an objective fact independent of my actual sincere application of the term, or else the term wouldn't carry any meaning. So I must be relying on my mastery of a concept of phenomenal similarity to which my personal usage conforms over time—a concept whose applicability to me is independent of my application of it to myself, in a way that underwrites the objective meaning of my own personal application of it.

Concepts can be objective in more than one way, but phenomenological concepts seem in fact to secure their objectivity through an internal connection to behavior and circumstances. That is how we establish that someone else has the concept of sensation, and that is how an individual knows that he himself has mastered a phenomenological concept—by confirmation from others who can observe that he uses it correctly. It is also how we tell that we ourselves or someone else has forgotten what a phenomenological term means and has misapplied it. The concept that we apply introspectively to ourselves is the same concept that others apply to us—and we to others—observationally.

To have the concept of pain, a person must apply it to his own sensation in the circumstances that enable others to apply it to him. This conjunction is the only way to identify the concept. The third-person conditions are not sufficient, but they are (conceptually) necessary. Someone doesn't have the phenomenological concept of pain unless he can apply it introspectively in accordance with certain standard circumstantial and behavioral conditions. These include its tendency to signal damage and to provoke avoidance in an otherwise intact organism.

The reference of a phenomenological term is fixed, then, by its immediate phenomenological quality, whose identification depends on its functional role. A given functional role might be occupied by different phenomenological qualities in different organisms—or conceivably there could be a system in which the same functional role was not occupied by a conscious experience at all. And my hypothesis is that when a functional role helps to fix the reference of a sensation term, the term refers to something whose immediate phenomenological quality and physiological basis are both essential properties of it, properties without which it could not exist.

This is parallel to the case of water: There could be a watery liquid ("behaviorally" indistinguishable from water) that wasn't the compound H_2O and therefore wasn't water; but in the world as it is, the essential gross properties of water are entailed by its being H_2O, and that is what water is. Similarly, it is conceivable that there could be a state functionally equivalent to pain in a mechanism with a completely different internal constitution, and if it were both physically and phenomenologically different, it would not be the same sensation. But in us, the behavior that helps to fix the reference of "pain" is produced by a state whose phenomenological and physiological properties are both essential, and that is what pain is.

So the proposal is that mental states would have a dual essence—phenomenological and physiological—but we still don't understand how this could be, since our modal intuitions go against it. In particular, we still have to deal with the apparent conceivability of an exact chemical-physiological-functional replica of a conscious human being that nevertheless has no subjective phenomenological "interior" at all—a zombie, in current jargon. This is an illusion, according to the proposal, but it still has to be dissolved. The task of defending a necessary connection between the physical and the phenomenological requires some account of how a connection that is in fact internal remains stubbornly external from the point of view of our understanding.

Colin McGinn gives a similar description of the situation in his essay "The Hidden Structure of Consciousness," though he puts it in terms of the distinction between the "surface" of consciousness and its true nature, inaccessible to us either by introspection or by external observation:

> My position is that the hidden structure of consciousness contains the machinery to lock consciousness firmly onto the physical world of brain and behaviour and environment, but that the surface of consciousness encourages us to believe that these links are merely contingent. When you cannot perceive (or conceive) necessary links you are apt to think there are not any, especially when you have racked your brains trying to discover them. This is a mistake, but a natural one. Cognitive closure with respect to necessary links is misinterpreted as contingency in those links.[15]

By "the surface of consciousness," I take him to mean the way it appears from the first-person standpoint—whether we are experiencing our own or imagining someone else's. This seems to be both something we have a very clear grasp of and something logically quite unconnected with the physical workings of the brain, even though there are obviously causal connections. McGinn holds that both these appearances are illusory in a way we are prevented from seeing because we cannot get beneath the surface of consciousness.

V. What's Wrong with the Conceivability Argument

Though I believe McGinn is right about our present situation, I think we can advance beyond it once we acknowledge that our immediate first-person grasp on the phenomenology may be logically incomplete. But is that a real possibility? Perhaps our concepts of consciousness and the brain, although not containing full information about these two types of thing, are still adequate to allow us to know a priori that no necessary relation between them can be discovered no matter how much more we

---

15. McGinn, *The Problem of Consciousness*, pp. 106–7, fn. 23.

learn about their deeper constitutions. Perhaps the difference in type is such as to set limits on the paths along which fuller knowledge of the nature of these things can develop.

This is what seems forced on us by the clarity with which we appear to be able to conceive absolutely any physiological process existing unaccompanied by conscious experience. The vivid imaginability of a totally unconscious zombie, resembling a conscious being only in its behavior and physical constitution, seems not to depend in any way on the details of that constitution. That is because conceiving that the system has no consciousness is completely independent of conceiving anything about its physical character. The latter is a conception of it from the outside, so to speak, as a spatiotemporal structure, whereas the former is a conception of it from the subjective point of view, as having no subjective "inside" at all. The two types of conception are so completely unrelated that the first seems incapable of ruling out the second: All I have to do is imagine the physical system from the outside and then imagine it from the inside—as not having any inside in the experiential sense. That is, I project my own point of view into the zombie and imagine that there is nothing of that kind going on behind its eyes at all. What could be more clearly independent than these two conceptions?[16]

But it is just the radical difference between these modes of conceiving that may undermine the result. I want now to argue not directly for the necessary connection between mind and brain but rather for the position that even if there were such a necessary connection, it would still appear through this kind of conceivability test that there was not. The process of juxtaposing these two very different kinds of conception is inherently misleading.

In testing philosophical hypotheses by thought experiments, one should be wary of intuitions based on the first-person perspective, since they can easily create illusions of conceivability.[17] The zombie thought experiment clearly depends on the first-person perspective, because although it is an intuition about a being other than oneself, it depends on taking up that being's point of view in imagination or, rather, finding that it has no point of view that one can take up. In this case the very disparity between the two forms of conception that gives rise to the strong intuition of conceivability should make us suspicious. The absence of any conceptual connection when phenomena are grasped by such disparate concepts may conceal a deeper necessary connection that is not

16. This argument has recently been given much prominence by David Chalmers, *The Conscious Mind* (New York: Oxford University Press, 1996). It was thinking about Chalmers's book that stimulated me to write this essay. And although we come to very different conclusions, there is a great deal in his book with which I agree.

17. See Sydney Shoemaker, "The First-Person Perspective," in *The First-Person Perspective and Other Essays* (Cambridge: Cambridge University Press, 1996).

yet conceptual because not accessible to us by means of our present forms of thought.

To see this, consider how I might investigate reflectively the relations among phenomenology, behavior, and physiology with respect, say, to the taste of the cigar I am now smoking. What I must do first is to regard the experience as a state of myself of whose subjective qualities I am immediately aware, which also has certain publicly observable functional relations to stimuli and discriminatory capacities. Even at this first stage there is already the risk of a natural illusion of conceptual independence with respect to these functional relations, because they are concealed in my introspective identification of the experience. But it is an illusion because introspective identification is itself one of those mental acts that cannot be completely separated from its functional connections (e.g., the capacity to distinguish this taste from that of a cigarette). Recognizing this, I can see that the Cartesian thought experiment of imagining myself having this experience without ever having had a body at all is an unreliable guide to what might really be the case. It depends on the concealment of the necessary conditions of reference of the phenomenological concept that I am employing to think about the experience. That is the point I take from Wittgenstein.

But now what of the relation between the experience and its physiological basis? Here I seem to be able to imagine either myself or someone else tasting exactly this flavor of cigar—and its having all the usual functional connections as well—although my brain or the other person's brain is in a completely different physiological state from the one it is actually in. Indeed it seems imaginable, though unlikely, that when I offer a friendly cigar to an exotic visitor from outer space who has a completely different physiology, it should taste the same to him. But here, too, the imagination is a poor guide to possibility because it relies on an assumption of the completeness of the manifest conditions of reference of the concept (now taken to include functional, as well as phenomenological, conditions).

The first thing to acknowledge is that if there were a necessary connection between the phenomenology and the physiology of tasting a cigar, it would not be evident a priori on the basis of the ordinary concept of that experience, since the possession of that concept involves no awareness of anything about the brain. It isn't just that, like the criterial connections of mental concepts to typical behavior and circumstances, the relation to the brain is *hidden from view* in my first-person use of the concept: The relation is completely absent from the concept and cannot be retrieved by philosophical analysis. Nevertheless, if there is such a relation, *having* the full concept (including the first-person aspect) would require having a brain, indeed a brain with exactly the right physiological characteristics, and the brain would be directly involved in the act of imagination—though its involvement would be completely outside the range of my awareness in employing the concept. To imagine a mental state from the inside would be what I have elsewhere called an act of *sympathetic* imagination—putting myself in a conscious state that *resembles* the thing imagined—and it would be impossible to do this without putting my brain in a corresponding physical state.[18]

This shows that I cannot rely on the apparent imaginability of the separation of phenomenology and physiology to establish the contingency of the relation, since I can know in advance that this act of imagination would seem subjectively the same whether the relation was contingent or necessary. If the relation is necessary, then I have not really succeeded in imagining the phenomenology without the physiology. The imagination here is essentially ostensive, and I cannot point to one without pointing to the other.

If the relation is necessary, then someone is mistaken if he says, concentrating on his present sensation of tasting a cigar, "I can conceive of *this* experience existing while my brain is in a very different state." He is mistaken because he is actually referring, by "this experience," to something that is at the same time a specific brain state. And if the relation is necessary, then someone is also mistaken who says, "I can conceive of the brain state that is in fact the physical condition of my tasting the cigar as existing without any such sensation existing." He is mistaken because he is actually referring, by "the brain state," to something that is at the same time the experience. He does not really succeed in detaching the one from the other in imagination, because he cannot demonstratively pick out either of them separately, even though the lack of visible connection between the two ways of picking out the same thing conceals this from him.

This does not show that the relation is necessary, but it does show that the familiar subjective thought experiment doesn't prove that the relation is contingent. The thought experiment would come out the same way whether the relation was necessary or contingent.

I think we can still rely on such thought experiments to refute the most common types of *conceptual* reductionism. Even if there is some kind of entailment of the mental by the physical-functional, it is not analytic or definitional: There is no hidden conceptual contradiction in the description of a zombie, even if in reality a zombie is logically impossible. Our mental concepts do not, for example, exclude the possibility that mental states are states of an immaterial soul and that there could be a fully functioning physical replica of a human body without a soul. As I

---

18. See Nagel, "What Is It Like to Be a Bat?" *Philosophical Review* 83, 1974; reprinted in *Mortal Questions* (Cambridge: Cambridge University Press, 1979), fn. 11. This was an earlier response to the modal argument against materialism. See also Christopher Hill, "Imaginability, Conceivability, Possibility and the Mind-Body Problem," *Philosophical Studies*, 87 (1997).

have said, this does not rule out a conceptual link in the other direction—from the mental to the behavioral—on account of the public criteria for the application of mental concepts, which go with their distinctive first-person/third-person character. But while third-person criteria are necessary for the operation of mental concepts, they are not sufficient. In any case, those criteria are functional rather than physiological, and the issue here is the relation between mental states and the brain, not between mental states and behavior. Here there is obviously no conceptual connection, and this tempts us to think that their separation is conceivable. But the inference is unwarranted.

The following things seem prima facie conceivable which are pretty certainly impossible in a very strong sense:

1. A living, behaving, physiologically and functionally perfect human organism that is nevertheless completely lacking in consciousness, that is, a zombie
2. A conscious subject with an inner mental life just like ours that behaves and looks just like a human being but has electronic circuitry instead of brains

The apparent conceivability of these things reveals something about our present concepts but not about what is really possible. Analytic psychophysical reductionism is false, but there is independent reason to believe that these are not logical possibilities, and if so, our concepts are missing something. They don't lead to contradiction—it's not as bad as that—but they fail to reveal a logical impossibility.

Contrast these thought experiments with the a priori inconceivability of a number having parents. The latter involves a straightforward clash between concepts, not merely a disparity. No number could enter into the kind of biological relation with a predecessor that is a necessary condition of being a child or offspring. In that case, we see a contradiction between the conditions of numberhood and the conditions of being the child of anything or anyone. In the relation of consciousness to the physical world, by contrast, our concepts fail to reveal a necessary connection, and we are tempted to conclude to the absence of any such connection. Our intuition is of a logical compatibility, not of a logical incompatibility. We conceive the body from outside and the mind from inside, and we see no internal connection, only an external one of correlation or perhaps causation.

Conceivability and inconceivability are the main evidence we have for possibility and necessity, but they can be misleading, and conceivability that depends on the relation between first- and third-person reference is particularly treacherous terrain. The first-person view of our experiential states may reveal something that is not just contingently related to their physical basis, despite appearances. The physical description of the brain states associated with consciousness may be an incomplete account of their essence—merely the outside view of what we recognize from within as conscious experience. If anything like that is true, then our present conceptions of mind and body are radically inadequate to the reality and do not provide us with adequate tools for determining whether the relation between them is necessary or contingent.

VI. A New Concept

How am I to form the conception that the relation might actually be necessary—as opposed to merely acknowledging that I can't discover a priori that it isn't? I have to think that these two ways of referring—by the phenomenological concept and the physiological concept—pick out a single referent, in each case rigidly, but that the logical link cannot be discovered by inspecting the concepts directly: Rather it goes only through their common necessary link to the referent itself.

The idea would have to be, then, that there is a single event to which I can refer in two ways, both of them via concepts that apply to it noncontingently. One is the mental concept that I am able to acquire in both first- and third-person applications because I am a subject of this state, which has the special character of consciousness and introspective accessibility—the state of tasting a cigar. The other is a (so far unspecified) physiological concept that describes the relevant physical state of the brain. To admit the possibility of a necessary connection here, we would have to recognize that the mental concept as it now operates has nothing to say about the physiological conditions for its own operation, and then open up the concept to amplification by leaving a place for such a condition—a place that can be filled only a posteriori, by a theory of the actual type of event that admits these two types of access, internal and external, from within and from without. But this description of the task tells us nothing about how to carry it out.

What will be the point of view, so to speak, of such a theory? If we could arrive at it, it would render transparent the relation between mental and physical, not directly, but through the transparency of their common relation to something that is not merely either of them. Neither the mental nor the physical point of view will do for this purpose. The mental will not do because it simply leaves out the physiology and has no room for it. The physical will not do because although it includes the behavioral and functional manifestations of the mental, this doesn't enable it, in view of the falsity of conceptual reductionism, to reach to the mental concepts themselves. The right point of view would be one that, contrary to present conceptual possibilities, included both subjectivity and spatiotemporal structure from the outset, all its descriptions implying both these things at once, so that it would describe inner states and their functional relations to behavior and to one another from the phenomenological inside and the physiological outside simultaneously—not in parallel. The mental and physiological concepts and their reference to this same inner phenomenon would then be seen as secondary and each partial in its grasp of the phenomenon: Each would be seen as referring to something that extends beyond its grounds of application.

Such a viewpoint cannot be constructed by the mere conjunction of the mental and the physical. It must be something genuinely new; otherwise it will not possess the necessary unity. It would have to be a new theoretical construction, realist in intention and contextually defined as part of a theory that explained both the familiarly observable phenomenological and the physiological characteristics of these inner events. Its character would be determined by what it was introduced to explain—like the electromagnetic field, gravity, the atomic nucleus, or any other theoretical postulate. This could only be done with a truly general theory, containing real laws and not just dispositional definitions; otherwise the theoretical entity would not have independent reality.

If strict correlations are observed between a phenomenological and a physiological variable, the hypothesis would be, not that the physiological state causes the phenomenological, but that there is a third term that entails both of them but that is not defined as the mere conjunction of the other two. It would have to be a third type of variable, whose relation to the other two was not causal but constitutive. This third term should not leave anything out. It would have to be an X such that X's being a sensation and X's being a brain state both follow from the nature of X itself, independent of its relation to anything else.

Even though no transparent *and direct* explanatory connection is possible between the physiological and the phenomenological, but only an empirically established extensional correlation, we may hope and ought to try as part of a scientific theory of mind to form a third conception that does have direct transparently necessary connections with both the mental and the physical, and through which their actual necessary connection with one another can therefore become transparent to us. Such a conception will have to be created; we won't just find it lying around. A utopian dream, certainly, but all the great reductive successes in the history of science have depended on theoretical concepts, not natural ones—concepts whose whole justification is that they permit us to give reductive explanations.

But there is another objection—that such extravagance is unnecessary. Why wouldn't a theory be sufficient that systematically linked mental phenomena to their physical conditions without introducing any concepts of a new type? That is the approach favored by John Searle, who maintains that a purely empirical theory would enable us to see that mental states are higher-order *physical* states of the brain, caused by lower-order physiological states to which they are not reducible.[19] Searle, too, wants to avoid dualism without resorting to functionalist reductionism, but I don't think his way of doing it succeeds. The problem is that so long as the mental states remain characteristically subjective and radically emergent, there is no basis for describing them as physical or physically constituted.

This is not just a verbal point. The mental-physical distinction cannot be abolished by fiat. I agree with Searle that the correct approach to the mind-body problem must be essentially biological, not functional or computational. But his proposal is still, as I understand it, too dualistic: In relating the physiological and the mental as cause and effect, it does not explain how each is literally impossible without the other. A causal theory of radically emergent higher-order properties would not show how mind arises from matter by necessity. That is the price of sticking with our existing mental and physical concepts.

The inadequacy of those concepts is revealed by their incapacity to display a necessary connection that obviously must exist. Only new concepts that turn the connection into a conceptual one can claim to grasp the phenomena in their basic nature.

Clearly not just any concept that we can create, which has both mental and physical implications, would reveal a necessary connection between the two. In some cases, we will only have created a conjunctive concept, relative to which the two categories are analytically, but not necessarily, connected. For example, even if Cartesian dualism were true, we could introduce the concept of a human being as the combination of a body and a soul. In that case there would be one thing, a human being, whose existence entails both mental and physical characteristics, but this would not mean that one can't exist without the other, any more than the concept of a ham sandwich shows that bread can't exist without ham.

What is the difference between these purely conjunctive, analytic connections and the more metaphysically robust type of concept that reveals true necessity? Physical science is full of examples of the latter. The clearest are found in the atomic theory of matter. The hypothesis that familiar substances are composed of invisibly small particles, whose motion is responsible for the observable manifestations of temperature and pressure, made it possible to see that the positive correlation between changes in temperature and pressure of a gas at constant volume was not a contingent but a necessary connection. Likewise, the chemical analysis of air, and of fire as rapid oxidation, reveals it to be a necessary truth that a fire will go out if enclosed in a small, airtight space. The postulation of electromagnetic fields, similarly, made it possible to see many previously mysterious correlations, such as the capacity of a mov-

19. See John Searle, *The Rediscovery of the Mind* (Cambridge, Mass.: MIT Press, 1992).

ing magnet to induce an electric current, as necessary consequences of the nature of the component phenomena—though in this case the new concept requires a greater leap from prescientific intuition than the direct analogy with the familiar part-whole relation that yields atomism.

One of the things that is true in these cases is that the "single" postulated underlying phenomenon explains the manifestations of each of the superficially distinct phenomena in a way that makes it impossible to separate the explanation of the one from the explanation of the other. The very same atomic (or molecular) agitation that accounts for increased pressure against the walls of the container accounts for increased temperature of the gas within. The process of oxidation that constitutes the fire eventually binds all the free oxygen in the airtight container, thus entailing its own termination. So the new account of the correlated phenomena makes their separability no longer conceivable.[20]

In addition, the postulated underlying basis explains more things than it was introduced to explain. Atomic theory was the avenue to the endless developments of chemistry; the theory of electromagnetism led vastly beyond the curious phenomena of lodestones and electrostatic charge from which it began. It is clear that such postulates cannot be analyzed in terms of the manifestations on the basis of which they were introduced, since they imply so much more that is not implied by those manifestations themselves. For all these reasons, the unification accomplished by such concept formation is not merely verbal or conjunctive. It is the genuine discovery that things that appeared distinct and only contingently correlated are in fact, in virtue of their true nature, necessarily connected.

So the discovery of a genuinely unifying, rather than conjunctive, basis for the relation between mind and body would require the postulation of something that accounted for them both in terms of the same activity or properties or structure or whatever. And its reality would be confirmed if it could also account for things other than those it had been postulated to explain or their direct implications—other, previously unremarked psychophysical correlations, for example. That would require more than an inference from observed correlations to psychophysical laws, which in turn predict further correlations. It would mean finding something that entailed such laws as the logically necessary consequence of its essential nature.

It is a real question whether there is something already present in our current concepts of mental and physical—some unbridgeable gulf—that precludes their both being accounted for in the requisite unified way by a common basis. The atomistic method, of accounting for a property of the whole by explaining all its physical manifestations in terms of

---

20. Given the character of modern physics, all these necessities have to be understood probabilistically.

the activities of the parts, is not sufficient here, because there is more to be explained than the observable physical manifestations of mental processes.

Merely adding phenomenological qualities to brain states as an extra property is not enough, since it would imply that the same brain state might exist without that property. It has to follow from what these states really *are* that they have both these types of properties. If we are going to take reduction in physics and chemistry as our logical model, we have to recognize, as was explained earlier, that the necessary identity of water with H_2O or fire with oxidation or heat with molecular motion depends on another necessary connection. It requires that the manifest properties by which we prescientifically identify water or fire or heat must be explained without residue, and in their essential respects entailed, by the reducing account. This upward entailment (that all the distinguishing marks of heat are in fact exhaustively explained by molecular motion) is essential for the validity of the downward entailment (that heat is identical with molecular motion and cannot exist without it). The only way we can discover that heat *is* molecular motion—so that if something felt the same to us but was not molecular motion it would not be heat—is to discover that in our world the actual complete account of the features by which we identify heat pretheoretically is given in terms of molecular motion and that this account is complete in the sense that it entails what is essential in those features.

In the mind-body case, there is no direct entailment in either direction between the phenomenological and the physiological, and at present we don't have the concept of a third type of state or process that would entail both the phenomenological and the physiological features of an experiential episode like tasting chocolate. But that is what would be required to warrant the conclusion that tasting chocolate had this physiological character necessarily, or vice versa. Only if we discovered such an actual common basis would we be able to say that a zombie is impossible, as water that is not H_2O is impossible, or fire that is not oxidation.

If we did discover such a thing, it would perhaps still be conceivable that something should look outwardly like a living human being with a functioning brain but not have consciousness. But such a system would have to be constituted out of different material and would therefore not, despite appearances, be a physical duplicate of a human body that merely lacked consciousness. On the supposition that, in us, the psychophysical connection is necessary, the brain of such a creature could not be made of what our brains are made of and would be similar only in its external appearance—just as there might be a different colorless, odorless, tasteless liquid that was not H_2O and therefore not water.[21]

21. This leaves us with a further question. Suppose we did discover such a common basis. Would there not then be an analogue, for the zombie case, of the possibility of an-

VII. Under Mind

I have described these conditions for the existence of a necessary connection between phenomenology and physiology very abstractly. They do not yet offer any suggestion of what kind of concept might entail both and thus reveal their common foundation. It would have to be the concept of something that in its essence has, and cannot fail to have, both a subjective inside and a physical outside.

Let me at last, after this very long windup, offer an extravagant conjecture. I suggest that we take the macroscopic relation between mental processes and their behavioral manifestations, which I have said is conceptual but not necessary, as a rough model for a deeper psychophysical connection that *is* necessary—pushing embodiment inward, so to speak. The gross and manifest relations between consciousness and behavior would thus be reinterpreted as a rough indicator of something much tighter in the interior of the brain, which can be discovered only by scientific inference and which explains the manifest relations in virtue of its usual links to the rest of the body. Perhaps, for example, the reason for the relation between pain and avoidance at the level of the organism is that at a deeper physiological level, the state that generates the appropriate observable behavior in an intact organism by the mediation of nerves, muscles, and tendons is an essentially subjective state of the brain with an *unmediated, noncontingent* "behavioral expression" of its own. It would be a single state that is necessarily both physical and mental, not a mere conjunction of the two.

Does this "pushing down" of the relation between mind and its behavioral manifestations make sense: Could there be a tighter version of

---

other liquid that resembles water in its manifest qualities but that is not water because it is not H_2O? Can we imagine something like that with respect to consciousness and the brain?

The question can be divided in to two parts. First, even if our conscious states were in fact brain states, couldn't we imagine a different physical system that to external observation resembled a human being in all behavioral and physiological and chemical respects but consisted of intrinsically different material that lacked consciousness? Second, couldn't we imagine a different conscious subject with experience that subjectively resembled human pain but that was not pain(!) because it was not a brain state but, say, a state of an immaterial soul?

I believe that in both of these cases, unlike the water case, there is no reason to think that we have imagined any possibility at all. Even if such alternative systems were possible, our use of our own imagination of the presence or absence of subjective experience could give us no evidence of it. If the connection between our minds and our brains is indeed necessary, then our imagination provides no way of peeling off the experience from its physical embodiment, or vice versa, as argued in the previous section. We have no way of conceiving of the presence or absence of the purely mental features of experience by themselves. By contrast, we do have a way of conceiving of the presence or absence of the perceptual appearances of water by themselves, since those appearances involve a relation to something else, namely, the perceiver.

the relation below the level of the whole organism? Well, to begin with the first level down, these relations should certainly be reflected in some form in the case of a separated but still operating brain—the classic imaginary "brain in a vat"—deprived of its body but still receiving inputs and producing outputs and functioning internally otherwise like an embodied brain. Its mental states (I assume it would have mental states) would bear a relation to its purely electronic inputs and outputs analogous to those of a normal person to perceptual inputs and behavioral outputs—but without the contingency due to dependence on the usual external connections.

The next question is whether the same is true of half brains. In the case of individuals with brain damage, or those with split brains, each functioning cerebral hemisphere seems to interact with the brain stem in a way that expresses behaviorally the somewhat reduced conscious activity associated with the partial brain. I believe the remarkable split-brain results have a philosophical significance that has not been sufficiently appreciated.[22] They show that both the brain and the mind are in some sense composed of parts and that those parts are simultaneously physical and mental systems, which can to some extent preserve their dual nature when separated. In an intact brain, the two halves do not lead distinct conscious lives: They support a single consciousness. But the fact that each of them can support a distinct consciousness when separated seems to show that the normal unified consciousness is composed of mental parts embodied in the physical parts. These parts are "mental" in a derivative but nonetheless real sense.

If this phenomenon of composition can be seen to exist at the gross level of bisection, it makes sense to conjecture that it may be carried further and that some form of more limited psychophysical unity may exist in smaller or more specialized subparts of the system, which in ordinary circumstances combine to form a conscious being of the familiar kind but may also in some cases be capable of existing and functioning separately. The strategy would be to try to push down into the interior of the brain the supposition of states that loosely resemble ordinary mental states in that they combine constituents of subjective mental character (in an extended sense) with behavioral or functional manifestations— with the difference that here the "behavior" would be internal to the brain rather than being mediated by links to the body, an intrinsic, non-contingent feature of the state rather than a relation to something outside of it. And they need not be spatially defined subparts but might include other sorts of subsystems or operations that are not strictly localized.

22. I have discussed those results in "Brain Bisection and the Unity of Consciousness," *Synthese*, 20, (1971); reprinted in Nagel, *Mortal Questions* (Cambridge: Cambridge University Press, 1979).

Such hypothetical subparts of consciousness would not be subjectively imaginable to us. They would be subjective only in the sense that they are inherently capable of combining to constitute full states of consciousness in an intact organism, even though they have no independent consciousness when they are so combined and may or may not have independent consciousness when they occur separately. The compositional character of consciousness is evident not only from bisected brains but also from the description of people with the sort of brain damage that causes behaviorally spectacular and subjectively alien mental changes. Certain cases of agnosia are like this, as when a person can pick a pen out of a group of objects if asked to do so but can't say, if shown a pen, what it is and can't show how it is used, although he can when he touches it. This is due to some cut between the visual, tactile, and speech centers, and it isn't really imaginable from the inside to those who don't suffer from it.[23]

A theory of the basis of the mental-physical link might begin from the component analysis suggested by the deconnection syndromes. Some such pushing down of the link to a level lower than that of the person is necessary to get beyond brute emergence or supervenience. Even if crude spatial divisions are only part of the story, they might be a beginning. More global but functionally specialized psychophysical subsytems might follow. The conceptual point is that both the mind and the brain may be composed of the same subsystems, which are essentially both physical and mental, and some variants of which are to be found in other conscious organisms as well.

The idea of a third type of phenomenon—essentially both mental and physical—which is the real nature of these subprocesses, is easier to grasp if one thinks of the mental aspect as irreducibly real but not subjectively imaginable from an ordinary, complete human viewpoint. It would be conceivable only by inference from what can be observed—inference precisely to what is needed to explain the observations. Constituents inferred to explain simultaneously both the physiological and the phenomenological data and the connection between them would not be classifiable in the old style either as physical or as mental. We would have to regard the physical results of combining such constituents in a living organism—results we could observe both behaviorally and physiologically—as providing only a partial view of them.

Such a compositional theory would be one possible way, and perhaps the only way, to give content to the idea of a necessary connection between the physiological and the mental. To me it seems clear that any necessary connection must be a matter of detail and not just global. The necessary connection between two things as complex as a crea-

23. See Norman Geschwind, "Disconnexion Syndromes in Animals and Man," *Brain*, 88 (1965), for an extensive discussion of such disorders.

ture's total mental state and its total physiological state must be a consequence of something more fundamental and systematic. We can't form the conception of a necessary connection in such a case just by stipulating that they are both essential features of a single state. The inseparability must be the logical consequence of something simpler to avoid being a mere constant conjunction that provides evidence of necessity without revealing it. Necessity requires reduction, because in order to see the necessity we have to trace it down to a level where the explanatory properties are simply the defining characteristics of certain basic constituents of the world.

Our ordinary sensation concepts paint these states with a broad brush. We all know that in our own case there is much more detail, both phenomenological and physiological, than we can describe in ordinary language. The systematic though imprecise relation at the level of the organism between mind and behavior is captured by ordinary mental concepts, but it is only the rough and macroscopic manifestation of objective, lawlike conditions that must lie much deeper. And the detailed macroscopic relation between mind and brain may be necessary, though it appears contingent, because it is the consequence of the noncontingent physiological manifestations of component states at a submental level.

This hypothesis invites several questions. First, would the states I am imagining at the basic level really be unified, rather than raising again the question of the relation between their mental and physical aspects? Second, can we really make sense of the idea that each mind is composed of submental parts? Third, what is the relation between the physicality of these submental processes and the account of what happens in the brain in terms of physics and chemistry alone?

The first question requires us to distinguish a manifestation of a property that is truly essential, revealing an internal, noncontingent relation, from one that is due to a merely contingent, external relation.

All our working concepts require that there be some form of generally available access to what they refer to, and that means that any concept of a type of process or substance, or of a property, mental or physical, will refer to something that is systematically connected to other things, allowing different people from their different points of view to get a handle on it. This is the grain of truth in verificationism. It is true whether the property is liquidity or heat or painfulness. There are no natural kinds without systematic connections to other natural kinds.[24]

---

24. This position is much more fully and precisely expressed and defended by Sydney Shoemaker in his remarkable essay, "Causality and Properties," in *Identity, Cause and Mind: Philosophical Essays* (Cambridge: Cambridge University Press, 1984), with which I agree entirely. He also points out that it is a consequence of this view, fully worked out, that causal necessity is a species of logical necessity.

All properties that we can think about have to be embedded in a web of connections, and I suspect that this is even true of properties we can't think about, because it is part of our general concept of a property.

Sometimes the properties that permit us to make contact with a natural kind are external, contingent properties. This, I have said, is true of the ordinary behavioral manifestations of mental states, which permit us to have public mental concepts. It is also true of the manifest properties by which we fix the reference of many other natural kind terms. But the closer we get to the thing itself, the more unmediated will be its manifestations, its effects, and its relations to certain other things. Eventually we arrive at effects that are directly entailed by the essential properties of the natural kind itself. The mass and charge of a proton, for example, without which it would not be a proton, have strict consequences for its relations to other particles, similarly specified. Even in describing radically counterfactual situations, we have to suppose these essential relations preserved in order to be sure we are talking about the same property or thing. Some dispositions are necessary consequences of a thing's essential nature.

Let us look more closely at the familiar physical case. The manifest properties of ordinary physical objects—their shape, size, weight, color, and texture, for example—already have necessary consequences for their interactions with other things whose properties are specified with sufficient precision. The properties are not reducible to those external relations, but the consequences are not merely contingent. An object simply would not weigh one pound if it did not affect a scale in the appropriate way, in the absence of countervailing forces. But all these necessary connections at the gross level have implications for the type of analysis at the level of physical theory that can reveal more fully the intrinsic nature of such an object. An analysis in terms of microscopic components, however strange and sophisticated its form, must in some way preserve these necessary external relations of the properties of the manifest object. The properties of the parts may be different—a crude mechanistic atomism, although a natural pre-Socratic speculation, has proved too simple—but they must have their own necessary consequences for interaction with other things, of a kind that in combination will imply the relational properties of the larger entity that they compose. However far we get from the manifest world of perception and common sense, that link must not be broken. Even if some of the properties of the whole are emergent in the sense of not being predictable from the separately ascertainable properties of the parts, the emergent phenomena still consist of or are constituted by the collective behavior of the parts.

Something similar is needed if our starting point is not the manifest world of inanimate physical objects but the world of conscious creatures. In a case like thirst, for example, the subjective quality and the functional role are already internally connected in the ordinary concept. It is the concept of a phenomenological state that has typical physical manifestations. The full intrinsic character of the state has to be discovered. But the ordinary concept already contains, in rough form, an idea of the kind of state it is—just as an ordinary substance concept like water already contains, in rough form, an idea of the kind of thing it is, setting the possible paths to further detailed discovery of its true nature, which have led to the development of physics and chemistry.

The hypothesis of psychic atoms that are just like animals, only smaller, is not even a starter in this case, because we don't have ready a coherent idea of larger conscious subjects being composed of smaller ones—as the early atomists had the perfectly clear geometrical idea of larger physical objects or processes being composed of smaller ones. But the more abstract idea of a form of analysis of conscious organisms whose elements will preserve in stricter form the relation between mental reality and behavior should constrain and guide the development of any reductive theory in this domain. There must be some kind of strict inner-outer link at more basic levels that can account for the far looser and more complicated inner-outer link at the level of the organism. And, of course, the idea would have to include a completely new theory of composition—of mental parts and wholes. (As I have said, the parts and wholes would include not just chunks of the brain and their smaller components but nonspatially defined processes and functions as well.)

My conjecture is that the relation between conscious states and behavior, roughly captured in the way ordinary mental concepts function, is a manifest but superficial and contingent version of the truth—namely, that the active brain is the scene of a system of subpersonal processes that combine to constitute both its total behavioral and its phenomenological character, and each of those subpersonal processes is itself a version of a "mental-behavioral" relation that is not contingent but necessary because it is not mediated by anything.

This differs from traditional functionalism, coupled with an account of the physiological realization of functional states, in that the "realization" here envisioned is to be not merely physiological but in some sense mental all the way down—something that accounts for the phenomenology as well. The combination of these postulated processes would entail at more complex levels not only the observable behavior and functional organization but also the conscious mental life conceptually related but not reducible to it. We are looking for a realization not just of functional states but of mental states in the full sense, and that means the realization cannot be merely physical. The reductive basis must preserve, in broad terms, the logical character of the mental processes being reduced. That is just as true here as it is in reductions of purely physical substances, processes, or forces.

The problem of adequate unity in the inferred explanatory concept—the problem of how it can avoid being a mere conjunction of the phenomenological and the physiological—can be addressed by seeing it as a purification of the ordinary concept of mind, with the sources of contingency in the mental-behavioral connections gradually removed as we close in on the thing itself. States of this kind, if they exist, could be identified only by theoretical inference; they would not be definable as the conjunction of independently identifiable mental and physical components but would be understandable only as part of a theory that explains the relations between them.

I leave aside the question of how far down these states might go. Perhaps they are emergent, relative to the properties of atoms or molecules. If so, this view would imply that what emerges are states that are in themselves necessarily both physical and mental, not just mental states attached to nonemergent physical states. If, on the other hand, they are not emergent, this view would imply that the fundamental constituents of the world, out of which everything is composed, are neither physical nor mental but something more basic. This position is not equivalent to panpsychism. Panpsychism is, in effect, dualism all the way down.[25] This is monism all the way down.

I said there were three questions about the proposal. The second was how we could conceive of a single mind resulting from the combination of subpersonal components. On that issue, we have very few data to go on, only the split-brain cases. Further experiments to investigate the results of combining parts of different conscious nervous systems would be criminal if carried out on human subjects—the only kind who would be able to tell us about the experiential results. (There's a piece of science fiction for you.) But the contents of an animal mind are complex enough so that the idea of composition seems a fairly natural one, though who knows what kinds of "parts" the combinable components might be. We certainly can't expect them in general to be anatomically separable. The now common habit of thinking in terms of mental modules is a crude beginning, but it might lead somewhere and might join naturally with the creation of concepts of the sort I am suggesting, which entail both physiology and phenomenology. The real conceptual problems would come in trying to describe elements or factors of subjectivity too basic to be found as identifiable parts of conscious experience. I will not try to say more about compositionality at this point.

The third question was about the relation between explanation that employed such concepts and such a theory, on the one hand, and traditional, purely physical explanation, on the other. The idea is that such a theory would explain both the phenomenology and the physiology by

25. See Thomas Nagel, "Panpsychism," in *Mortal Questions* (Cambridge: Cambridge University Press, 1979).

reference to a more fundamental level at which their internal relation to one another was revealed. But wouldn't that require that there be no account of the physical interactions of a conscious organism with its environment, and of its internal physical operation, in terms of the laws of physics and chemistry alone? Whether or not such an account is possible, the denial of its possibility would certainly seem a dangerously strong claim to harness to any hypothesis of the kind I am suggesting.

My quick response to this question is that there is no reason to think that the explanations referring to this psychophysical level need conflict with purely physical explanations of the purely physical features of the same phenomena, any more than explanations in terms of physics have to conflict with explanations in terms of chemistry. If there is a type of description that entails both the mental and the physical, it can be used to explain more than what a purely physical theory can explain, but it should also leave intact those explanations that need to refer only to the physical. If there are special problems here, they have to do with the compatibility between psychological and physical explanations of action, and freedom of the will. Those problems are serious, but they are not, I think, made any more serious by a proposal of this kind, whereby the relation between the mental and the physiological is necessary rather than contingent. Indeed, such a proposal would probably dispose of one problem, that of double causation, since it would imply that at a deeper level the distinction between mental and physical causes disappears.

VIII. Universal Mind

All this is speculation of the most extravagant kind, but not for that reason impermissible. Armchair protoscience as the philosophical formulation of possibilities is an indispensable precondition of empirical science, and with regard to the mind-body problem we are not exactly awash in viable possibilities.[26] I have described in abstract terms the logical character of a different theory and different concepts. Their creation, if possible at all, would have to be based on empirical research and theoretical invention. But one feature such a theory should have that is of the first importance is a universality that extends to all species of conscious life and is not limited to the human. That just seems to me to be common sense about how the world works. The mind-brain relation in us must be an example of something quite general, and any account of it must be part of a more general theory. That conception ought to govern us even if

26. See "Philosophical Naturalism," Michael Friedman's presidential address to the Central Division of the American Philosophical Association, *Proceedings and Addresses of the American Philosophical Association*, 71 (1997).

we have to start with humans and creatures very like them in gathering evidence on which to base such a theory.

This has an important consequence for the basic theoretical terms it will employ, the terms that entail both the phenomenological and the physiological descriptions of inner states. They must be understood to imply that experiences have a subjective character, without necessarily allowing the theorist to fully understand the specific subjective character of the experiences in question—since those experiences may be of a type that he himself cannot undergo or imagine and of which he cannot therefore acquire the full first- and third-person mental concepts. The terms will therefore have to rely, in their full generality, a good deal on what I have elsewhere[27] called "objective phenomenology"—structural features like quality spaces that can be understood and described as aspects of a type of subjective point of view without being fully, subjectively imaginable except by those who can share that point of view.

If such a theory is ever developed, the reason for believing in the reality of what it postulates, like the reason for believing in the reality of any other theoretical entities, will be inference to the best explanation. The relation between phenomenology and physiology demands an explanation; no explanation of sufficient transparency can be constructed within the circle of current mental and physical concepts themselves, so an explanation must be sought that introduces new concepts and gives us knowledge of real things we didn't know about before. We hypothesize that there are things having the character necessary to provide an adequate explanation of the data, and their real existence is better confirmed the wider the range of data the hypothesis can account for. But they must be hypothesized as an explanation of the mental and the physical data taken together, for there will be no reason to infer them from physiological and behavioral data alone. As Jeffrey Gray observes:

> The reason the problem posed by consciousness seems so acute, at least to nonfunctionalists, is the following: nothing that we know so far about behaviour, physiology, the evolution of either behaviour or physiology, or the possibilities of constructing automata to carry out complex forms of behaviour is such that the hypothesis of consciousness would arise if it did not occur in addition as a datum in our own experience; nor, having arisen, does it provide a useful explanation of the phenomena observed in those domains.[28]

The most radical thing about the present conjecture is the idea that there is something more fundamental than the physical—something

27. Nagel, "What Is It Like to Be a Bat?"
28. Jeffrey A. Gray, "The Contents of Consciousness: A Neuropsychological Conjecture," *Behavioral and Brain Sciences*, 18 (1995), 660.

that explains both the physical and the mental. How can the physical be explained by anything but the physical? And don't we have ample evidence that all that needs to be postulated to get ever deeper explanations of physical phenomena is just more physics? However, I am not proposing that we look for a theory that would displace or conflict with physical explanation of the ordinary sort, any more than it would conflict with ordinary psychological explanation of actions or mental events. Clearly the processes and entities postulated by such a theory would have to conform to physical law. It's just that there would be more to them than that. What reveals itself to external observation as the physiological operation of the brain, in conformity with physical law, would be seen to be something of which the physical characteristics were one manifestation and the mental characteristics another—one being the manifestation to outer sense and the other the manifestation to inner sense, to adapt Kant's terminology.

This leaves open the question of the level and type of organization at which the stuff becomes not just dead matter but actually conscious: Its mental potentialities might be completely inert in all but very special circumstances. Still, it would have to explain the mental where it appears, and in a way that also explains the systematic connections between the mental and the physical and the coexistence of mental and physical explanations, as in the cases of thought and action. And this conception would, if it were correct, provide a fuller account of the intrinsic nature of the brain than either a phenomenological or a physiological description or the conjunction of the two.

To describe the logical characteristics of such a theory is not to produce it. That would require the postulation of specific theoretical structures defined in terms of the laws that govern their physical and mental implications, experimentally testable and based on sufficiently precise knowledge of the extensional correlations between physical and mental phenomena. The path into such a theory would presumably involve the discovery of systematic structural similarities between physiological and phenomenological processes, leading eventually to the idea of a single structure that is both, and it would have to be based on vastly more empirical information than we have now.

It would have to be graspable by us, and therefore would have to be formulated in terms of a model that we could work with, to accommodate psychophysical data that we do not yet have. But it would not be simply an extension of our existing ideas of mind and matter, because those ideas do not contain within themselves the possibility of a development through which they "meet."

I have suggested one possible form of an approach that would permit such convergence, but it would not permit us to transcend the division between subjective and objective standpoints. The aim is rather to integrate them all the way to the bottom of our worldview, in such a way that neither is subordinate to the other. This means that what Bernard Williams calls the "absolute" conception of reality[29] will not be a physical conception but something richer that entails both the physical and the mental. To the extent that we could arrive at it, it would describe subjective experience in general terms that imply its subjectivity without necessarily relying on our capacity to undergo or fully imagine experiences of that type. This means that our grasp of such an absolute conception will inevitably be incomplete. Still, it would include more than a purely physical description of reality.

Whatever unification of subjective points of view and complex physical structures may be achieved, each of us will still be himself and will conceive of other perspectives by means of sympathetic imagination as far as that can reach, and by extrapolation from imagination beyond that. The difference between the inside and the outside view will not disappear. For each of us, the site and origin of his conception of the world as a unified physical-phenomenological system will always be the particular creature that he himself is, and therefore the conception will have a centered shape that is at variance with its centerless content. But that need not prevent us from developing that content in a way that captures the evident unity of what in our own case we can experience both from within and from without.

Previous efforts at reduction have been too external and in a sense too conservative. We need a conceptual creation that, by revealing a hidden necessary connection, makes conceivable what at present is inconceivable, so it won't be possible to imagine such a theory properly in advance. But it won't be possible even to look for such a solution unless we start with an incomplete conception of it. And that requires the willingness to contemplate the idea of a single natural phenomenon that is in itself, and necessarily, both subjectively mental from the inside and objectively physical from the outside—just as we are.[30]

29. Bernard Williams, *Descartes* (New York: Penguin, 1978).
30. Some portions of this essay derive from my article "Conceiving the Impossible and the Mind-Body Problem," *Philosophy*, 73 (1998), 337–352.

Index

Necessity, 194–235
Neutrality, 97–9, 135–7
Neutral monism, 209–10
Newton, Isaac, 169, 188
Nietzsche, Friedrich, 158, 160, 174
Nozick, Robert, 36, 82–3, 119
Nussbaum, Martha, 56–62

Objective phenomenology, 233
Objectivity, 170–4, 175–86, 187–93
Okin, Susan, 57, 131n
Original position, 80, 122–4
Orwell, George, 87
Overlapping consensus, 106

Panpsychism, 231
Parfit, Derek, 117n
Perfectionism, 96
Personal versus political, 104–6,
    107–112
Plato, 157
Platonism, 185
Pluralism, 96–101, 105–6, 135–7
Pogge, Thomas, 85
Political correctness, 8, 20–2
Popper, Karl, 168
Pornography, 26, 42, 50–1
Post, Robert C., 26n
Postmodernism, 163–7, 170, 173–4
Pragmatism, 157–62
Privacy, 3–30
Property dualism, 203
Ptolemy, 169
Public reason, 99
Pure procedural justice, 95, 114, 118
Putnam, Hilary, 158, 212n

Quantum theory, 171–3
Quine, W. V., 158, 169, 175
Quinn, Warren, 36–8

Rawls, John, 57, 75–106, 107, 110,
    115–24, 135–7, 142
Raz, Joseph, 39n, 42, 97n, 134–40
Realism, 154
Reasons, 153, 160, 168–70
Reduction, 196–202, 221–4
Relativism, 154, 159, 168–70, 173–4
Relativity, 171–3

Religion, 57–9, 76, 83–4, 110, 137–8
Responsibility, 115, 123–4, 129
Rights, 31–52, 90, 100
Romanticism, 65
Rorty, Richard, 157–62
Ross, Andrew, 163
Rousseau, Jean-Jacques, 55, 75, 87
Rushdie, Salman, 137
Russell, Bertrand, 19, 63–71, 209–10

Sandel, Michael, 84
Sartre, Jean-Paul, 70
Savage, C. Wade, 209n
Scanlon, T. M., 43, 147–54
Scheffler, Samuel, 36
Schoenman, Ralph, 69–70
Searle, John, 158, 221–2
Secondary qualities, 187–93
Sellars, Wilfrid, 158
Sen, Amartya, 57
Serrano, Andres, 25
Sex, 17–9, 22–3, 27–30, 45–51, 53–5,
    56–62, 65–6, 98
    and inequality, 128–32
Sexual harassment, 51, 59
Shalit, Wendy, 53–5
Shoemaker, Sydney, 194n, 216n,
    228n
Simmel, Georg, 4
Skepticism, 175–86
Smart, J. J. C., 210
Sokal, Alan, 163–74
Sound, 204–5
Spinoza, Baruch, 209
Split brain, 226
Stalin, Joseph, 65, 68
Starr, Kenneth, 27
Strawson, Galen, 208n
Stroud, Barry, 187–93
Supervenience, 207–8
Swoyer, James, 212n
Sympathetic imagination, 218

Thomas, Clarence, 23, 28
Thomson, Judith Jarvis, 36
Toleration, 42–52, 96–101, 134–8
Tripp, Linda, 27

Utilitarianism, 94, 103, 135, 148, 151